Rights in Rebellion

Rights in Rebellion

Indigenous Struggle and Human Rights in Chiapas

Shannon Speed

Stanford University Press
Stanford, California

Stanford University Press
Stanford, California

Printed in the United States of America on acid-free, archival-quality paper

Library of Congress Cataloging-in-Publication Data

Speed, Shannon, 1964-
    Rights in rebellion : indigenous struggle and human rights in Chiapas / Shannon Speed.
      p. cm.
    Includes bibliographical references and index.
    ISBN-13: 978-0-8047-5733-1 (cloth : alk. paper)
    ISBN-13: 978-0-8047-5734-8 (pbk. : alk. paper)
    1. Mayas—Mexico—Chiapas—Government relations.   2. Mayas—Mexico—Chiapas—
Politics and government.   3. Mayas—Mexico—Chiapas—Civil rights.   4. Human rights—
Mexico—Chiapas.   5. Government, Resistance to—Mexico—Chiapas.   6. Chiapas
(Mexico)—Politics and government.   7. Chiapas (Mexico)—Social conditions.   8. Chiapas
(Mexico)—Race relations.   I. Title.
    F1435.1.C492S74 2008
    323.1197'4207275—dc22   2007019284

Typeset by Westchester Book Group in 10/14 Minion

For Camila, with love.

Contents

List of Figures and Maps

Figures

Maps

Acknowledgments

THE PROJECT THAT RESULTED in this book has been under way for eleven years. As is inevitable with such a long-term undertaking, there are more people to thank for their help along the way than I can possibly include here.

My primary debt of gratitude is to the many people I worked with in Chiapas. The people of the community of Nicolás Ruiz were open with me despite the tensions the community was experiencing, and they tolerated my many questions and confusions. Rubén Moreno Méndez and Herón Moreno Moreno, community human rights defenders from Nicolás Ruiz, provided me with invaluable help in my research in a variety of spheres. Special thanks are due to the authorities of the *Presidencia Municipal* and *Bienes Comunales* of Nicolás Ruiz for facilitating my research in the community as well as in the archives and historical documents. I am very grateful to everyone at the *Red de Defensores Comunitarios por los Derechos Humanos*. My experience with this organization of highly committed indigenous and nonindigenous human rights defenders is at the base of much of my thinking about Chiapas, human rights, indigenous rights, and autonomy. I would also like to thank Ted Lewis of the Mexico Program of Global Exchange for providing me the opportunity to work at Global Exchange in San Cristóbal and for his openness to my combined activist-research activities. My fellow comrades at Global Exchange, especially Amanda Brown-Stevens, Chris Gilbreth, and Jutta Meier-Weidenbach, provided insightful analysis as well as much-needed laughter in tense times. A variety of human rights activists dedicated time to interviews and conversations with me that provided important background for this book. I especially thank Gustavo Castro, Martha Figueroa, Gerardo González,

Onésimo Hidalgo, Marina Patricia Jímenez, Mercedes Olivera, Mercedes Ozuna, and Jorge Santiago.

Miguel Angel de los Santos is multiply implicated in this work, as a human rights activist, founder and coordinator of the *Red de Defensores*, attorney for Nicolás Ruiz, thoughtful analyst of rights issues, and my husband. Much of my fieldwork over the years was facilitated by his long-established relations of trust with communities and individuals in his native Chiapas and my analysis has been strongly informed by our countless discussions, especially in the context of the work of the *Red*. In addition, he gave me a beautiful daughter, Camila, who is my inspiration in life. Although our paths have parted, he will always have my deepest gratitude, respect, and affection.

In Chiapas, I was fortunate to have an institutional home at the *Centro de Investigaciones y Estudios Superiores en Antropología Social* (CIESAS-Sureste) and I gratefully acknowledge the support and intellectual community that institution has provided me over the years, under the successive directorships of R. Aída Hernández, Lourdes de Léon, Graciela Freyermouth, Carolina Rivera, and Jan de Vos.

The ideas expressed in this book are the result of dialogue with many friends and colleagues over the years. Indeed, these ongoing discussions have so formed my thinking about the issues in this book that I can think of the analysis expressed here only as a collaborative product. Many have also provided comments and close reads of different parts of the manuscript over the years. I especially thank Jennifer Bickham-Méndez, Maylei Blackwell, Araceli Burguete, Emma Cervone, Jane Collier, Kathleen Dill, Melissa Forbis, Pablo Gonzalez, Mark Goodale, Charlie Hale, Aída Hernández, Xochitl Leyva, Mariana Mora, Vivian Newdick, Kathia Nuñez Patiño, Alvaro Reyes, Victoria Sanford, Rachel Seider, María Teresa Sierra, Carol Smith, Lynn Stephen, and Angela Stuesse. My work has especially benefited from years of intellectual engagement with Charles R. Hale, who has filled a variety of roles as my teacher, mentor, colleague, and friend.

Special thanks are due to Lynn Stephen, Neil Harvey, Mark Goodale, and an anonymous reviewer at Stanford University Press for their insightful comments on this manuscript, which undoubtedly made for a vastly improved final version. I am also eternally grateful to Kathleen Dill and Angela Stuesse, who went above and beyond the call of duty, reading successive chapters of the manuscript as I finished them and providing line-by-line comments and suggestions.

This book started out as a doctoral dissertation, and I was very fortunate to have a doctoral committee that was tolerant of, indeed encouraged, my unusual trajectory through graduate school (much of which was carried out from the field) and my activist research commitments. Carol A. Smith has been a wonderful dissertation director, mentor, friend, and *comadre*. Her wisdom and her unique ability to express it in straight language have been invaluable to me. Stefano Varese and Martha Macri of the Department of Native American Studies were also sources of critical feedback and vital support. Aída Hernández of the CIESAS also served on my dissertation committee, and her work and our ongoing collaborations over the years have greatly shaped my work. She is an inspiration and a dear friend.

UC Davis also provided a fantastic group of graduate student colleagues, and the discussions and debates of those years, in classes and through the Hemispheric Initiatives group, still inform my thinking in many ways: Kathleen Dill, Alex Greene, Jennifer Bickham-Méndez, Circe Sturm, Sarah England, Silvia Escárcega, Holly Ober, Chistian Erickson, Ileana La Bergere, and Donald Moore.

The research for this book was conducted with support from a Social Science Research Council–MacArthur Foundation Fellowship on Peace and Security in a Changing World and three Mellon Faculty Summer Research Fellowships from the Teresa Lozano Long Institute of Latin American Studies at the University of Texas at Austin. Writing was supported at different stages by an American Anthropological Association Minority Dissertation award, a Ford Minority Dissertation Fellowship, a postdoctoral fellowship from the Kellogg Institute at the University of Notre Dame, a University of Texas Deans Fellowship, two University of Texas Summer Research Assignments, and a Ford Diversity Postdoctoral Fellowship. I gratefully acknowledge this support.

Several parts of this work have been published elsewhere. Parts of Chapters 2 and 6 first appeared as "In Our Own Defense: Globalization, Rights and Resistance in Chiapas," *Political and Legal Anthropology Review (PoLAR)* 25(1): 69–89, co-authored with Alvaro Reyes. Parts of Chapter 3 first appeared in "Limiting Indigenous Autonomy: The State Government's Use of Human Rights in Chiapas," *Human Rights Quarterly* 22(4), co-authored with Jane Collier. A small portion of Chapter 4 appeared in a different form in "At the Crossroads of Human Rights and Anthropology: Toward a Critically Engaged Activist Research," *American Anthropologist* 108(1): 66–77, and another portion appeared in "Global Discourses on the Local Terrain: Human Rights and Indigenous Identity in Chiapas," *Cultural Dynamics* 14(2): 205–28. Sections of Chapter 5 were published as "Rights at the Intersection: Gender and Ethnicity in Nicolas Ruiz," in *Dissident Women: Gender, Ethnicity and Cultural Politics in*

Chiapas, Shannon Speed, R. Aída Hernández, and Lynn Stephen, eds., University of Texas Press, Austin. Finally, some parts of Chapters 2 and 7 will appear in a different form in "The Zapatista Juntas de Buen Gobierno: Exercising Rights, Reconfiguring Resistance," in *The Practice of Human Rights: Tracking Law in Transnational Contexts,* Mark Goodale and Sally Merry, eds., Cambridge University Press. I am grateful to the publishers of these journals and books for granting me permission to reproduce these portions here.

In the final stages of writing in Austin, a core group of friends provided the support that kept me sane (relatively speaking) and allowed me to keep on going. Thanks to Jennifer Bickham-Méndez and William and Sofia Méndez, for in-house friendship, company, and solidarity. Thanks to Kathy Dill, for red wine. Thanks to Charles R. Hale and Melissa Smith, for the gift of massage at a crucial juncture. I am lucky to have my fabulous friends and neighbors George Kinard and Dinah Sbelgio Kinard, who grew a new life as I "grew" the book. Jenny Walker Gates and Andrew Gates provided much-needed laughter and an ergonomic chair. Lara Byrd and Lyric Mitchell provided emergency childcare, as well as friendship. Special thanks go to Amber Vasquez, sweet and intelligent girl, for keeping Camila company while her mother was missing in action, and to Albert Vasquez, who provided emergency dinners, flowers, and fun.

These acknowledgments could not be complete without an expression of my deepest love and gratitude to my parents, William and Iris Speed, who raised me to make my own decisions, to believe in myself, and above all to celebrate life.

Acronyms and Abbreviations

ACNUR   Alto Comisionado de las Naciones Unidades para las
           Refugiados (U.N. High Commission on Refugees)

APPO   Asamblea Popular del Pueblo Oaxaqueño (Popular Assembly
           of the Oaxacan People)

CCRI-CG   Comité Clandestino Revolucionario Indígena–Comandancia
           General (Clandestine Indigenous Revolutionary
           Committee–General Command)

CDHFBC   Centro de Derechos Humanos "Fray Bartolomé de Las Casas"
           ("Fray Bartolomé de Las Casas" Human Rights Center)

CEDH   Comisión Estatal de Derechos Humanos (State Human
           Rights Commission)

CEDIAC   Centro de Derechos Indígenas A. C. (Center for Indigenous
           Rights)

CEPAL   Comisión Económica para América Latina y el Caribe
           (Economic Commission for Latin America and the Caribbean)

CFE   Comisión Federal de Electricidad (Federal Electricity
           Commission)

CIEPAC   Centro de Investigación Económicas y Políticas de Acción Co-
           munitaria (Center of Economic and Political Research for
           Community Action)

CIESAS   Centro de Investigaciones y Estudios Superiores en

	Antropología Social (Research Center and Graduate Studies in Social Anthropology)
CNC	Confederación Nacional Campesina (National Peasant Confederation)
CNDH	Comisión Nacional de Derechos Humanos (National Human Rights Commission)
CNI	Congreso Nacional Indígena (National Indigenous Congress)
CNPA	Coordinadora Nacional Plan de Ayala (National Coordinating Group "Plan de Ayala")
CNPI	Consejo Nacional de Pueblos Indígenas (National Council of Indigenous Peoples)
COAO	Coalición de Organizaciones Autónomas de Ocosingo (Coalition of Autonomous Organizations of Ocosingo)
COCOPA	Comisión de Concordia y Pacificación (Commission for Concordance and Pacification)
CODAIF	Comité Diocesano de Ayuda a Inmigrantes Fronterizos (Committee of the Diocese for Assistance to Border Immigrants)
CONAI	Comisión Nacional de Intermediación (National Mediation Commission)
CONPAZ	Coordinación de Los Organismos No-Gubernamentales por la Paz (Coordination of Nongovernmental Organizations for Peace)
DPI	Departamento de Protección Indígena (Department of Social Action, Culture, and Indigenous Protection)
EZLN	Ejército Zapatista de Liberación Nacional (Zapatista National Liberation Army)
FAT	Frente Amplio de Trabajo (Broad Labor Front)
FNCR	Frente Nacional Contra la Represión (National Front Against Repression)
ILO	International Labor Organization
IMSS	Instituto Mexicano de Seguridad Social (Mexican Social Security Institute)

INEGI	Instituto Nacional de Estadística, Geografía, y Informática (National Institute for Statistics, Geography, and Data Processing)
INI	Instituto Nacional Indigenista (National Indigenist Institute)
INM	Instituto Nacional de Migración (National Immigration Institute)
MIRA	Movimiento Indigena Revolucionario Anti-Zapatista (Anti-Zapatista Indigenous Revolutionary Movement)
NAFTA	North American Free Trade Agreement
NGO	Nongovernmental Organization
OAS	Organización de Estados Americanos (Organization of American States)
ONUSIDA	UN HIV/AIDS Commission
PAN	Partido de Acción Nacional (National Action Party)
PGR	Procuraduría General de la Républica (Attorney General's Office)
PNR	Partido Nacional Revolucionario (National Revolutionary Party)
PRA	Programa de Rehabilitación Agraria (Program for Agrarian Rehabilitation)
PRD	Partido de la Revolución Democrática (Party of the Democratic Revolution)
PRI	Partido Revolucionario Institucional (Institutional Revolutionary Party)
PROCEDE	Programa de Certificación de Derechos Parcelarios y Titulación de Solares Urbanos (Program for Certification of Land Rights)
RAN	Reqistro Agrario Nacional (National Agrarian Reqistry)
SAM	Sistema Alimentaria Mexicana (Mexican Nutrition System)
SEDESOL	Secretaría de Desarrollo Social (Secretary of Social Development)
SIPAZ	Servicio Internacional por la Paz (International Service for Peace)
SRA	Secretaría de la Reforma Agraria (Department of Agrarian Reform)
UNHCHR	United Nations High Comission on Human Rights

Rights in Rebellion

Preface: Activist Research in the Chiapas Conflict

I CONDUCTED THE RESEARCH for this book over a period of nine years, from 1995 to 2004. I have defined my approach to this work as "activist research," though this term may suggest a preconceived and programmatic approach that it did not actually entail. In fact, my activist research included several different types of political-academic engagements over the course of my time in Chiapas, as well as an evolving understanding of the benefits and complications of an activist commitment in the research process. I took an activist approach for several interrelated reasons: my own long-standing commitment to activism for social justice, the circumstances on the ground in Chiapas, and the need to address the variety of ethical and practical concerns of anthropology as a discipline and in relation to the production of knowledge more generally. It is my belief that activist research does more than allow anthropologists to be "good progressives." Critically engaged activist research can also potentially contribute to the transformation of the discipline itself because it entails an overt positioning of the researcher vis-à-vis the research subjects, integrates those subjects into the research process, and recognizes and validates ways of knowing and theorizing social processes other than academic ones. In doing so, activist research allows us to address (though not resolve) the politics of knowledge production and may provide insights that could not be generated through traditional research. I have given myself the luxury of the space of this preface for a consideration of these assertions through my own research process, not to provide an ideal example of activist research, but rather to offer material for further discussion and debate.

Why Activist Research? Anthropology and the Politics of Knowledge Production

I came to the discipline of anthropology as an activist, certain that further academic study interested me only to the extent that it made for better understandings of "the political" and thus for better possibilities for social change. I had found an ideal program: my cohort in Socio-Cultural Anthropology at UC Davis was made up of activists of a variety of stripes, and the training we received included a continual regrounding of theoretical debates in the political realities of social struggle, just as it continually complicated our notions of social struggle and social change through complex and challenging theorization. Yet I came to anthropology largely unfamiliar with the discipline and its debates: my academic background was in international relations and area studies. It was as I learned more about these debates and developed a commitment to anthropological practice that the decolonization of the discipline became intimately bound up with my other political goals.

In the early 1990s, anthropology was grappling with several decades of internal and external critiques of anthropological theories and methodologies that had caused the discipline to question and redefine some of its most basic precepts. These critiques were launched from various quarters: not only from our postcolonial research "subjects,"[1] but also from feminist, postmodern, critical race, and postcolonial theorists, who charged that anthropologists' ostensibly neutral ethnographic descriptions often reproduced discourses that served to naturalize social inequalities. Critical analyses pointed to the historical collusion of the social sciences, and in particular the discipline of anthropology, with colonial power, by producing representations that supported colonialist logics and rationalities (Asad 1973; Gough 1968; Said 1978). Such critiques came not only in the realm of high theory but also from postcolonial research subjects themselves, who were increasingly vocal and contestatory in their engagements with anthropologists.[2]

In the same period, scientific epistemology came under fire from a variety of perspectives, including feminist, postmodern, and poststructuralist theorists (Baudrillard 1988; Foucault 1972; Haraway 1989; Harding 1986; Kuhn 1962). The notion of anthropology as a social "science" was challenged and the validity of claims to a knowable truth regarding human cultures was seriously undermined (Berreman 1981). Critical analyses in these fields made clear that anthropologists' own cultural and political perspectives shape our ethnographic descriptions, belying our supposed objectivity. Feminists demonstrated that anthropological studies had androcentric and eurocentric biases and assumptions and that dominant conceptions and practices of knowledge attribution, acquisition, and justification systematically disadvantaged women and other subordinated groups (E. Anderson 2006). Feminists made patently clear that our representations of others were products of our own social positioning, our own "situatedness" in relation to those people and cultural dynamics we chose to represent (Haraway 1988; hooks 1995; Minh-ha 1989; Moraga and Anzaldúa 2002 [1989]).

Further, this was not simply a question of whether we could or could not accurately know and describe our research subjects: our subjective representations had concrete and at times powerful effects on those we represented in our work. Analyses of anthropology's complicity with colonial and postcolonial administrations revealed the ways objectivism had been used to obscure the political uses of the knowledge anthropologists produce. This included both unintentional reproduction of discourses of power and overt political engagements, such as spying for government agencies under the guise of fieldwork (Horowitz 1967; Price 2000; Wolf and Jorgeson 1970).

These multiple critiques and the discipline's introspection were severe enough to be termed "the crisis of representation" (Clifford and Marcus 1986), and this "crisis" led to serious rethinking of the anthropological project in ways that would address the critiques and yet salvage anthropology's unique contribution to human knowledge. This was not an easy task, particularly for those who wished to make anthropology useful and relevant beyond the academe. While the critiques of positivist objectivity and the politics of representation were important for the discipline of anthropology, they also had disturbing relativist underbellies. That is, if all knowledge claims are suspect and no one can know what's "really true," then all truth claims could be understood as equally true and valid or, alternatively, all simply reducible to underlying relations of power (C. R. Hale 1999). As an activist and an anthropologist, I struggled for epistemological footing on terrain where the most "radical" theorists were busily deconstructing metanarratives and challenging capital "T" truth claims—undertakings I fully agreed with yet found terribly demobilizing. I sought a path forward through the detritus left behind by deconstruction that was not dangerously full of U-turns veering back toward positivist objectivity and unreflexive empiricism.

Anthropology Beyond the "Crisis"

Most anthropologists have recognized and accepted the basic constructivist insight about the politically situated nature of all knowledge production, including how research agendas are set, what questions are defined as legitimate, and what counts as theoretically valid knowledge production. For many, reflexively "situating oneself" in relation to the research subjects and the work has become an indispensable part of anthropological practice, vital to recognizing and addressing the politics of knowledge production.

For a smaller group of anthropologists, reflexivity did not go far enough in addressing the question of power dynamics in research and knowledge production. A variety of approaches have been taken over the years that entail some form of political commitment on the part of the anthropologist to the people with whom one works. Particularly in Latin America, advocacy models such as the organization Cultural Survival, founded in 1972 by Harvard anthropologist David Maybury-Lewis, envisioned anthropologists' role as one of representing, defending, and supporting the members of disenfranchised groups who were unable to promote their own interests (see Maybury-Lewis 1990; Lutz 2005). The cultural survival model of advocacy engagement has remained small but strong within anthropology, despite some critiques of paternalism and a relatively limited geographic focus on South American Indians. In a different vein, "participatory action research" redefined research relationships by striving for horizontal interactions in which research problems were defined by co-researchers (academics and people involved in the processes under study), who engaged in cycles of mutual reflection and redefinition of problems and goals based on a Freirean pedagogical model (Fals Borda 1979; Fals Borda and Rahman 1991; Greenwood and Levin 1998). Some scholars emphasized the need to decolonize the relationship between researcher and research subject (C. R. Hale 2007; Harrison 1991; Mutua and Swadener 2004; L. T. Smith 1999); others specifically called for a form of anthropology that was committed to some form of human liberation (Gordon 1991; Harrison 1991; Scheper-Hughes 1995).

Influenced by these currents, I came to the research project in Chiapas with dual aspirations that went beyond an academic interest in understanding the dynamics of neoliberal globalization, the discourse of human rights, and indigenous resistance in Chiapas. I was also interested in participating in that struggle and allowing my own insights to emerge from engagement. Finally, I sought, at a minimum, to engage in an anthropological research practice that addressed the politics of knowledge production.

For me, this approach entailed making explicit my own positionality as both researcher and activist, as well as the views that I hold (e.g., that universal human rights exist), even while recognizing the socially constructed and historically contingent nature of such claims. It required finding the places where my own politics overlapped with those of certain actors in Chiapas and attempting to build an activist research project in that space of overlap. Finally, it involved working to make the political decisions involved in knowledge production in collaboration with the people who were the subjects of this research. Over the course of years my approach was constantly evolving as I grappled with the rapidly shifting situation on the ground in Chiapas, my own personal circumstances, and the continual rethinking of the work that this approach entailed.

My own commitment to ongoing struggle for social justice shaped my engagement with anthropology and the kinds of questions I was interested in researching. Indeed, the fact that I was in Chiapas was because of the recently launched indigenous uprising and the high-profile social struggle there. As a mixed-descent Native American (Chickasaw, Choctaw, and European) and an active citizen of the Chickasaw Nation, I hold a strong personal commitment to seeking justice for Indian peoples. Yet, I was born and raised in Los Angeles, not in an indigenous cultural context. I do not speak a Native language and because of my phenotype I am not readily identified by others as Indian. While my family history is intimately linked to the history of oppression of Indian peoples, I have not suffered personal discrimination or racism as a Native American.

My already complex identity was further complicated in Mexico. Here, my positionality shifted to that of "gringa," a modification of my identity that invokes the power relationships inherent in north-south border crossings and denotes phenotypic and cultural difference as well as a series of gender stereotypes (see A. Adams 1997; Nelson 1999). Furthermore, until very recently in Mexico, everyone from government officials to leftist intellectuals to indigenous communities themselves understood indigenous identity to be based on language and dress. Hence the comment I heard more than once during my work in Chiapas that someone "used to be indigenous" but no longer was, because upon leaving the community that person had lost his or her indigenous language and stopped wearing traditional dress. (This particular historical construction of indigenousness is analyzed further in Chapter 4.) Whether or not I had chosen to identify myself to the indigenous people I worked with as

Native American (in general, I did not), they would have found it difficult, if not impossible, to identify me as such. Furthermore, an attempt to align with them politically on this basis, even if it had been possible, would have served to occlude the power dynamics inherent in our alliance.

For these reasons, I approached my activist work and research in Chiapas as "solidarity" work in Mohanty's (2003) sense, entailing:

> [M]utuality, accountability, and the recognition of common interests as the basis of relationships among diverse communities. Rather than assuming an enforced commonality of oppression, the practice of solidarity foregrounds communities of people who have chosen to work and fight together. (2003:10)

More than simple alliance with others in a universalizing way ("we are all workers/women/indigenous people"), it is a politics in which we recognize difference and different forms of oppression, yet form our politics around common, overlapping goals.

This form of political alliance is distinct from the "solidarity" of a previous era, in which I worked alongside many other *solidario/as* in Nicaragua supporting the Sandinista revolution and in San Francisco in support of the leftist struggle in El Salvador. The solidarity work of the 1980s was geared to opposing U.S. imperialism by supporting movements or governments that challenged it. However, all too often it entailed a paternalistic element of "helping" others in their struggles and left unexamined the relations of power inherent in this kind of political action. Nelson (1999) analyzes the problematic nature of gringa solidarity in Latin America, which she argues is often comfortably unreflexive about "forms of self-fashioning" that construct the *solidarias* as "good gringas" in the field of action of pure "good guys" and "bad guys," and the manner in which such relations of solidarity have "complicity in the on-going production of relations of oppression."

Mohanty's formulation is directed toward a feminist solidarity, and thus is centrally concerned with overcoming the problematic solidarity of "sisterhood" in which diversity and difference were erased (Anzaldúa 1987, 1990; Lorde 1984; Mohanty 1988; Moraga and Anzaldúa 2002 [1989]). This can also be usefully applied to leftist solidarity of a former era in which it was assumed that we were all part of one struggle and that focusing on or emphasizing difference only weakened that struggle. This conceptualization of effective resistance conveniently erased the particular forms of oppression suffered by different social actors and thus the distinct relations of power between them (potentially reproducing those relations in the process). Feminists of color and intersectionality theory have provided clear analyses of the manner in which distinct social actors experience different and often multiple intersecting and interlocking forms of oppression (Collins 1991; Crenshaw 1991; Sudbury 1998). Mohanty's use of solidarity assumes that these multiple experiences of oppression exist, but Mohanty argues that there is possibility of alliance across them, at points of overlap, without erasing that difference. Such a solidarity must be tied, Mohanty argues, to a decolonization of feminist theory and practice, to undermine the structures of power that work to reproduce hierarchies of power in solidarity relationships.

I sought, in pursuing activist research in Chiapas, the areas of coincidence between my own feminist, antiracist, and anticapitalist politics and those of indigenous people waging a social struggle that forefronted many of these same goals. In general terms, the areas where they coincided were easy to identify. In concrete practical terms, they were often much more difficult. Several of the chapters in this book reflect the terrain of overlap on which my research was carried out. But this was never an uncomplicated terrain, as Chapter 4 in particular reflects. Throughout, the stark differences in power and privilege between me and the indigenous people I worked with reminded me continually of the need to pursue decolonizing practice in anthropology.

Decolonizing Anthropology

What constitutes decolonizing practice? Undoubtedly, there are many approaches one might take. For me, activist research provides a vehicle for addressing some of the most important issues. One is the overt recognition of and continued reflection about the differential power relations that exist in the research relationship. Reflexivity about the researcher's race, class, gender, and political and economic situatedness in relation to those she works with, along with attempts to take into account how these affect her research and analysis, is vital to addressing this issue. Ideally, such reflexivity implies a continual interrogation of the relations of power inherent in research relationships. Activist research builds on and extends this decolonizing move. In fact, Charles R. Hale (2007) argues that formulating explicitly activist research alliances, making our political commitments explicit up front, and maintaining the social dynamics of the research process open to an ongoing dialogue with the research subjects are simply taking "positioning" to its logical conclusion. Critical analysis that is informed by an explicit politics has to grapple with those politics overtly, rather than cede to the tendency to downplay their role. Critical analysis is continually drawn back to political grounding, whereas political strategy is continually challenged and potentially strengthened by the insights of critical analysis.

The second aspect of a decolonized anthropology involves a distinct kind of relationship with those research "subjects" / political allies, one in which they are not the "*materia prima*"³ of the research but rather are theorists of their own social processes whose knowledge differs from but is equally valid and valued as anthropological knowledge and theorizing. A collaborative engagement with research subjects, based on an explicit political alliance and shared goals, can contribute to a distinct kind of research relationship in which knowledge production is in some way shared.

This is important not only because some anthropologists wish to approach their subjects differently. Most anthropologists, certainly those who work with previously colonized peoples, confront the fact that their research subjects are neither interested in being researched for abstract purposes nor "saved" by well-intentioned gringos or any other academics, for that matter. My experience in Chiapas has been that indigenous people expect you to situate yourself—they want to know who you are, why you are there, and what you bring with you in terms of political disposition, what you plan to get out of your relationship with them, and how your work will serve their overall goals. Perhaps obviously, positioning yourself is not a strategic question of how to get access to the people and information you want but rather one of the professional ethics involved. Anthropologists today must answer ethical questions not only for themselves or in response to abstract questions on human subject review forms; such questions will in many cases be raised vigorously by the people involved in our studies.

The Rocky Road of Activist Work in Chiapas

In Chiapas in the mid-1990s, the open conflict and highly polarized political landscape made it impossible to work as a neutral researcher without defining myself in some way. My "research subjects," the people in the communities and organizations with whom I worked, would not have allowed it. And in the conflicted communities of Chiapas, it quickly became obvious that their position was, "If you aren't with us, you're against us." Without aligning yourself politically, it would thus be nearly impossible to get anyone to talk to you, being, as it were, the enemy.

Whether or not I had chosen to position myself as an activist, I would have been positioned politically by others. I had a project about human rights, in a conflicted area where rights are hotly contested and regularly violated. In the popular political imaginary, there was a generalized and definitive alignment of "human rights" with Zapatista support. All one needed to know was that you were "from human rights" (which actually involved a complex chain of relationships among the communities, the Catholic diocese of San Cristóbal, the Fray Bartolomé human rights center, NGOs, and individual activists that is analyzed in later chapters) in order to define you as "on the side of the Zapatistas." There was no "neutral observer" stance available; human rights, and hence I, were located in a very particular place within the complex configurations of power and struggle.

It was clear to me from my first days in Chiapas that I would need to define my position as a researcher and an activist, integrate this into my project, and keep it front and center throughout my research period. Beyond the practical question of whether we must ally with our research subjects in order to get the work done, and the ethical question of whether we *should*, there is also the question of what it means for anthropological practice if we don't. For those concerned with decolonizing the research relationship, an activist engagement provides a way for mutual goals to be made explicit and defined in dialogue between researcher and research subject. This does not mean that it will be an equal dialogue; relations defined in larger fields of power still determine this relationship. However, it necessitates the acknowledgment of and dialogue about those power relations in the definition of a shared project.

Shortly after beginning work in Chiapas, I took a position as the director of the San Cristóbal office of Global Exchange, a U.S.-based NGO that at the time was conducting mainly human rights observation and accompaniment work in Chiapas. My goals in doing this were several. First, I needed to ground myself in the day-to-day realities of human rights work in Chiapas. Second, this work allowed me to situate myself; I defined myself through that job as working to support indigenous rights and human rights, although I recognized that this automatically situated me as a Zapatista supporter in the eyes of many, if not most, people on all sides of the conflict (an interpretation that was not, in fact, erroneous). Third, it gave me something concrete to offer communities: my presence as an observer, or that of the volunteers from my organization, and a channel through which to get information about their human rights situations out to a larger "global" community. This was my first approach to activist research: having something to offer to the communities I was researching and simultaneously carrying out research on the same or related issues. It provided me a way to situate myself, to become immersed in the issues, and to give something back to the communities of study. I worked at Global Exchange for a year and a half, leaving shortly before the birth of my daughter in February of 1998.

Several months later, I began working as an advisor to the *Red de Defensores Comunitarios por los Derechos Humanos* (Community Human Rights Defenders' Network), which I will simply call the *Red*. This organization prepares representatives of indigenous communities in conflicted areas of the state to conduct legal defense of the rights of the people in their regions. Although it was not my original intention, the *Red* itself eventually became one of my field research sites, its *defensores* (the participants in the *Red*) becoming my research subjects. Initially, I thought of my work with the *Red* in a similar way to my work with Global Exchange—an involved way to engage my research subjects and provide them something in return for what they gave to me. But over time, I began to learn so much about the very processes I was trying to get at—the relationships among indigenous communities, this nonlocal discourse, and the legal structures of the state—that I realized the *Red* was becoming not just *one* of my sites of study but the primary one. From the *defensores* I learned why they and their regions were interested in human rights, how they understood them, what they saw as important in relation to human rights issues, what they hoped to gain from becoming human rights defenders. I saw, in action, the *defensores* become the vehicles, or bearers, of the external discourse of human rights to their communities as well as the vehicles of its redeployment. Through the *Red* I also developed an activist engagement in the community of Nicolás Ruiz, another principal site of research. Here, the mechanics of direct dialogue with community members around overlapping political goals led to insights about community identity and cultural change that I cannot be sure I would have gained in a more traditional research interaction.[4]

There was a difference between the activist research I did with Global Exchange and that with the *Red* because my work with the *Red* and my interactions with the *defensores* shaped my own vision of how I should approach the problem and what was interesting about it. My work with the *Red* also motivated me to attempt to do research and writing that are beneficial and empowering to the *defensores* and to their communities, based on their own vision of their goals and aspirations. In other words, this involved not just simultaneously doing research and activism on the same issues, but letting an engaged dialogue with research subjects help guide the project. One result of such an engagement is that the process and the end product of knowledge production are part of the "activism."

While activist research had its practical, ethical, and epistemological benefits, it also had its difficulties and quandaries. One practical issue for conducting research that was absolutely unavoidable in Chiapas was that of being positioned as a human rights activist and hence a Zapatista. If indigenous communities made this association and defined people this way, it is not hard to imagine that the federal and state governments and their respective security forces did so too. Once defined and associated with a human rights project, in some senses I became an actor in the conflict. This had the logical outcome of hindering my ability to conduct certain kinds of research, closing certain doors to me permanently, and putting my research project in constant risk of immediate termination.

A xenophobia campaign against foreigners in Chiapas was waged by the Mexican government beginning in the spring of 1997, with the detention and expulsion by the *Instituto Nacional de Migración* (INM) of ten European activists who provided human rights accompaniment to participants in a two-day march from the Northern Zone to the capital Tuxtla Gutiérrez to demand the release of indigenous Zapatista political prisoners.[5] Surveillance of foreigners and cancellation of tourist cards of foreigners found in the conflict zones continued throughout the year and accelerated intensely in early 1998, following the massacre at Acteal.[6] Between 1997 and 2000, dozens of people were summarily expelled, including anthropologists and people associated with Global Exchange. As I lay in bed recovering from a cesarean birth, people stopped by telling stories of immigration agents roaming the city of San Cristóbal on mopeds, stopping anyone who looked foreign and demanding their papers. Global Exchange became a prime target of the governmental policy of targeting foreign human rights workers, and editorials placed by the government in local newspapers accused the organization of everything from making money off the conflict to intervening in the politics of the country. Needless to say, the immigration question made doing research exceptionally difficult because of the threat of summary expulsion from the country. Once marked as a human rights worker (i.e., Zapatista), I could no longer travel freely to indigenous communities, interview any government or military sources, or have an open affiliation with any research institute.[7]

Multi-sited Ethnography

The complications of militarization, paramilitarization, and immigration restrictions as rigorous as they were arbitrary—especially the roadblocks set up by all three groups on roads throughout the state, and particularly in the Zapatista base areas—affected my choice of field sites and eventually the whole shape of my research project. At the outset, I had intended to do a community study, examining how the globalized discourse of human rights and the heavily imposed norms of the state were playing out in a local setting. I changed communities several times over the course of as many years, as the conflict spread from region to region, and militarization, then paramilitarization, then immigration control covered broader and broader swaths of the state. This was frustrating and disheartening as I tried to conduct coherent research, and on more than one occasion I despaired of ever being able to carry out my project. Yet, I found that one positive aspect of this ever-shifting field was that it gave me a strong sense of the diversity of understandings at the local level, from region to region, community to community, and even within communities. This book is not, then, an ethnography of a community, or a region, or a state. It is multi-sited, following the discourse of human rights through various terrains (Marcus 1995) and more importantly through the spaces of dialogue between them.

As various observers have noted, globalization has altered both what cultural anthropologists are concerned with and how they go about studying it (Kearney 1995; Marcus 1995). As anthropologists have trained their analytic lens on processes such as transnational capitalism, migration, diaspora, media, science and technology, and traveling forms of cultural production such as art and music, there has been a concurrent move away from traditional single-site ethnography and toward multi-sited research. Studies of deterritorialized subjects and subjectivities have proliferated, impelling anthropologists to seek "new paths of connection" and to express them on a "differently configured spatial canvas" (Marcus 1995:98). Various conceptualizations have been elaborated, from Appadurai's (1990) abstracted "scapes" to Marcus's schematic "follow the people, thing, or metaphor" (1995). The research for this book involved multiple, overlapping sites of observation, and participation, allowing me to cross-cut the inherent dichotomy of the global and local and to get at processes constituted in multiple and fractal terrains.

One principal "site" of this study, as I have said, was the *Red de Defensores Comunitarios por los Derechos Humanos*. The community of Nicolás Ruiz was another. This community from the Central Region of the state (about three hours south of San Cristóbal, most of it on a dirt road) had the advantage of not being located on the other side of a military or immigration checkpoint. An extremely conflicted community, it does have its own state police encampment, but it was possible to enter the community without passing through the camp. Intracommunity conflict, tied to the larger conflict and counterinsurgency in the state, left a death toll of over one hundred people between 1996 and 2000 and earned the municipality the dubious title "Tierra Sin Ley" (Gurguha 2000). The office of the *Presidencia Municipal, Bienes Comunales,* and the people of Nicolás Ruiz were extremely open and greatly facilitated my research there.

Some of my data are from other parts of the state, particularly the conflicted Northern Zone, with which I came into direct contact as director of Global Exchange, and later through the *Red de Defensores*. I also observed a great deal while residing in San Cristóbal, particularly dynamics within the human rights "community" and among the elite residents of San Cristóbal (*Coletos*). All of this was participant observation and contributes to my data and shapes my analysis.

For obvious reasons, it was difficult to "follow the discourse" onto the terrain of the state. I had originally intended to interview state officials from the (then governmental, now quasi-independent) National Human Rights Commission (CNDH), the attorney general's office (PGR), members of the judiciary, and party leaders and members of Congress from both official and opposition political parties, to elicit information regarding shifting state discourses regarding human rights; various "state" perceptions of international human rights work; the particular forms which the mobilization of rights claims has taken in Chiapas; and overt state responses to the reconfigurations in power relations being brought about by new forms of global-local interaction.

Unfortunately, showing up to interview them ("Hello, I'm a foreigner who's writing about human rights in Chiapas") would at that time have been—possibly quite literally—turning myself in to the authorities for expulsion. I was able to interview a representative of the state human rights commission (the CEDH) on one occasion and had informal discussions with people who worked at the CNDH. I was also able to engage in a year of legal studies at the *Universidad Autónoma de Chiapas* in San Cristóbal as part of a two-year, cross-disciplinary training and research fellowship I received from the SSRC-MacArthur Program in International Peace and Security in a Changing World.

This allowed me to gain knowledge of the Mexican legal system with regard to human rights. But more importantly, it provided me an understanding of state legal discourse regarding these rights. This allowed me to situate the interaction of globalized discourses and local actors in the framework of the discourse and legal regimes of the nation-state and to explore their dialogic interaction and mutual constitution. I also carefully followed the prolific and ever-shifting public discourse of state officials regarding human rights.

Transforming the Discipline

Of course, there are many tensions and contradictions inherent in activist research that are more complex than practical issues of this kind. What to do when research collaborators' perspective on what should be included in the analysis differs from one's own, whether our "interventions" in local processes alter them in harmful ways, and whether (or when) activist research serves to alleviate researchers' guilt about the power imbalances inherent in research relationships without resolving them are all questions each researcher must deliberate in his or her own research situation. I have written about some of these issues elsewhere (Speed 2006a). Nevertheless, despite the contradictions and dilemmas posed by activist research, it offers better possibilities for addressing the problematic nature of anthropological knowledge production than do the alternatives of continuing to rely on a nonexistent objectivity or a retrenchment in the realm of the theoretical and the textual, allowing cultural critique to stand alone as anthropology's contribution and avoiding the messier engagement with increasingly vocal and critical research subjects.

Above, I suggested that there are dual forces at work in the decolonization of the discipline: one from the researcher and one from the research subjects. I want to suggest in closing that the researchers' engaging in a politics of reflexivity, while vitally important rendering visible the power dynamics at work in anthropological research, is nevertheless not enough to move the discipline beyond the neocolonial framework it is bound by. A critical engagement with our research subjects, which makes them part of the process of knowledge production itself, is a vital component of a decolonized anthropology. The tension between political commitment and critical reflection will always exist to one extent or another. Activist research has the benefit of bringing that tension to the fore, maintaining it under scrutiny as part of the project, and thus potentially transforming it into a productive tension.

A Final Note About Names

The trust invested in me by people in the communities because of my role as activist also meant that I was given a good deal of information potentially dangerous to them should I publish it. I have tried to be careful in my writing. I have omitted any information I feel would place the people whom I worked with in danger, now or at some potential future political juncture. Following conventional anthropological practice, I have given pseudonyms to the people who spoke with me, with the exception of some public figures and those individuals who specifically requested that I use their real name. Pseudonyms always appear in quotation marks, for example, "Juan." These pseudonyms stand throughout the text to remind us that the discourse we are following is grounded in very real dynamics for the people the names represent.

1 Introduction: Human Rights and Chiapas in the Neoliberal Era

Rights save neither men nor a philosophy that is reterritorialized on the democratic State. Human rights will not make us bless capitalism.

Deleuze and Guattari (1994:107)

We do not ask the government to recognize our rights. The rights that they say we have are useless to us. Those that we are already living, our right to autonomy, does exist, even though the bad government doesn't recognize it.[1]

"Angelica"[2]

I HAD BEEN WORKING AS AN ACTIVIST ANTHROPOLOGIST[3] in Chiapas for only a short time in mid-1996 when I had a couple of conversations that sparked my interest in the questions that would later form the basis of my research. The first was a casual conversation with a colleague, sociologist and indigenous-rights activist Araceli Burguete. She was telling me about an incident a decade earlier in which she was shot in a botched assassination attempt. Her comment on the matter was, "The funny thing is, I did not think of this as a violation of my human rights. If it happened today, I would have decried this, and the NGOs (nongovernmental organizations) would have denounced it as a human rights violation. But back then, we just didn't understand things in that way."[4]

The second conversation was with a man I will call "Sebastian," a community leader from a well-organized Zapatista base area. I had just taken the position as the coordinator of the local office of Global Exchange in San Cristóbal, and he had come to introduce himself to me because, he explained, "human rights organizations support us; they protect us. We know that this is why you [meaning foreigners] are here: because our struggle is the same one; we [meaning the Zapatistas] are struggling for the human rights of indigenous peoples."[5]

As Araceli's comment suggested, even a few short years earlier, acts of political violence, a constant in the region since long before the largely indigenous

Zapatista uprising began in 1994, had come to be understood by most people in the area in a particular way—as human rights violations. And "Sebastian's" interpretation of human rights, at once a recognition of human rights organizations as a source of support, at the same time cast us as being part of a broad, unified struggle for human rights in which we were all taking part. It caught my attention that "Sebastian" framed national and international solidarity, as well as his own activities, in terms of human rights.

I had come to Chiapas following the Zapatista uprising both as an activist and as a doctoral student with an interest in indigenous resistance, social movements, and the generalized shift from class-based to identity-based forms of struggle in Latin America. Chiapas was a logical place for me to be. The Zapatista uprising that began two years before was the public launching of a social

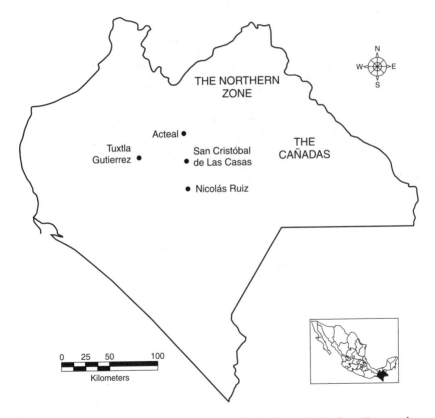

Map 1.1 Chiapas: San Cristóbal de Las Casas, Nicolás Ruiz, the Northern Zone, and the Cañadas region.

movement made up mainly of indigenous people that elaborated a complex rhetoric of nationalist, campesino, anti-neoliberal, and indigenous rights–based claims, disseminated transnationally in a remarkable use of new information and communications technologies. It had already generated much debate about its character as a "new" social movement, a "postmodern" revolution.

These conversations and others like them highlighted for me the extent to which human rights as a discourse[6] of liberation was being adopted by the left in the place of other discourses to describe all kinds of political participation, and which was also, it seemed, being incorporated by indigenous people into their understandings of their movement and their goals. Notably, however, it was not just activists and indigenous people who were wielding a discourse of human rights, as a third conversation made clear a short time later. In late 1996, I spoke with a representative of the state-level Human Rights Commission (CEDH) regarding the paramilitary violence devastating Chol communities in the Northern Zone of the state. I asked what the CEDH would do to protect the rights of those who were being violently expelled from their communities by the paramilitary groups aligned with the ruling party. "We make pamphlets," he told me. "And we may have workshops. Our job is to educate them, because they don't know anything about positive law. They don't know what human rights and individual guarantees are. They fight among themselves and they kill each other."[7] There are multiple layers to this comment, the dynamics of which I will examine in later chapters. Here, I want to point out that what might have seemed appropriate—the government engaging in education about human rights—also staked out the position of the state and its legal system as the official granter and defender of rights: not indigenous people, and not the NGOs that were mushrooming at a remarkable pace throughout the country. This mattered because it was this type of struggle over rights—particularly the discourse of human and indigenous rights—that formed that framework for the renegotiation of relations between the state and indigenous people as the state shifted its form of rule from corporatism to neoliberalism. Human rights was a discourse of state legitimation in the context of neoliberalization *and* a prominent discourse of opposition to neoliberal policies and forms of governance.

Eventually, the questions raised by those three conversations turned into the principal questions that guided the research for this book: how is the globalization of the discourse of human rights affecting local identities and forms of resistance? What is the relationship between neoliberalism and human rights?

How are different social actors appropriating the discourse of human rights and redeploying it in support of their own struggles? How do concepts of rights get redefined in that process? Over the course of nearly a decade, I have continued to work in Chiapas and focus on these questions.

Concentrating on the recent period of social conflict that began with the launching of the Zapatista uprising in 1994, I look closely at the role of human rights within that conflict. While I take as a point of departure that human rights discourses have problematic roots in Western thought and potentially suspect relationships to current global forms of power, I explore how human rights discourses are understood, appropriated, and mobilized by different actors in specific local settings in Chiapas. I examine the history and political positionalities of these actors and consider how these give shape to particular local articulations of human rights. I analyze the ways in which local engagements with human rights affect local identities and social relations as well as alter the field within which local groups interact with the state. I argue that certain local appropriations and reinterpretations reconfigure the concept of human rights in fundamental ways, and that ultimately these redeployments may be challenging to neoliberal discourses and structures of power. In its broadest sense, this book is a study of neoliberal globalization and indigenous resistance, taking Chiapas as the case study and the whole range of actors deploying human rights discourse as the research subjects. I am concerned with the ways in which local peoples, particularly indigenous peoples, are elaborating new forms of resistance to the shifting fields of power in the new global order.

Human Rights in the Chiapas Conflict

Chiapas was an excellent site for looking at these questions. Human rights violations and human rights defense work did not suddenly materialize in Chiapas with the uprising in 1994. For decades, human rights violations had been extensive, as local power holders and the state engaged in repressive tactics (Amnesty International 1986; Human Rights Watch 1997). Human rights as a discourse had also been present since the mid-1980s. In processes discussed at length in Chapter 2, human rights discourse gained a foothold in Chiapas beginning in the 1980s through the work of the Catholic Diocese of San Cristóbal de Las Casas on behalf of the thousands of Guatemalan refugees who poured into Chiapas fleeing genocidal state violence, and of protestant organizers in defense of the rights of indigenous people violently expelled from their highlands communities due to religious or political dissent (CNDH 1995; Kovic 2005).

However, from January 1994 on, there was a change in both the form and the intensity of human rights abuses and human rights activism. The start of the uprising marked the commencement of a dramatic incursion of nonlocal actors into the indigenous communities in areas designated as "conflict zones." This incursion included the various security forces of the state including the Mexican federal army, state police, and federal police, who set up camps and occupied communities. Such militarization, and the paramilitarization that followed, brought about increases in the number and types of human rights violations. The flow of nonlocal actors into communities also included a range of activists and organizations endeavoring to monitor the response of the Mexican government and its security forces to the uprising, including permanent peace camps to provide constant accompaniment in occupied communities. The increased interaction between members of indigenous communities, various state agents and apparatuses, and national and international human-rights activists has made Chiapas a unique site for exploring the relationship between "the global," "the local," and the nation-state,[8] and the articulation of human rights and indigenous resistance. Furthermore, because much of this interaction took place on a terrain marked by human rights—as a discourse of liberation by local actors, as a mode of social control by agents of the state, and as a unifying theme for activists and others in civil society—human rights constitutes an axis crossing through a variety of social processes.

Over twelve years of shifting conflict and political action, the Zapatistas and their base supporters have maintained their movement as a fundamental actor on the Mexican political landscape. Though the movement was local, their demands for democracy, social justice, and human dignity resonated for many throughout Mexico and the world. By effectively mobilizing "global discourses"—particularly of human and indigenous rights—they galvanized a broad transnational movement of solidarity and human rights activists to support them. In fact, Chiapas in many senses has become the quintessential "globalized movement" against oppression and injustice in the current context of neoliberal globalization.

This is in part because the movement was spurred to action by Mexico's entry into the new global order emerging in the wake of the Cold War. During the preceding seven decades, Mexico's ruling party, the *Partido Revolucionario Institucional* (PRI), had consolidated its rule through a corporatist relation with its populace. The authoritarian, nationalist state incorporated and regulated different (potentially oppositional) segments of the population, circumscribing their ability to challenge state authority by establishing the state as the source of their legitimacy and livelihood.

This corporatist tendency developed in tandem with strong assimilationist policies designed to make Indians into Mexicans. Policies of the early post-Revolution governments sought to consolidate the nation by creating a "national consciousness" and through cultural homogenization (Mallon 1994). Assimilationist policies and the national discourse of *mestizaje*, or racial mixing, worked to redefine them and draw them into a homogeneous "Mexican" population. The emergent national discourse of *la raza cósmica* (the cosmic race), a blend of Indian and Spaniard into one national *mestizo* culture and identity, rendered Indians by definition a part of Mexico's past. In the national imagination, indigenous peoples contributed to the "racial mix" that, along with Spanish people, constitutes the current ethnicity of the Mexican population, but were no longer understood to exist as peoples who maintain their languages, cultures, and communities.[9] The state agency charged with indigenous affairs, the National Indigenist Institute (INI), from its founding in 1948 through the late 1970s, had as its principal mission to assimilate indigenous peoples (Hernández Castillo 2001a).[10] In some areas where *mestizaje* had less impact—notably the Highlands of Chiapas—the state effectively appropriated local indigenous power and authority structures, linking them to state power and the welfare of the ruling party and creating what Rus has called "Revolutionary Institutional Communities" (see Rus 1994b).

But as Mexico began to shift to new economic models, new forms of rule needed to be established. Corporatism was state-heavy, entailing state intervention in the economy and significant spending on maintaining corporatist entities and social services. These aspects of state corporatism were incompatible with the neoliberal mandate to downsize the state, limiting its role in the economy and reducing investment in mediating social inequality. The neoliberal restructuring begun in the 1970s and accelerated during the regime of Carlos Salinas de Gortari (1988–94) effectively brought Mexico into the emergent global order and ended decades of corporatist rule. These reforms included the opening up of industries nationalized after the Revolution to foreign investment, ending state protections on agricultural products, and terminating agrarian reform. This meant, for many, the end of any hope of balancing out social inequalities through direct petitioning of the state, the demise of hope for land, of subsistence agriculture as a way of life—in sum, the termination of the established relationship with the national state. The same set of reforms signaled this change in other ways, recognizing for the first time the pluricultural composition of the nation, a discursive shift that led away from agrarian redistribution and toward state multiculturalism (processes that will be discussed more thoroughly in the following chapters).

The Zapatista uprising was, in many ways, a recognition by indigenous communities that the terms of rule had changed and an assertion of their intention to play an active role in the renegotiation of their relationship to the state in the context of neoliberal globalization. These factors are a part of what cast the Zapatistas as the new champions of the struggle against the restructuring of power in globalized form. But it was also the manner in which they carried out this struggle, mobilizing "the global" to their own defense in the context of heated repression from the state.

Despite the incipient shifts apparent in the forms of governance, the ruling party responded to the uprising with its long-established practice: when cooptation fails, step up to repression. But the government was unable to end the uprising, despite dramatic militarization (by some estimates, close to 70,000 troops of the Mexican Army were stationed in Chiapas at the height of militarization in 1998) and low-intensity warfare, including paramilitarization (as many as twenty pro–ruling party paramilitary groups emerged, resulting in hundreds killed, tens of thousands internally displaced, and hundreds of political prisoners in just a few years) (CIEPAC 1999). The movement's survival is due, in part, to the fact that the Zapatistas globalized their movement. They have done this in several ways—most importantly for this study through the mobilization of globalized discourses such as human rights, women's rights, and indigenous rights.

By staying in action, the Zapatista uprising has had significant effects on both the national and the global arenas in the course of the last ten years. On the global terrain, the Zapatista uprising contributed to consolidating a disarticulated left that was in search of a new form of struggle for social justice in the emerging global order. Despite the many limitations on its advances, the movement continues to exist and to inspire many to resist oppression and injustice in Mexico and elsewhere in the world.

In Mexico, the uprising challenged the PRI's hegemonic rule and contributed to a serious legitimation crisis, which by the year 2000 had resulted in the electoral victory of a non-PRI presidential candidate, Vicente Fox, of the right-of-center *Partido de Acción Nacional* (PAN). However, despite some initial hopes, the Fox government was not any more effective than its predecessor in meeting the demands of the Zapatistas. While disappointing, the failure of the Fox administration to respond to Zapatista demands was not surprising, as the PAN is to the right of the PRI in terms of its political, economic, and social policies. It is even more wedded than was the PRI to the neoliberal capitalism as an ideology and as a practice.

Also, the Zapatista movement contributed to bringing indigenous peoples into the national consciousness and indigenous rights onto the national agenda, where they had long been excluded through assimilationism and the myth of *mestizaje*. The uprising and its aftermath, particularly the 1995–96 negotiation of the San Andrés Accords on Indigenous Rights and Culture, also gave impetus to the consolidation of a national indigenous movement. The accords themselves represented a dramatic shift in the playing field, one in which representatives of the federal government sat down at the negotiating table with indigenous people to hammer out agreements on a range of issues, including constitutional recognition of indigenous autonomy. While the signed accords were later ignored by the federal government and the much-delayed legislation for constitutional reform on indigenous rights resulted in 2001 only in a law emptied of significant content (these processes are discussed in more detail in Chapters 2 and 7), it is nevertheless important to remember what a dramatic departure from previous state dealings with indigenous peoples their negotiation represented.

Perhaps most important for our central concerns in this book, by staying in action for over a decade, the Zapatista movement has had time to develop and put into practice its own conceptualizations of human and indigenous rights, its own autonomy, and its own form of resistance that is challenging to established power relations both with the state and with global capital. This resistance is powerful, I will argue in this book, not because it is backed by the guns of the Zapatista Army (which were always limited in any case), and not, or at least not only, because the movement has globalized by appropriating globalized discourses. Their resistance is powerful because they have appropriated and redeployed those discourses in new forms, based on their own political subjectivities and goals.

Conceptualizing Human Rights: From Western Imperialism to Global Dialogues

What does it mean to reconceptualize human rights? The concept of human rights, despite its fixity in today's international legal regimes, has been much debated in philosophy, law, and even anthropology. The concept, in its current internationally accepted form of "universal" rights, has been particularly vexing for anthropology. Anthropology's engagement with universal human rights has been marked by the discipline's "persistent concern with identifying and valorizing cultural difference" (V. Adams 2002:81), in other words, recognizing that different cultures conceived of such questions in distinct ways and that none was "more right" than another. Cultural relativism has been an important mode of thought in anthropology since the days of Franz Boas, Ruth Benedict, and Margaret Mead. This relativism has often led anthropologists to reject the appropriateness of judgments about specific cultural practices from a universal framework, arguing instead that they could be understood only in the context of the internal cultural logics of the social groups to which they pertain (for discussion, see Donnelly 1989; Downing and Kushner 1988). Indeed, a relativist position was officially adopted by the Executive Board of the American Anthropological Association (AAA) in the canonical AAA Statement on Human Rights (1947). In this document, penned by Melville Herskovits, the association expressly rejected anthropological participation in the U.N. human rights activities (the Universal Declaration of Human Rights was ratified the following year) and asserted its view of the primacy of culturally defined norms over universal norms, which would inevitably be an imposition of Western values.

This last point is significant. Anthropology's engagement with human rights has been troubled not so much by the philosophical contradictions inherent in universalism and relativism as by the potential cultural imperialism of universalizing "Western," liberal cultural values to indigenous and "non-Western" societies (An'Naím 1992; Bell 2000; deGaay Fortman 1987; Pannikar 1992).[11] Conscious that the concept of universal human rights is historically rooted in the Western philosophical and legal traditions, many have considered universal human rights standards as "an artifact of Western cultural traditions raised to the status of normativity" (Merry 1997:28). Merry thus suggests that this relativism was not apolitical but rather reflected a form of anti-imperialism: "The parallels with imperialism have been too close for anthropological comfort. . . . These anthropologists wanted to avoid ethnocentrism . . . an approach that made sense in an imperialist world" (1997:28).

As the discourse of human rights globalized, it was understood by some as an ever more pernicious form of imperialism, now with a global reach. As several analysts have noted, this debate has been problematic both practically and theoretically for many anthropologists, who found themselves limited in their ability to respond to violations of the human rights of their research "subjects" and unable to theoretically engage a discourse which was becoming ever more globalized and thus increasingly significant in the areas where they work (V. Adams 2002; Doughty 1988; Merry 1997; Messer 1993, 1995; Nagengast 1994; Nagengast and Turner 1997).

By the mid-1980s, the corpus of research on human rights was growing quickly, and important articles took note and called for more such research (see Messer 1993, 1995; Nagengast and Turner 1997).[12] The growth in rights research was undoubtedly a product of the dynamic expansion of the discourse of human rights throughout the world. With the fall of the Berlin Wall, the political narratives of socialism and communism also lost currency. This was the juncture at which the discourse of human rights, along with that of neoliberal democracy, truly globalized. It is often stated that human rights is an enlightenment discourse that gained broad currency after World War II with the United Nations Universal Declaration (Brysk 2002; Donnelly 2003 [1989]). However, the discourse did not become truly globalized until the post–Cold War period, when it spread on a par with the discourse of neoliberal democracy. Human rights were part and parcel of the "end of history," the ultimate triumph of a certain brand of democracy in the world.[13] Precisely as the triumphalist march of neoliberal capitalist democracy moved forward over the ruins of socialist projects and authoritarian governments, rights struggles became the primary form of contestation to state power and social injustice. In the void left by the grand political narratives for social change, "rights" became the terrain on which virtually all movements for social justice and equality were waged (see Grandin 2004). This pushed virtually all political struggle into the legal realm, so much so that within a decade analysts would state, "So saturated by legalism is contemporary political life, that it is often difficult to imagine alternative ways of deliberating about and pursuing justice" (Brown and Halley 2002:19).

The transition from resistance discourses based on ideals of social transformation to discourses based on identity and law has been a concern of anthropologists and other social theorists. While some have argued convincingly that identity and rights-based struggles can generate important social change (Alvarez et al. 1998), others have highlighted the regulatory force of rights and the manner in which rights legitimate and support existing forms of power, whether those of the state or of the capitalist system (Brown 1995; Gledhill 1997; Goodale 2005). This dual role of rights has led Santos (1998; Santos and Rodríguez-Garavito 2005) to theorize the unique position of human rights in the "tension between social regulation and social emancipation." Highlighting the duality, Merry (2006) recently demonstrated how human rights law is used to force states to be accountable in the defense of certain rights while at the same time reinforcing and expanding state power.

These studies go beyond the paralyzing universalism-relativism debate, taking the globalization of human rights as a fact and exploring the complex articulations of human rights and neoliberalism in the current juncture of global capitalism. But in a sense the questions are the same as the ones asked by analysts in the older debates. All are concerned with the effects of discourses of law—by definition discourses of power—on subordinated peoples, and the extent to which those individuals and groups have agency (the ability to act according to one's will) in their engagements with such discourses. Are local conceptions of rights and justice erased by the arrival of human rights discourse? Are people constructed as political subjects by the discourse in ways that serve state power? These questions are particularly salient in Chiapas, where the shifting relationship between the state and indigenous people and, indeed, the shifting forms of capitalism are taking place in a discursive framework of rights.

Neoliberal Capitalism, the State, and Human Rights

Though it is globalized as a discourse and firmly rooted in international legal regimes, the concept of human rights remains inseparable from the nation-state. Human rights are, as Wilson states, "a product of the historical process of the rise of the modern nation-state, through which the development of apparatuses and technologies of violence and individualistic forms of political economy created the conditions within which human rights became possible and necessary" (R. Wilson 1997:10). State violence remains the most widespread form of human-rights violation and state institutions most often are the site within which contestation through rights claims takes place. The state and its institutions remain the arena within which most rights claims are made and state legal systems are, at the present time, the only juridical bodies with enforcement power in the adjudication of such claims.

Much attention has been placed on the relative decline in the sovereignty of the nation-state in processes of globalization. Various analysts have signaled the ways in which globalization implies an erosion of the nation-state, its autonomy undermined by the transnationalization of capital, culture, and even civil society. The power and control of nation-states have been limited in some spheres as global ruling bodies emerge, as capital escapes the reach of particular national laws and restrictions, and as the subjectivities of "the ruled" are increasingly deterritorialized or transnationalized. But states are also being reconfigured in relation to new social and power relations in globalization (Basch et al. 1993; Guehenno 1995; Hardt 1998). This reconfiguration process is notable in Latin America, where states have neoliberalized, adjusting to the needs of rule in the global era.

Neoliberalization, in the minimalist definition, entails the restructuring of the economy to limit state intervention in order to provide a "free" market. Common elements of such restructuring are the elimination of state subsidies to domestic industries, reduction of trade barriers, and the elimination of restrictions on foreign investment in national resources and industries. Structural adjustment policies, long advocated by international financial bodies such as the World Bank and the International Monetary Fund, require the reduction of social welfare and assistance programs as a cost-cutting, state-reducing measure. Thus the state must downsize its social welfare undertakings and remove all restrictions on the economy designed to protect those citizens with fewer resources, a process epitomized by the "structural adjustment" measures. The shrinking state can no longer mediate social inequality through welfare and social services or through the maintenance of corporatist agencies that served to keep populations invested in the well-being of the government in power. Corporatist rule is incompatible with neoliberalism, which requires the state to retreat from its role in social mediation and leave relations between groups within society largely to be defined by market forces (Gill 2000).

How, then, does the state control its population? State divestment of responsibility for the mediation of social inequality functions within the "cultural logics" of late capitalism (Jameson 1991). These "logics" have many important attributes, chief among them notions of managerialism, entrepreneurship, self-help, and forms of citizenship that emphasize self-regulation and responsibility (Postero 2001). In what Foucault termed "governmentality," the rationalities of neoliberal governance are imbued throughout the social body (Deleuze 1994; Foucault 1991). The self-regulating populace then controls itself, engaging in appropriate behaviors (including acceptable forms of resistance). Nikolas Rose describes the process of the emergence of "late capitalism": "The relation of the state and the people was to take a different form: the former would maintain the infrastructure of law and order; the latter would promote individual and national well-being by their responsibility and enterprise" (Rose 1999:139). Rose thus suggests that there are two aspects of neoliberal governance, subject formation and controlling law. One of the neoliberal state's primary functions is ensuring that the market can and does operate freely. One of the principal ways that the state does this is by maintaining "stability," in particular through the maintenance of law and order—one of the reasons the "construction of rule of law" has played a vital role in state reorganization in Latin America (Seider forthcoming). But law also provides a space for subject making, often in ways that allow the state to be a neutral or invisible agent in that subject construction.

One way this happens is through the intervention of intermediary bodies, especially NGOs. In the context of the state devolution of responsibility for mediating social relations to civil society, NGOs have emerged and flourished. A variety of theorists have suggested that NGOs fall within the same neoliberal logic, taking over the state's managerial role (Feldman 1997; Guehenno 1995; Hardt 1998; Joseph 2002). In Latin America, the process of neoliberalization has entailed leaving behind former strategies of governance, from authoritarianism to corporatism. Thus, the rise of NGOs is tied in popular conceptions to processes of democratization and increased political freedom and participation by citizens. But even as the flourishing of NGOs has opened spaces of participation within which neoliberal policy might be contested, NGOs are nevertheless deeply informed by the logics of neoliberal governance. NGOs, in fact, often reproduce these logics and do the work of disseminating them to diverse segments of the population through training programs, workshops, and other undertakings which have at their root conceptions of rational, self-managing citizens (Postero 2001).

How do human rights fit into this picture? Because of the now fairly obvious negative impact that these policies and practices have had on large numbers of people (as reflected in the growing poverty and income disparity),[14] some authors have suggested that the parallel spread of neoliberalism and the discourse of human rights is due either to a response to increasing need as the welfare state is left behind (Donnelly 2003 [1989]) or to horizontally spreading resistance to the harsher consequences of neoliberalization (Ignatieff 2001).[15] These theorists understand the relationship between the globalization of human rights and that of neoliberalism to be fundamentally antagonistic, a process in which neoliberal policies, being antithetical to human rights, create conditions of increasing oppression, and civil society increasingly turns to human rights discourse and doctrine to defend itself. Thus the fact that human rights has emerged as an important discourse of resistance movements all over the world is understood as a response to the negative impacts of neoliberal globalization. Quite often, this conceptualization is shared by human rights activists. Such theorizing tends to reproduce the positive/negative dichotomy characteristic of much work on globalization, suggesting that there is "bad globalization" and "good globalization," as the "from above" variety is most often critiqued (global capital and the institutions created to defend and advocate for it such as the World Bank, the International Monetary Fund, etc.) and the "from below" variety is often celebrated (transnational advocacy networks, new social movements, etc.).

It is undoubtedly tempting to view the process of the spread of human rights discourse and practice as a dual process: one in which democratizing and neoliberalizing governments necessarily adopt the discourse, and a correlated grassroots process in which civil society organizes to challenge the state, and particularly in the language of human rights (Donnelly 2003 [1989]; Falk 2002; Ignatieff 2001). While this may in fact be the case, or some aspect of it may be, it is important to interrogate these relationships more thoroughly to avoid falling into the dangerous assumption that struggles for rights are automatically contestatory to state power, that when they come "from below" they invariably challenge neoliberalism as a project, and that the propagation of and local appropriation of such discourses will always or necessarily result in greater social justice. Some, in fact, may be exactly the form of acceptable resistance that neoliberal states have purposefully created the space for.

Indigenous Rights and Neoliberal Multiculturalism

The spread of the discourse of human rights has given new form to indigenous resistance throughout the Americas. The emergence of human rights discourse in Latin American states coincided with events such as the organizing around the 500-year anniversary of the "discovery" of America by Europeans, peace processes in several countries, the decline of the socialist alternative, and significant indigenous uprisings (e.g., Chiapas). In this context, human rights discourse provided a new moral language and legal framework for pursuing indigenous claims (Dean and Levi 2003; Seider 2003; Stavenhagen 2003; R. Wilson 1997). The emergence of indigenous rights movements in a number of countries is one of the most important dynamics in Latin America today (Bengoa 2000; Jackson and Warren 2005; Postero and Zamosc 2004; Warren 1998; Warren and Jackson 2002; Yashar 1998). As with human rights struggles more generally, it is easy to view indigenous rights movements as fundamentally challenging to the state and anti-neoliberal in their orientation. After all, the demand for group rights challenges the individualist basis of liberal systems, collective landholding hinders privatization, and so on. Yet, as with human rights, the relationship may be slightly more problematic.

In the 1990s, in tandem with neoliberal economic reforms, some Latin American states adopted a multiculturalist discourse, and constitutional reforms recognizing indigenous rights were undertaken in a number of countries, among them Bolivia, Ecuador, Colombia, Brazil, and Mexico (Assies, van der Haar, and Hoekema 2000; Van Cott 2000). The "politics of recognition" model of multiculturalism entails state recognition of the legitimacy of claims to differential identity of minority groups, and potentially some rights based on belonging to that group (Kymlicka 1996; Taylor 1994). The multicultural constitutional reforms are often understood as a highly positive change brought about by the push "from below" that indigenous movements represent. But while the indigenous movements have undoubtedly played an important role in forcing the states' hand (and in some cases do provide challenges to neoliberal logics and policies), the multicultural indigenous rights reforms are not *only* responses to indigenous mobilization and demands. They are also intimately linked to processes of neoliberalization (Postero 2006).

Multiculturalism as state policy in Latin America is also part of the larger neoliberal project, which as we have seen encompasses both economic restructuring and new governance practices. It entails a shift from previous assimilationist approaches to governing diversity, to a new recognition of distinct groups within society, and the allowance of some measure of self-regulation for these groups. A number of analysts have shown how multicultural reforms work to reinforce the underlying goals of neoliberal economic and political strategies and limit the force of indigenous organizing (Gustafson 2002; Hale 2002; Postero 2001, 2006). For example, Charles R. Hale (2002) suggests that the discourses of multiculturalism, in this case in the hands of the dominant bloc in Guatemala, may serve to limit the terms and the potential of indigenous resistance. In Hale's analysis, "neoliberal multiculturalism"[16] functions to limit the challenge of collectivities, in part by dividing indigenous people, articulating them as those who are "acceptable" and those who are "unacceptable" to the state. More than just divide and conquer, such policies lead indigenous people to invest their energies in demonstrating their authentic belonging to the recognized group and away from focusing on real inequalities in Guatemalan society that need redress.[17]

Postero (2001) has demonstrated how in Bolivia the "indigenous subjects of neoliberalism" get constituted through the state's multicultural practices, which work to structure indigenous political participation in ways that imbue them with rationalities proper for adequate—and acquiescent—integration into economic markets. Postero shows how state policies and international NGO-sponsored trainings inculcate concepts of individuality and self-regulation. Multiculturalism thus cedes rights to indigenous people, but with the effect of remaking them as subjects less likely to frontally challenge neoliberal economic and political policies.

Even the recognition of collective group rights, often understood to be fundamentally opposed to liberal individualism, may be an integral part of neoliberal subject formation and the construction of neoliberal rule. Gill (2000) argues that in democratization processes the use of repression and force to maintain political power undermines legitimacy and credibility, making it necessary for states to find other ways to gain legitimacy and maintain control. To do so, they may increasingly deploy political strategies and discourses of inclusiveness to draw in different segments of the population. The neoliberal mandate for reduced state intervention in social life makes necessary the participation of all subjects in the work of managing and regulating society, and thus renders both inclusive policies and processes of subject formation the priorities of rule. The granting of collective rights may function within this logic by potentially rendering large groups of people beholden to the state, reinforcing the state's position as the power that can grant and take away rights, legitimating the legal system that upholds state power, and finally, by creating a framework for groups within society to engage in limited self-governance (without ceding state power).

In 1992, Mexico certainly seemed to be on the same neoliberal multicultural track as many other Latin American countries. Vying openly for a privileged place in the new global order, the constitutional reforms implemented in preparation for the North American Free Trade Agreement (NAFTA) included changes to Article 4, which was altered to recognize that Mexico was a "multicultural nation." The "positive" aspect of recognizing pluriculturality in this packet of reforms has sometimes been perceived as contradictory, or the one good (if limited) element in a set of modifications that was largely quite negative for indigenous people.[18] Like the analysis that human rights are the "good" side of globalization processes, this perspective renders multiculturalism something to embrace, disentangling it from the "bad" neoliberal economic reforms. In fact, many in Mexico, including indigenous groups and others struggling for social change, strongly advocate for multicultural reform—understood in this instance as a reorganization of society in ways that allow recognition of and respect for cultural difference. But considering the close relationship of these new recognitions of cultural difference with the neoliberal project, multiculturalism as a goal of social struggle becomes considerably more problematic.

Of course, not all indigenous people are pursuing or interpreting their rights in this way. Notably, the Zapatistas' relationship to state reform has been limited and cautious, despite their pursuit of constitutional reform. And since the legislative debacle that this reform resulted in, they have advocated a form of indigenous rights that is not granted by the state and is challenging to, rather than legitimating of, state power (this is the subject of Chapter 7).

Indigenous People and Human Rights: Dialogic Engagements

As we have seen, anthropological debates about human rights share a common concern with cultural studies debates about the effects of globalization processes: how global discourses affect local cultures. Similarly, though from a different perspective, analyses of the effects of neoliberal globalization and the neoliberal multicultural state are concerned with how local subjectivities are formulated through discourses of power. Anthropologist Veena Das has asserted that globalization does not necessarily mean universalization. A historicized and in-depth look at these dynamics in Chiapas supports this assertion. While the discourse is relatively new in Chiapas and its usage now nearly obligatory, what we see on the ground is an appropriation and rearticulation of the concept based on local histories and political subjectivities. This does not mean, of course, that there are not effects. In adopting and utilizing the discourse of rights, in many cases there is a reshaping of local identities and practices. However, this is not to say that local subjectivities are determined by global and state discourses: it is clear that indigenous communities are not passive receivers of predatory globalizing "Western" discourses which overwhelm their cultures and identities, nor are they simply products of state effects. What I will show throughout the book is that there is a good deal of agency involved in that engagement. Indigenous people actively take part in the dual process of reconstituting globalized discourses and reasserting local identities in the context of struggle and negotiation with the Mexican state. In these reassertions, they also alter the discourse of rights in ways that can be reactionary, progressive, or radically challenging to the discourses and structures of power within which they are articulated.

In trying to conceptualize these processes of interaction, I have found some concepts adopted from Mikhail Bakhtin helpful, particularly the notion of dialogic interactions, or "dialogisms." Bakhtin (1981) argued that every speech act implied a dialogic process, a response to others. Our discourse exists only in the context of previous or alternative discourses and is in dialogue with them. Mannheim and Tedlock (1995) usefully apply this to culture, arguing that cultural systems and practices are constantly produced, reproduced, and revised in dialogues among their members and in dialogue with other cultures and cultural expressions.

I argue throughout this book that local mobilizations of the globalized discourse of human rights are products of this kind of complex dialogic interaction. The appropriation by local groups of global discourses is not an acritical and mechanical process, but a dialogic and creative one, in which "local" people participate actively, bringing in their local histories, understandings, and goals (which are already the products of such interaction). I offer this as a counter to the argument that they are the victims, and their cultures the casualties, of predacious global discourses. In particular in Chapters 3 and 4, I consider how cultural understandings and identities of various groups have emerged and shifted over time in dialogue with the differing discourses of changing interlocutors, principally the state, actors associated with the Zapatista movement, and human rights activists. In Chapter 3, we see how such dialogic engagements play out, resulting in vastly distinct understandings and usages of the human rights based on distinct local histories and political subjectivities. Chapter 4 considers how one community's engagement with the discourses and external actors involved with human and indigenous rights contributed to reshaping its identity and reformulating its resistance in particular ways.

Internal Dialogisms: Collective and Individual Rights

Positing the "local" community against "external" actors suggests an internal unity that rarely exists in the indigenous communities of Chiapas. Such renderings obscure internal wrestling over the ongoing processes of reshaping culture and identity. That is, culture and identity are continuously reformulated not only in relation to outside actors and discourses but also in internal dialogues between members.

One area where internal contentions have played out in human rights terms has been around issues of individual and collective rights. The introduction of human rights discourse has in some areas meant the introduction of a discourse of individual rights where no such concept previously existed (or at least no such concept was incorporated into community norms). One good example of this is the issue of women's rights. In most indigenous communities until quite recently, women understood their roles to be defined in relation to collectivities: the family, the community, and so on. The notion that an individual woman had rights she could assert against her family's or community's demands scarcely existed. Women could go to community authorities to try to pressure an abusive husband or in other family conflicts, but rarely did women assert rights defined and adjudicated outside the community context. Many women told me that the Women's Revolutionary Laws, a list of basic women's human rights issued by the Zapatistas at the time of the uprising, was the first they had ever heard of such a concept.

At the same time, in Chiapas and elsewhere, the indigenous rights movement has made strong claims to collective rights, based on the priority of maintaining their *usos y costumbres* (traditional practices and customs). In the autonomy debate, many have suggested that these *usos y costumbres* are not generally democratic (in the Western liberal theory sense) and often are violatory of individual rights, especially those of women. Thus group cultural rights are positioned against individual gender rights in both academic writings and public discourse. In this debate, the cultural rights of collectivities come into conflict with the individual rights of specific members of the group when collectively defined norms are violated by individual desires or actions. Whose right should take precedence, the individual's right to freedom of choice or the collectivity's right to defend its cultural norms? Globalized human rights discourse largely remains "contingent on notions of subjectivity that are primarily individualist" (V. Adams 2002:401) and consequently in the debates among liberal political theorists, even those advocating a politics of recognition, the individuals' rights prevail (see, e.g., Kymlicka 1997). More important, the state has mobilized individual rights as a way to curb collective autonomous practices (Speed and Collier 2000a). In Chapter 5, I explore this question through the lens of a conflict among women's groups in the community of Nicolás Ruiz, suggesting that in many cases indigenous women are rejecting the "benevolent" hand of the state in protecting their rights against their culture and are choosing instead to struggle from within their cultural context to effect change in gender norms and practice.

Tools as Weapons: Identity, Rights, and Indigenous Resistance

Thus, while I argue that globalization is opening spaces for new forms of resistance, it should be clear that identity, diversity, and rights-based resistance are not in and of themselves necessarily something to celebrate. They may, in fact, be so closely tied to the globalization of neoliberal capitalism that their existence—their discourses of resistance—serve to support it, providing controllable outlets for social dissent at the same time that they reinscribe its logics.

Yet, the extent to which these processes of hegemony building and subject formation are effective has yet to be established. There are continued challenges to the state from indigenous people even where the most "progressive" and the most "neoliberal" reforms have been implemented. Notable in this respect is Bolivia, where despite extraordinary multicultural reforms in recent years, mobilizations against the privatization of water and gas led by the indigenous movement paralyzed the country in different moments, leading finally to the fall of President Sánchez de Lozada (Postero 2004). In December 2005, Evo Morales was elected president in Bolivia, making him the first indigenous president in Latin America. My research in Chiapas also suggests that resistance is not so easily containable. In Chapters 6 and 7, I explore the ways that discourses that are products of hegemonic ideologies—such as human rights—can turn into counter-hegemonic discourses when brought to bear in the right circumstances ("Every tool is a weapon if you hold it right").

Book-at-a-Glance

In Chapter 2, I look at the history of the concept of human rights in Chiapas, from the Catholic Church's liberation theology beginning in the 1970s to the rise of NGOs in the 1980s and to the Zapatista uprising of the 1990s. I am particularly concerned in Chapter 2 with tracking the roots of different conceptions of human rights and relating them to current complexities of understandings among different groups involved in the conflict, including the state, paramilitary groups, and Zapatista supporters.

Chapter 3 problematizes the globalization of the discourse of human rights, considering the implications of its origins in Western Enlightenment–era understandings as well as its current comfortable fit within ideologies of neoliberal capitalism, for indigenous people in Chiapas. I explore the divergent uses of the discourse of human rights in the Chiapas conflict and their dialogic emergence in relation to distinct historical experiences and political positionalities.

Chapter 4 explores the effects of these dialogic engagements on community identity and resistance. It takes, as a case in point, the community of Nicolás Ruiz, an internally divided and highly conflictive town and municipality in the central region of the state. In Nicolás Ruiz, where people ceased to call themselves indigenous decades ago, indigenous identity is reemerging. I explore the recent historical experience of Nicolás Ruiz to show how its discourse of ethnic identity has been constructed in dialogue with the discourses of other social groupings, including the state, as well as the EZLN (*Ejército Zapatista de Liberación Nacional*, the Zapatista National Liberation Army) and human rights activists, and the discourse of human and indigenous rights that has increased in prominence since the Chiapas conflict began.

In Chapter 5, I explore the intersection of human rights and gender, addressing the debate regarding collective assertions of rights (as indigenous people) and the rights of individuals within that collectivity (such as women). It has been argued that the collective assertion of the right to defend "traditional" cultures is in conflict with the individual rights of members of the group that may be violated by those traditions. Considering the situation of women in Nicolás Ruiz, as well as women associated with the Zapatista movement in other parts of the state, I argue that indigenous women are pushing beyond the theoretical dichotomy of individual and collective rights by insisting on defending their communities' right to define and maintain their customs, even as they work to redefine aspects of those customs which are oppressive. This chapter also problematizes the concept of community as homogeneous, suggesting that questions of "rights" are contested and negotiated within communities as well as with external social actors.

In Chapter 6, I turn to the question of the implications of the origins and nature of global rights discourses, and the local diversity they produce, for the forms of resistance that base themselves in these discourses. I ask whether such resistances are ultimately bound within hegemonic globalizing discourses and constrained to forms of resistance that reinscribe them. I look here at the experience of the *Red de Defensores Comunitarios por los Derechos Humanos* and argue that this project and the larger movement for autonomy of which it is a part are redeploying globalizing discourses in ways that ultimately subvert the global order of power. I return to the argument about dialogic interaction, arguing that rights-based discourses and the forms of resistance they engender are shaped by relationships of domination and are formulated and reformulated in an ongoing dialogue with discourses of power. I highlight the ways in which, through what they bring to that dialogue, they also have the potential to challenge those relations of power and domination.

Chapter 7 builds on the discussion in Chapter 6, examining the Zapatista *Juntas de Buen Gobierno* (Good Governance Councils) formed in August 2004 in the Zapatista autonomous regions. The *Juntas* are an example of how, in the absence of possibilities for constructive dialogue with the state aimed at translating human and indigenous rights into concrete and effective policies, new forms of local governance are being created in order to exercise these rights. In the process, the actors involved are redefining concepts such as "autonomy" and "rights" as existing prior to and regardless of their recognition by the state. The Zapatistas' assertion is that these rights exist in their *exercise*, not their establishment in the legal regimes of the state. By eliminating the state as the external referent for rights, such conceptual reframings are challenging not only to the state but also to liberal conceptualizations of rights and their relationship to the law. The chapter concludes that people in the Zapatista autonomous municipalities are appropriating globalized discourses such as human and indigenous rights, reconfiguring them based on their own experiences and needs, and re-presenting them in ways that challenge the logics of the neoliberalizing state.

In Chapter 8, I conclude by summarizing the arguments made in the preceding chapters regarding the questions of globalization as homogenization/diversity; how such diversity emerges in dialogue with discourses of the state and "the global"; and how the forms of identity engendered by rights-based resistance intersect and come into contradiction; and I will consider in broader terms the overarching question regarding resistance in globalization: is rights-based resistance (and all resistance?) bound within the hegemonic "globalized" discourses which support the very system of oppression and relations of domination they seek to contest? That is, do they, in the very act of resisting, reinscribe the logics of the power they oppose? I argue that, while power is everywhere and imbued throughout the social body, resistance is coterminous with power. In the current context of globalization, resistance always has the potential, through the constitutive power of social struggle, to challenge sovereign power by utilizing the tools at hand and asserting alternative logics.

2 Global Discourses on the Local Terrain: Grounding Human Rights in Chiapas

> Juridical rights and juridical systems always refer to something other than themselves. Through the evolution and exercise of right, they point toward the material condition that defines their purchase on social reality.
>
> *Hardt and Negri (2001:22)*

IT WAS A RAINY AFTERNOON in San Cristóbal de Las Casas, a torrential rain that turned the streets into rivers and washed up under the doors in thin waves. The weather suited our mood, as we sat in the office of the Community Human Rights Defenders Network gloomily analyzing and discussing the Law on Indigenous Rights and Culture recently approved by the Mexican Congress. We were grim. The law set indigenous rights back more than a decade, to before the signature and ratification of the ILO Convention 169 by Mexico in 1991. "Celerina," a young Tzeltal woman from the Morelia region, spoke. "It doesn't matter," she said. "Our autonomy doesn't need permission from the government; it already exists. That's why the government no longer wants laws that permit pluricultural society to thrive."[1]

"Celerina's" comment caught my attention, particularly her assertion of indigenous people's right to autonomy as existing prior to and irrespective of its establishment in law. This notion was at odds with the legalistic discourse of human rights NGOs and activists and seemed mildly suggestive of conceptions of natural rights. Were indigenous people conceptualizing rights in new ways? I will consider that question over the course of this book. In this chapter, I begin by exploring the history of human rights as a discourse and practice, outlining the multiple trajectories of the concept on the ground in Chiapas, including natural law and the Catholic Church; positive law, the state legal regime, and NGOs; and the emergent indigenous rights and autonomy movement. I emphasize how the conceptual threads of natural law, particularly the notion of rights as extant prior to and regardless of their establishment in formal structures of law, are intertwined with conceptions of rights inhering in positive law, such as the right to "equality of individuals before the state," and the state as the sole authority "guaranteeing" these rights. I will then look at how indigenous people, as "Celerina's" comment indicates, are elaborating a distinct conceptualization of rights tied to a larger project of autonomy that is quite distinct from that of the state and its legal regimes.

The Catholic Church and the Natural Law Tradition

The concept of human rights has three trajectories in Chiapas, one with a religious orientation disseminated through the Catholic Church, another with a positivist legal orientation propagated by the agencies of the state and NGOs, and a third centered around the concept of "indigenous rights," articulated in a variety of forms by different indigenous groups. The last trajectory, which sometimes coincides with but remains fundamentally distinct from the prior positions, is closely tied to the positions adopted by the Zapatistas.

Although there is a good deal of blurring and overlap in human rights practice, the first two lines of legal thought correspond to two distinct conceptual frameworks and justifications for the existence of "human rights." One views rights as innate, natural, and prior to any judicial normativity; the second posits that rights cannot not exist prior to their establishment in law.

In Chiapas, the interweaving of strands of natural and positive law is largely a result of the dynamic role the Catholic Church has played in the development of human rights discourse and practice. The Church began its defense of the indigenous peoples of Chiapas as early as the sixteenth century with Bartolomé de Las Casas's famous theses on the "humanity" of the indigenous subjects of the Spanish Crown. However, activists and academics working in Chiapas over the last several decades seem to agree that the modern discourse and practice of human rights were given their strongest impulse in contemporary Chiapas in the mid-1980s, through the Catholic Diocese of San Cristóbal de Las Casas, under the leadership of Bishop Ruíz.[2]

Samuel Ruíz García became the bishop of the Diocese of San Cristóbal[3] in 1960. After a process of his own conversion from his former conservative views, by the early 1970s he was training catechists and giving masses with a strong liberation theology bent. Of this process Bishop Ruíz has said, "I came to Chiapas to convert the poor, but they are the ones who have converted me" (cited in Womack 1998:49). Liberation theology gave the Church's discourse a strong element of criticism of the structures of domination, exploitation, and political control of the poor. Kovic (2005) suggests that "the option for the poor" was the progressive Church's human rights discourse. She notes that liberation theologians purposefully utilized a discourse of "the rights of the poor" rather than of "human rights," to emphasize that the equality assumed in liberal rights theory did not exist and to highlight the structural and institutional economic violence that kept it from existing.

Because the indigenous people of Chiapas were clearly "the poorest of the poor," the "option for the poor" soon evolved into the "option for the indigenous" and *teología india* (Indian theology) emerged (Ruíz García 1999:61). *Teología india*, which developed in Chiapas, the Sierra Norte de Puebla, and other indigenous areas of the country, is most strongly associated with the Diocese of San Cristóbal and Bishop Ruíz. It is based on a strong valorization of indigenous culture and, notably, the understanding that human beings of all cultures are equal before, and have equal access to, God (Kovic 2005; Meyer 2000; Ruíz García 1999). The impact of the teachings of the

Figure 2.1 Samuel Ruíz García, retired bishop of the Diocese of San Cristóbal, was an important figure in bringing human rights discourse to indigenous communities. Jutta Meier Wiedenbach.

diocese and its catechists on indigenous communities was significant, giving indigenous communities new possibilities for organizing themselves and defending themselves. Many feel the work of the diocese prepared the road for later alliances between groups such as the one that would later become the EZLN (though Ruíz himself rejects armed struggle) (de Vos 2002; Meyer 2000).

The conceptualization of human rights, which evolved in the Catholic Church, has varied little in its affinity with natural law. The discourse that is currently disseminated through the Church had its earliest formulation in the writings of the first bishop of Chiapas, Bartolomé de Las Casas, and can be summarized with his famous statement, "The nature of men is the same and all are called by Christ in the same way" (de Las Casas 1974 [1542]).[4] All men are equal in the eyes of God. By situating God as the highest authority, rather than the sovereign or state, it follows that the rights of human beings always already exist, regardless of their establishment in the laws of sovereign. Bishop Ruíz affirmed this position by citing Pope John Paul II: "the rights of your peoples are *prior to any right established in human laws*" (Discourse in Latacunga II, cited in Ruíz García 1999:69, emphasis mine).

The Catholic Church was responsible for the establishment of the earliest human rights organizations based in Chiapas, which were formed in the early 1980s in the context of the arrival of thousands of Guatemalan refugees fleeing their country's scorched earth campaign. According to García Aguilar (1998a), the primary antecedent of today's human rights organizations was the *Comité Diocesano de Ayuda a Inmigrantes Fronterizos* (CODAIF), a project of the Catholic Church registered in 1986 to assist Guatemalan refugees. Three years later, the "Fray Bartolomé de Las Casas" Human Rights Center (CDHFBC) was founded. Also a project of the diocese, this organization, still the most active in the state, was the first specifically dedicated to human rights work and represented the formalization of the diocese's commitment to human rights work. Bishop Ruíz has been its president since its inception, continuing in that role even after retiring as bishop and leaving the state in 1999.

The CDHFBC, and the other Church-based human rights organizations that followed it, had a clear mandate to pursue human rights cases through the legal norms and structures established in national and international law.[5] The organization had two discourses of human rights, retaining a moral argument that emerged from natural law in its educational materials for indigenous communities and often in its public statements, while utilizing the discourse of

Mexican and international human rights law to denounce and to pursue legal redress in cases of rights violations.

Positive Law: Human and Indigenous Rights in the Mexican Legal Regime

While the Catholic Church formed the first human rights organization based in Chiapas, other organizations had periodically had a presence in the region beginning in the late 1970s. These organizations operated based on a positive law model, essentially as early NGOs, and they likely had some influence on the form the Church's organization took, integrating a positive law approach. Below, I turn to an examination of the positive law trajectory in conceptions of human rights, situating it in the context first of evolving Mexican legal regimes, and then of the organizations that work within this framework.

From Modern Liberalism to Neoliberalism in Mexican Law

Early Mexican constitutions were based on the classic liberal notion of "natural rights" developed by Enlightenment thinkers such as Locke and Hobbes in which certain rights were vested in human beings by virtue of the fact that they are human. These rights were understood to establish limits on existing political powers by asserting that there were natural rights and fundamental laws of governance that not even kings could overstep. Notable about these rights is that they are vested in the individual and exist prior to their formal recognition or acceptance by the sovereign. The sovereign, in fact, was beholden to them.

The precursory "Consitutional Decree for the Liberty of Mexican America" (also known as the Constitution of Apatzingán), issued in 1814 (although it never became law), stated in Article 24: "The happiness of the people and of every citizen consists of the enjoyment of equality, security, property, and liberty. The full preservation of these rights is the object of the institution of government and the only end (objective) of political association" (Terrazas 1996:51). Note that in this framing rights exist prior to the state, and it is the role of the state to ensure that its citizens can enjoy them. These ideas were also integral to the 1824 Federal Constitution of the United States of Mexico, which took its federalist framework and much of its language from the American Constitution.

There was a debate at the time of the writing of the Federal Constitution of 1857 between those who defended natural law doctrine and those who held a positivist philosophy, arguing that rights were not in the nature of man but were derived from positive law (C. A. Hale 1990). At that time, natural law conceptions prevailed. This constitution, the first to actually mention "the rights of man," demonstrated in its language its roots in the French and German thought of the late eighteenth century. It drew inspiration from the French Declaration on the Rights of Man, and it was undoubtedly heavily influenced by the American Constitution as well (Carozza 2003; C. A. Hale 2000; Terrazas 1996).[6] But, like its predecessors, it took "the rights of man" to have their origin in natural law (Terrazas 1996). In Article 1, the 1857 Constitution was clear: "The Mexican people recognize that the rights of man are the basis and the objective of social institutions. Consequently, it declares that all laws and authorities of the country must respect and support the guarantees granted by this constitution." Social institutions and the law were thus products of rights, rather than the other way around. The natural rights of man were primary; political power, social organization, and law existed to further these rights.

But rights discourses were moving in the direction of a distinct role for government. With the spread of secular legal realism, it was no longer tenable to justify moral rights by appeal to a natural order. There was a shift from natural rights, which need not be enforceable by law in order to exist, to legal rights, which exist only when a preestablished legal rule provides an individual an entitlement enforceable by law. Thus, modern rights exist and can be appealed to only when they are established in positive law. When rights become a function of the law, the Kantian notion of duty on another party becomes a legal duty of states to fulfill that entitlement or refrain from denying it. This is a significant shift, which effectively puts the ability to establish rights in the hands of the sovereign (in the contemporary period, states) at the same time the sovereign is (or states are) charged with protecting them.

Mexico became a modern liberal state in the decades following the Mexican Revolution. The Constitution of 1917 imposed a new system in which positivist theory prevailed. Law was in accord with, but not subject to, the rights of man. The opening statement of the Constitution of 1917, "Every person in the United Mexican States shall enjoy the guarantees granted by this Constitution," makes clear that while individualist notions of rights are to be retained, they are guarantees granted by the state, through its laws. The transition of the definition of rights to "guarantees" reinforced the fundamental role of the state: one cannot have guarantees without a guarantor. The establishment of rights in the Mexican Constitution as a system of state "guarantees" to its citizens defined the paternalist state as the exclusive entity ensuring the existence and enforcement of those rights, and the law as the only legitimate site of their establishment.

The Mexican Constitution of 1917 also established social rights based on premises of social justice and human dignity. This was consistent with emergent modern liberalism: the individual continued to be privileged but a variety of social and economic rights were added to the basic moral and political ones. Modern liberalism would of course reach its apex during the years of the New Deal and the welfare state, in which the state was understood to play an important role in mediating social inequality. But the 1917 Mexican Constitution was one of the earliest documents to enshrine such rights in law. [7] It included such a broad social rights platform that, in fact, it has often been characterized as socialist. However, far from being a socialist document, it retained the liberal individualist orientation of rights and maintained intact the full range of liberal civil and political rights of the earlier constitutions. Here the establishment of social rights did not imply group or collective rights. Rather, these were rights that pertained to individuals within particular constituencies. This is distinct from the notion of group rights, as they would pertain to an entire group, such as indigenous peoples.

The Constitution of 1917 was a product of the Mexican Revolution and social rights were necessary to address the demands of the groups that had formed the base of the Revolution, especially the marginalized populations of campesinos and workers. These rights were particularly manifested in Articles 27 and 123: land and labor law. Article 27 declared land and subsoil resources to be national property. The right to own land and to exploit the subsoil, therefore, could be granted and taken away by the state. This article was intended to address the serious problem of land concentration (it is estimated that as little as 1 percent of the population in Mexico owned as much as 97 percent of the land at the end of the *Porfiriato* in 1910), and put controls on private property and foreign ownership (Lewis 2002).[8] Importantly, Article 27 allowed the expropriation of large landholdings in order to create small individual or communal properties, called *ejidos*. Article 123 established the eight-hour work day, created protections for women and children, and established the right to form labor unions and to strike.

The Constitution of 1917 provided the legal framework for the state-citizen relationship in the post-Revolutionary period. Notably, the social rights it established did more than placate the demands of the revolutionary masses. The new constitution also shifted conceptualizations of rights and rights-bearing subjects away from the agentive individual and onto "the needy individual," requiring state protection and assistance, which paved the way for paternalistic political practice (Gourevitch 2004). The privileging of state relationships with particular groups of individuals, such as peasants and workers, would be key to the corporatist relationships that would uphold state power. Thus the relationship between the state and civil society that was consolidated in the post-Revolutionary period was a paternalist, corporatist, state-dominated relationship, established within a framework of positive law. This form of governance, in general terms, would characterize Mexican politics for the next several decades.

Constitutional Reform: Into the Neoliberal Era

The form of governance established by the Constitution of 1917 began to change with the neoliberal restructuring which began in the 1970s and gained momentum after the debt crisis of the mid-1980s (Hernández Castillo 2001a). A complex of constitutional reforms designed to neoliberalize the economy were implemented in 1992, creating the conditions for Mexico to enter the new global order. It was at this key juncture that the state formally altered its relationship with the population, ending corporatist rule. Articles 27 and 123 were significantly impacted in the reforms. For example, the amendment to Article 27 formally ended over seventy years of land redistribution, ending the state's obligation to redistribute land and opening previously inalienable *ejido* lands to privatization (Bartra 1991; Collier 1994c; Cornelius and Myhre 1998).[9] Following World Bank policy recommendations, the "new agrarian law" of 1992 sought to promote the functioning of land markets by liberalizing rental and sale among members of an *ejido*, to increase investment incentives, and to improve governance and regulation in the countryside (Teichman 2004).[10] Indeed, while the *Secretaría de la Reforma Agraria* continued after 1992, its stated mission was principally to "preserve the rule of law" (by dealing with ongoing conflicts) and to facilitate, through the National Agrarian Registry (RAN), the private titling of lands through the Program for Certification of Land Rights (PROCEDE) (Secretaría de la Reforma Agraria 2003).

Notably, in the same complex set of reforms, Article 2 recognized for the first time that the Mexican nation had a "pluriethnic composition sustained originally by its indigenous peoples." While it may seem disconnected from the neoliberal reforms—after all, it had little to do with liberalizing the economy—stipulating the pluriethnic composition of the nation was in fact *a key part of the reforms*, intended to facilitate the shifting relationship of the state to the population. While these reforms did not go far enough to set up a structure for doing so (reforms in some Latin American countries went further), they nevertheless signaled that the state would recognize a significant portion of the rural population as indigenous. This language opened the way for indigenous peoples to forge a new relationship with the state based on community recognition and commensurate rights, potentially facilitating some measure of local self-regulation. I suggest that the state's official recognition of the presence of an indigenous population in Mexico was fundamental to the establishment of new forms of governance compatible with neoliberalism. Thus, the constitutional reforms of 1992 dramatically altered the Constitution of 1917, eliminating the social contract it embodied and paving the way for a full-fledged neoliberal state. It accomplished this by creating a new legal framework for the relationship of the state to civil society, and especially to its indigenous population. The shift from modern liberalism to neoliberalism was formally under way.

Human Rights NGOs: Positive Law and Social Struggle

I have suggested that the rise in the numbers and the significance of NGOs is tied to processes of neoliberal globalization. Yet the initial emergence of human rights groups on the Mexican political landscape preceded neoliberalization processes and brought human rights claims into Chiapas even before the work of the diocese in the 1980s. In the late 1970s, a national movement emerged, demanding the truth about the disappeared and the release of political prisoners resulting from the violent repression of the student movement in 1968 and the dirty war against guerrilla movements in the early 1970s. Two groups, the Eureka Committee led by Rosario Ibarra and the *Frente Nacional Contra la Represión* (National Front Against Repression, or FNCR), formed in 1978 and 1979, respectively. These early human rights organizations got involved in Chiapas in response to the violent repression by landholders and the state government against campesino social organizations. In particular, they had a presence in the community of Venustiano Carranza, where four local activists had "disappeared" in 1974 following a military operation against a short-lived guerrilla movement, and campesino leaders and a non-local organizer, Arturo Albores, were unjustly detained and beaten in 1981–82 (Harvey 1998). A campaign to gain the release of these activists was led jointly by the FNCR and the national *Coordinadora Nacional Plan de Ayala* (CNPA), an independent campesino organization.[11] The campaign attracted the attention of Amnesty International, which carried out research in 1983 and 1984 for its report on human rights abuses in Oaxaca and Chiapas (Amnesty International 1986). The discourse of human rights in the case of FNCR and CNPA was framed in terms of class struggle in an authoritarian regime, where the state and law protected the class interests of the bourgeoisie and, in the case of Chiapas, the *cacique* landowners.[12]

In the 1990s, human rights organizations flourished in Chiapas. Particularly after the Zapatista uprising began in 1994, the number of NGOs increased dramatically, as national and international organizations also began to have a presence in the region. By the late 1990s, there were ten independent human rights organizations (García Aguilar 1998b),[13] five national human rights NGOs,[14] and at least nine international ones[15] with a permanent or periodic presence in Chiapas. The state and federal governments had also established their own human rights agencies.[16] The flourishing of NGOs in the state responded partly to the increase in rights violations and of public attention following the uprising, but also to the broader processes leading to the flourishing of NGOs in Mexico and around the world.

Human rights organizations generally have a legalist orientation and articulate their demands through a discourse of positive law. They are most often engaged in the work of calling upon states to create laws establishing rights and to enforce those rights already formulated in laws. They engage in a broad range of activities, but these are principally directed to pressuring states in the legal arena. While they may present significant challenges to states that are serious violators, they do not challenge the notion of the state/sovereign as the legitimate source of rights and the law as the sacred site of their establishment. The discourse of human rights that flourished in Chiapas in the 1990s was strongly based in positive law, and this second trajectory of the discourse (like the natural law discourse of the Church) has also had a great deal of influence in indigenous communities.

Indigenous Rights in Chiapas: A New Path?

How have these two discourses—natural law and positive law—come together in indigenous peoples' ideas about human rights? In this section, I want to suggest that the trajectories come together in a new and distinct conceptualization in particular instances in Chiapas, a suggestion I hope to sustain throughout the book. Of course, one of the principal arguments I will make about indigenous engagements with human rights is that they are multiple, diverse, and often vary based on micro-local political subjectivities. In this section, I am referring principally to Zapatista formulations of indigenous rights struggle, though these may, because of the prominence of the organization, have wider impact on others' understandings of rights.

During the 1990s and into 2001, indigenous people actively sought to participate in the restructuring of the Mexican legal framework through constitutional reform, part of their larger endeavor to reconfigure their relationship
with the state. National constitutional reform has been viewed as necessary and
important because of Mexico's historical relationship to its indigenous peoples.
Assimilationism and the discursive erasure of living indigenous peoples underpinned the system of political exclusion and economic exploitation and were
strongly supported by Mexican legal regimes. So total was this exclusion that
for more than seven decades following the writing of the Constitution of 1917,
the word *indigenous* was never mentioned, either in the constitution itself or in
constitutional jurisprudence (Hernández Navarro 1998). Not until July of 1991,
almost two years after Mexico ratified the ILO Convention 169 on Indigenous
and Tribal Peoples, was the Mexican Constitution reformed to recognize the
presence of indigenous peoples in the populace. Even then, the constitutional
reform offered little basis for the realization of indigenous rights, and legislation

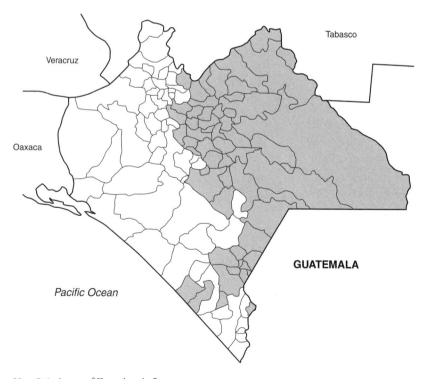

Map 2.1 Areas of Zapatista influence.

to enable their implementation was not developed. Moreover, the 1991 constitutional reform focused only on cultural rights, omitting reference to political rights, self-determination, or autonomy (Gómez Rivera 1997).

While significant indigenous organizing was already taking place (Mattiace 2003), the Zapatista uprising gave further impetus to the struggle for indigenous rights. Since 1994, indigenous peasants have increasingly cast their demands within a framework of legal autonomy. Nevertheless, the position of the Zapatistas on legal struggle for state recognition has been guarded, and it has shifted depending on the particular political moment. This made sense, given that their initial proposition was that the kind of social change necessary could not come about through the current political system in Mexico. Their initial demands went beyond legal reform measures to demands for reorganization of the state and society. However, over the course of several years, the movement increasingly prioritized the establishment of indigenous rights and autonomy, and at key points constitutional recognition and legal reform were critical aspects of that demand.[17] There were several reasons for this, but the most important was the fact that the only negotiated agreements signed by the Zapatistas and the government focused on indigenous rights and culture. These accords played an important role in shaping events and the movement's demands and therefore merit further discussion.

The San Andrés Accords: Legal Basis for Autonomy

Only twelve days after the EZLN uprising began, and under much national and international pressure, then-President Salinas de Gortari declared a unilateral cease-fire that effectively ended open hostilities between the EZLN and the Mexican Army and negotiations were initiated. It was a year of crisis for both Salinas and the PRI that extended far beyond the uprising in the south. A presidential election year, it was expected that the ruling party candidate, selected through the traditional *dedazo*, in which the sitting president designated his successor and his victory was assured through whatever means necessary, would win the election.[18] However, on March 23, 1994, the candidate, Luis Donaldo Colosio, was assassinated while campaigning in Tijuana. There was widespread suspicion that his own party had been responsible for his death.[19] In August his successor Ernesto Zedillo won in a contested election. The following month, José Francisco Ruíz Massieu, the secretary general of the PRI and the brother-in-law of outgoing president Carlos Salinas, who was shortly to become the PRI majority leader in the Chamber of Deputies (the lower house of congress), was assassinated. Again, there was widespread suspicion that people within the PRI were responsible for the political killing. Within weeks, a PRI congressman, Manuel Muñoz Rocha, was linked to the assassination.[20] The special prosecutor assigned to the case, Ruíz Massieu's brother, reportedly uncovered a massive conspiracy but resigned on November 15, 1994, after publicly accusing the PRI of blocking his investigation of the upper-level government officers whom he suspected of involvement.[21] This debacle seriously eroded confidence in the party and in the government as a whole both nationally and internationally. Reportedly, $1.5 billion of foreign investment left the country the day after Massieu's announcement.

On December 1, 1995, Ernesto Zedillo took office. Twenty days later, Mexico decided not to continue to support the overvalued peso against the dollar and the peso crashed, losing over 50 percent of its value overnight.[22] This precipitated an economic disaster and large-scale financial bailout by the United States and the IMF to the tune of $50 billion (Humphrey 2000). Far from being the free-trade poster child that Carlos Salinas had envisioned his country becoming through NAFTA, Mexico faced dramatic political and economic instability and the flight of international capital.

One of the perceived reasons for the ensuing capital flight was the social instability playing out in Chiapas. A now-infamous internal memo of the Chase Manhattan Bank was leaked and circulated heavily on the Internet and e-mail networks. The memo, entitled "Mexico Political Update" and dated January 13, 1995, stated, "While Chiapas, in our opinion, does not pose a fundamental threat to Mexican political stability, it is perceived to be so by many in the investment community. *The government will need to eliminate the Zapatistas to demonstrate their effective control of the national territory and of security policy*" (italics mine).[23] Under international pressure, in February 1995 the Mexican government launched a massive military mobilization against the Zapatista base area and attempted to arrest the high Zapatista leadership. It did not succeed, but the mobilization left many communities throughout the conflict zone heavily militarized and only heightened the sense of crisis in the country. The same month, Raul Salinas, brother of ex-President Carlos Salinas, was arrested in the Ruíz Massieu assassination.[24]

It was in this extraordinary context that the government and the EZLN approached negotiations in 1995. After the February military mobilization, to facilitate the peace talks, the Law for Dialogue, Conciliation, and Dignified Peace in Chiapas was passed. The law gave Zapatista leaders immunity from arrest as long as the EZLN remained under cease-fire and provided for the formation of an intermediary body for the dialogues made up of a rotating group of federal legislators from the three main political parties called the *Comisión de Concordia y Pacificación* (Commission for Concordance and Pacification, COCOPA). Another intermediary body, the *Comisión Nacional de Intermediación* (National Mediation Commission, CONAI), led by San Cristóbal Bishop Samuel Ruíz, was also formed. The CONAI was undoubtedly more trusted by the EZLN than the COCOPA.[25] The first direct meeting between the EZLN and the government took place on April 9, 1995, in San Miguel, Ocosingo.[26] The pre-dialogue process—deciding what to dialogue about—took most of 1995. The process was lengthy in part due to the Zapatistas' insistence that the proceedings be translated into the various languages of their members, and on consulting with the base communities before formalizing any decisions. The preliminary negotiations led to the agreement that actual negotiations would be structured in a set of four themes, the first of which was "Indigenous Rights and Culture," followed by "Democratization and Justice," "Well-Being and Development," and "Women's Rights" (Díaz-Polanco 1997). This structure reflects the fact that the EZLN had a much broader agenda than "Indigenous Rights" in its initial stages (and its public demands and declarations reflect this as well).[27] The first of these sets of talks, on "Indigenous Rights and Culture," took place between October 1995 and January 1996 in the community of San Andrés Larrainzar (renamed San Andrés Sakamch'en de los Pobres by the Zapatistas).

This set of talks ended with cautious optimism, and in February of 1996 the San Andrés Accords on Indigenous Rights and Culture were signed (Ce Acatl 1996). The accords recognize the rights of indigenous peoples to "develop their specific forms of social, cultural, political and economic organization," "to obtain recognition of their internal normative systems for regulation and sanction insofar as they are not contrary to constitutional guarantees and human rights, especially those of women," "to freely designate their representatives within the community as well as in their municipal government bodies as well as the leaders of their *pueblos indígenas* in accordance with the institutions and traditions of each *pueblo*," and "to promote and develop their languages, cultures, as well as their political, social, economic, religious, and cultural customs and traditions" (San Andrés Accords on Indigenous Rights and Culture 1999:35, italics mine). Notably, the accords included commitments to constitutional recognition of indigenous peoples (*pueblos indígenas*) and "the right to self determination exercised in a constitutional framework of autonomy" (Hernández Navarro and Vera Herrera 1998:58–59).

Much needed as they were in order to address centuries of oppression, in the particular political juncture in which Mexico found itself at the time of the signing, there was nothing especially radical about the accords. They were based largely on international law, especially the ILO Convention 169 (considered by many to be the most complete international agreement on indigenous rights), which Mexico had signed and ratified in 1990, making them law at the level of the constitution. Further, as a result of its constitutional reforms in 1992, Mexico had already made the shift from a corporatist, assimilationist model to a neoliberal, multicultural one, recognizing the pluriethnic makeup of the population. The accords, and the further constitutional reform that they mandated, were consistent with that transition, one that a number of Latin American countries were to make over the following five years.

The San Andrés Accords were viewed by many as a positive first step in the peace process. The negotiations to follow in the tables on Democracy and Justice, Well-Being and Development, and the Situation of Women in Chiapas were also widely recognized as fundamental to the process. However, in the six months following the signing of the San Andrés Accords, it became clear that the government was not willing to move forward on implementing them. As militarization increased and paramilitary groups surged in the communities of the conflict zone, all indications were that the government had chosen a path other than peace negotiations to end the uprising. The table on Democracy and Justice began in March 1996, but by the second session, in April, it seemed clear that the government was not serious about those negotiations. In a press release, the CONAI complained: "The Federal Government refused to talk, or bring advisers and independent guests to the second round of discussions centering on issues of Democracy and Justice." After the third session in July of 1996, the EZLN suspended the dialogue. In their August 29 announcement, the EZLN cited five conditions that the government would have to meet in order to return to the negotiating table:

1. The implementation of the agreements established in the San Andrés Accords, including the creation of the oversight body for the accords, the "Implementation and Verification Commission" and the fulfillment of the part of the San Andrés Accords that specifically addressed the issues of the indigenous rights and cultures (especially constitutional reform).

2. The presentation by the federal government of a proposal to specifically address issues of democracy and justice.

3. The liberation of the Zapatista political prisoners (an agreement signed by the government in the context of the Dialogue and Conciliation Laws signed in March 1995).

4. An end to the low-intensity warfare initiated by the government, including the disarming of paramilitary groups in the Northern Zone of Chiapas.

5. The designation of a governmental delegation with the capacity to help resolve the conflict with full respect of the Zapatista mediation body.

Attempting to salvage the negotiations process, the COCOPA prepared legislation to comply with the accords and forwarded it to the executive and the EZLN in November 1996.[28] The EZLN consulted with the legislative commission of the newly formed National Indigenous Congress and after this consultation agreed to the terms of the COCOPA initiative. The Secretario de Gobernación (Secretary of the Interior) signaled that the government would do the same, but a few days later President Zedillo rejected the proposal, stating, remarkably, that he had been unaware of the content of the agreements.[29] In January of 1997 President Zedillo submitted a counterproposal that significantly altered the principles of the San Andrés Accords. It was rejected by the EZLN, who withdrew into the jungle and began a period of "silence" that would last four years. Peace dialogues were never resumed. A few months later the CONAI dissolved, in recognition that "this phase of the peace process had ended."[30]

Forefronting Indigenous Rights, from National Demands to Local Autonomy

From that time on, the Zapatistas began forefronting their demands for indigenous rights. Along with other indigenous organizations throughout the country, they sought to make indigenous rights an issue of immediate national significance. But more importantly, as a result of the failed negotiations, they abandoned the effort to establish indigenous rights through the state. While the demand for state recognition would resurge after the ruling party lost power in 2000 (see Chapter 7), for the next three years the Zapatista communities would turn their autonomy process inward and build a conception of rights that existed even in the absence of government recognition. Thus the Mexican government's failure to comply with the accords that its representatives signed at San Andrés, and especially its failure to fulfill the express commitment contained in the accords to promote constitutional reform recognizing indigenous rights and some measure of autonomy, had important effects. First, it confirmed what the Zapatistas already asserted: that meaningful change would not come about through the established system of political power and the Mexican state. Further, on the rhetorical terrain, it gave the Zapatistas a strong weapon: they had negotiated in good faith, and the Mexican government had failed to honor its own agreement. Not surprisingly, this moved to the forefront of the Zapatistas' public discourse.

The elimination of the state option combined with other important dynamics to move indigenous rights and autonomy to the center of the Zapatista project. It has often been stated that the Zapatista uprising gave strong impetus to the formation of a national indigenous rights movment. But in a sense, the reverse is also the case: the consolidation of a national indigenous movement provided a strong national base of support for the EZLN, lending further impetus to their forefronting of indigenous rights and autonomy. Indigenous organizing and limited demands for autonomy certainly existed prior to the Zapatista uprising, though these groups and demands were largely disarticulated. During the 1950s and 60s, indigenous organizing in defense of culture and language was closely linked to state projects, particularly the INI (National Indigenist Institute) (Hernández Castillo 2001a). Important events, such as the 1974 Indigenous Congress organized by Bishop Ruiz and the 1975 National Congress of Indigenous Peoples in Patzcuaro, Michioacán helped to set new dynamics in motion that would lead to the formulation of indigenous demands that were independent of state projects. While both of these state-sponsored events represented attempts to co-opt and maintain control over indigenous people, they nevertheless brought indigenous groups together and created consciousness of shared oppressions, as well as initiating networks that would later be significant in the indigenous movement (Mattiace 1997). In particular, the Patzcuaro conference eventually led to the formation of the National Council of Indigenous Peoples (CNPI) which represented fifty-six ethnic groups from throughout the country. While pressure from the state to remain under PRI party influence led to tensions and by the late 1970s a number of Indian organizations would abandon the ranks of the CNPI to join the newly formed National Coordinating Group "Plan de Ayala" (CNPA), the CNPI had served as a space for autonomous (non-state) indigenous organizing to be formulated (Mattiace 1997). By the mid-1980s, spaces were opening for indigenous organizing and indigenous demands—in some cases including autonomy demands—within broader social organizations. The organizing efforts throughout the country and the continent around the quincentennial anniversary of Columbus' arrival to the New World added fuel to indigenous demands in Chiapas and in Mexico. The Zapatista uprising in 1994 served as a catalyst for these demands and for the articulation and consolidation of a broader national indigenous movement, particularly after the negotiations at San Andrés (see Hernández Navarro 1998).[31] This movement in turn provided a strong base of support for the EZLN, even when tensions emerged over various models for autonomy (most notably in the National Indigenous Forum convoked by the EZLN in 1996).[32]

Similarly, non-indigenous national and international support surely reinforced the forefronting of this aspect of the movement. The existence of international agreements on indigenous rights such as the ILO Convention 169, the growth in international support and advocacy groups supporting indigenous rights, and the general realignment of the left away from national liberation movements and toward identity-based struggles encouraged this focus. I am not suggesting that indigenous rights and autonomy became the focus of the Zapatista movement due to outside influence, but rather that this component of the movement, always present, was encouraged by national and international support. But, perhaps more importantly, it was the government's failure to recognize indigenous self-determination that motivated Zapatista leaders and base communities to pursue autonomy in the manner that they did, unilaterally.[33] Although the Zapatistas had established thirty-eight "municipalities in rebellion" in 1994, it was from 1997 onward, after the failure of the San Andrés Accords, that these municipalities emerged as a principal space for the organization of resistance and a strategy for indigenous political participation (González Hernández and Quintanar Quintanar 1999).[34] Zapatista communities formed autonomous regions and began their own processes of implementing local government through autonomous councils. They directed their energies to the task of developing—often in collaboration with national or international groups—their own systems of education, healthcare, agriculture, and more.

Thus, the San Andrés Accords, and the Mexican government's failure to implement them, contributed strongly to a shift in Zapatista rhetoric toward "indigenous rights," with autonomy as the principal manifestation of those rights. Significantly, however, not only did public statements shift, but also the *practice* of resistance shifted. The movement for "national liberation" had become a movement for indigenous rights. Even more significantly, "indigenous rights" were no longer being elaborated as a demand before the state. By unilaterally pursuing their autonomy projects, people in Zapatista base areas set themselves on a path that would imply a fundamental shift regarding rights, one that I argue represents a third trajectory of rights on the ground in Chiapas. This third trajectory is the one that "already exists," according to "Celerina," the Tzeltal woman whose words opened this chapter. That is, indigenous rights, including autonomy, exist in practice, regardless of their establishment in the legal regimes of the state. This argument will be given further consideration in the following chapters, particularly Chapter 7.

Conclusions

In Mexico, and Chiapas specifically, the discourse and practice of human rights have several distinct, though interrelated, trajectories: natural law, through the Catholic Church; positive law, through the Mexican legal system; and indigenous rights, through the autonomy projects of the indigenous communities of the state. Despite distinct philosophical underpinnings, the first two have been strongly intertwined in Chiapas due to the prominent role of the Catholic Church in both disseminating concepts of natural law and actively contributing to positive law practice. The discourse of the indigenous communities has shifted in dialogue with national and global forces, and in doing so a form of rights demand has emerged that has elements of both natural and positive law traditions, yet is based on a logic that is distinguishable from both. My intention in this chapter has been to provide background on the different trajectories of the discourse of rights in Chiapas, in order to lay the groundwork for the discussion and analysis that follow. In the chapters that follow, I will turn to an examination of how these underlying conceptions have played out in various ways in Chiapas during the conflict period that began with the Zapatista uprising.

3 "Neither Rights nor Humans": The Vicissitudes of Local Appropriation

IN EARLY 1997, I visited the Northern Zone as part of a delegation of the *Estación Norte*, a coalition of five human rights organizations that was focused on the violent conflict taking place in that region of the state.[1] We spoke with a number of people from one community about recent paramilitary violence that had caused a number of community members to be displaced. The comments of two men, who I later learned were cousins, stand out in their juxtaposition: The first said,

> It is good that you came. We sent Pedro to the Fray Bart [Human Rights Center] to advise them of what has happened: that they expelled us from the community, shot at us and burned our houses. We want the world to know the injustice we, the Chols of the Northern Zone, are suffering.

A short time later, his cousin (who had remained in the community) told us,

> You people from human rights should not have come—you have nothing to do here. This is our problem, and we Chols, we the people of our community, will handle it. We don't want Kaxlanes here. If human rights butts in, it will provoke more violence.[2] We do not tolerate human rights here.[3]

The distinct, in fact diametrically opposed, understandings of human rights reflected in these comments clarified something I had only begun to suspect: that while many people in Chiapas were utilizing the discourse of human rights, not everyone was interpreting it in the same way. In this chapter, I will consider the relationship of the globalization of the discourse of human rights to local cultures, subjectivities, and forms of resistance, through a broad look at some of the dynamics of human rights in Chiapas during the conflict period. In particular, I focus on how different social actors in Chiapas are appropriating the discourse of human rights, interpreting it based on their own experiences and understandings, and redeploying it in support of their distinct goals. As the quotes above indicate, there is a multiplicity of discourses of human rights operating in Chiapas, even in relatively localized settings such as "a community." This chapter considers a variety of social actors: EZLN-affiliated communities and independent organizations that understand human rights as a tool for their own defense in the context of social struggle; Chol paramilitary groups and *Ladino* elites—the *Auténtico Coletos* of San Cristóbal—that understand human rights as a weapon used against them, and the state government of Chiapas, which has mobilized the discourse of human rights to justify counterinsurgency and limit indigenous autonomy. I have chosen these social actors because they are diverse, and seen together they present a picture of the multiple understandings and appropriations of human rights that have taken place in Chiapas in the context of the conflict. In exploring these, what I hope to show is how each usage of the discourse is at once a result of its globalization and of local histories and political subjectivities—a product of dialogic interactions of the various social actors, including communities, organizations, the state, transnational activists, and global powers.

Zapatista Communities and Independent Organizations in the Conflict Zone

Since the start of the uprising, the EZLN has mobilized the discourse of human rights quite effectively. This was facilitated by the rise of human rights NGOs already underway in the state, the networks of actors linked to human rights work throughout the country and the world, and the availability of technology that allowed for rapid diffusion of information through those networks. In the wake of the uprising, the Zapatistas and their base supporters could count not only on organizations already in existence, such as the Fray Bartolomé Center, but also on new organizations that formed in response to increased need after the uprising, such as the *Coordinación de Los Organismos No-Gubernamentales por la Paz* (Coordination of Nongovernmental Organizations for Peace, CONPAZ), and international organizations that opened offices in San Cristóbal, such as Global Exchange and *Servicio Internacional por la Paz* (International Service for Peace, SIPAZ).

Figure 3.1 Militarization in the Lacandón: Military helicopter fly-overs and landings inside communities left the population living in fear. Jutta Meier Wiedenbach.

There are many examples of how utilizing a discourse of human rights, and the network of activists organized around human rights, worked to the Zapatistas' advantage. Because of the dramatic scale of the events, the military mobilization of February 1995 is a notable example. Driven by the financial and political crisis that characterized the opening of the Zedillo administration, and particularly the international pressure on Zedillo to resolve the conflict in Chiapas, the government launched a large-scale incursion into the conflict zone of the Lacandón and attempted to detain the Zapatista leadership. The EZLN sent out "communiqués" that were quickly picked up by the national and international press and circulated widely (and almost instantly) on the Internet, informing their national and international supporters that the Mexican Army was violating the rights of people in military-occupied communities. Protests were quickly organized in cities throughout Mexico and abroad, especially in the United States and Europe. These protests and other actions put pressure directly on the Mexican government and indirectly by exhorting other governments to pursue diplomatic channels to stop human rights violations. The Mexican government found itself compelled to limit its actions in the conflict zone and to release many of the indigenous people detained during the military mobilization.[4]

During these events, the power of "human rights" was quickly understood by people in the indigenous Zapatista base-support communities, who were already coming to see human rights as their primary line of defense. For this reason, the communities that remained occupied by the military following the February mobilization welcomed the formation of the civilian peace camps by the Fray Bartolomé Human Rights Center and CONPAZ. These camps were designed to have national and international human rights observers stationed in twenty-six communities to monitor the Mexican Army's adherence to the new peace and reconciliation law, which established the ground rules for their occupation of pro-Zapatista communities. The camps effectively provided an outside presence, which constrained the Mexican Army's ability to engage in actions that would violate residents' human rights, and people in the communities saw this as a vital form of protection. They strongly associated human rights workers with their own struggle, in part because of this protective role, and in part because those who went in as observers were almost invariably sympathizers with the Zapatista movement or at least with indigenous struggle more generally. For a long time, one of the only ways to get access to communities in the conflict zone was to go in as a human rights observer through the peace camps.

In July of 1995 I went to a civilian peace camp in the middle of the Cañadas.[5] I had spent several frustrated weeks in San Cristóbal, during which everyone I asked told me in no uncertain terms that I should not attempt to go to any communities in the conflict zone unless backed by a (locally) well-known organization or the Diocese of San Cristóbal. Finally, I wrestled a human rights observer credential out of the Fray Bartolomé Human Rights Center (they took the responsibility seriously and were very careful about whom they sent in, requiring letters of reference from organizations one had worked with and various other things I had not thought to bring with me). When I finally got the credential, they sent me on my way to the conflict zone with nothing other than a few words of instruction about how to find the trucks, instructions that meant little to someone who had never been there. I traveled nearly ten hours from San Cristóbal, most of it in the crowded back of an old truck on a very rough dirt road. After what seemed like an endless trip through mud, sun, and military camps, we passed a large river (the Jataté) with yet another military camp. Soldiers pointed big guns at us from camouflaged observation huts just off the road. A moment later, the truck came to a halt in the road in front of a small plaza with a basketball court, a church, and a meeting-house. I jumped down and stood blinking like a stunned animal in the unrelenting sun. Children peered at me from behind houses with big eyes and serious faces. I continued to stand there in the road, unsure how to proceed. The tension in the air was palpable. Finally, as I edged toward a small patch of shade at the side of the road, a man approached me. He peered severely into my face and asked, "*Vienes de derechos humanos?*" "Are you from 'human rights'?" "*Si, si,*" I told him quickly, scrambling to get out my credential. His face broke into a relieved smile. I was from human rights. I was on their side. I was one of them. He began to shake my hand, the sun ducked behind a cloud, and the children poured out from behind the buildings and gathered around me. They whisked me off to a house that had recently been designated for observers. Within an hour, I had fresh tortillas, avocados and limes, and a dozen or more children to keep me company.

Over the next several weeks, people demonstrated a remarkable trust in me and poured out a wealth of information to me as we sat around the "peace camp" in the evening cool after the men returned home from work, or in the homes of women who invited me over for mid-morning *pozol* (a corn beverage).

Figure 3.2 The army patrolling jungle roads as part of the low-intensity warfare campaign. Jutta Meier Wiedenbach.

In fact, they displayed such trust and told me so much that I began to fear for them. Finally, after a group of young men casually imparted a particularly sensitive bit of information to me, I blurted out, "Why are you telling me all this? You have no idea who I am! I could be anyone!" Fireflies danced around us in the dark as the young men laughed. A moment of silence passed before one man said, "*Pero, vienes de 'derechos humanos,' no?*" (But you are from "human rights," aren't you?).

Undoubtedly, the communities' trust of the diocese played a role in the trust they displayed to human rights observers "from human rights." For them, this credential tied you to the Fray Bartolomé Human Rights Center, and they had established relations of trust with the diocese built over the course of many years. Further, the Fray Bart took this trust seriously, which is why they were so very careful about whom they sent into the communities (a caution that, in the view of some, occasionally crossed the line into paternalism). But what really surprised me about this experience in the peace camp was the extent to which the communities' trust had been extended to all human rights observers, who were presumed to be trustworthy *compañeros*, even with potentially incriminating information, simply by virtue of the fact that they "came from human rights." Of course, this would not necessarily have been the case in all communities or even with all people in the community where I stayed, but the phenomenon was significantly widespread.

Another moment in which these dynamics stood out was when the government began to pursue a policy of dismantling Zapatista autonomous municipalities in 1998. In these *desmantelamientos*, the communities suffered the massive raids carried out jointly by the Mexican Federal Army, state and federal police, and immigration officers. In the cases of communities like Taniperlas, Amparo Agua Tinta, Diez de Abril, Nicolás Ruiz, and El Bosque, more than a thousand agents of these security forces went in, and violence and massive arrests were carried out. The communities were quick to call on human rights organizations and to denounce human rights violations in their own defense. For example, in the community of Nicolás Ruiz, "Ricardo" said, "We never knew anything about human rights, until the *operativo* [raid] of June 1998. . . . It was then that we realized that we had to learn about human rights to defend ourselves from the government, because [the government] doesn't want us around." The community hired a human rights attorney to defend the detained and later appointed two "defenders," one of them "Ricardo," to train with him in human rights defense work.[6]

Zapatista communities were not the only actors mobilizing human rights in this context. In the Cañadas, the discourse of human rights has also been mobilized by "independent" organizations that historically have confronted local ranchers, *Ladinos*, and elite groups in general. For example, in June of 1998 the *Coalición de Organizaciones Autónomas de Ocosingo* (COAO), a regional umbrella group of political organizations, demanded that charges be dropped against sixteen of its members who had been detained during the dismantling of the Zapatista autonomous municipality "Ricardo Flores Magón" (Taniperlas). The COAO supported its demand with a ruling by the Interamerican Human Rights Commission of the Organization of American States (OAS), which requested the prisoners' release be based on the violations of the detainees' rights in the course of the legal process (see Henríquez 1998; Leyva and Speed 2001).[7]

It is logical that, given the presence of the discourse of human rights and the ready network of activists prepared to mobilize in support of them, the EZLN, their base communities, and independent organizations which are aligned with them readily appropriated human rights to their needs in the context of the conflict. But in this same sense, it is logical that other social actors recognized the power of the discourse at this political juncture, while interpreting its meaning and uses very differently because of the particular history and current associations it holds. In the following sections, I look at two of these social actors: San Cristóbal elites and indigenous members of paramilitary groups. I examine these groups not because they are linked (I make no assertions here), but because they are very different groups which, due to their own histories, political positions, and goals, understand human rights quite distinctly from the groups we have just considered.

Alternative Engagements: From San Cristóbal to the Northern Zone

In 1994, with the emergence of the EZLN, Chiapas became so socially polarized that it often seemed there were only two positions: pro-Zapatista and anti-Zapatista. This has diminished over the last several years, though it has not disappeared altogether. The government and other social actors also recognize the power of the discourse of human rights and the networks it mobilizes. In one infamous analysis, conservative think-tank Rand analysts Ronfeldt and Arquilla (1998) argue that there is a *Zapatista social netwar*. This slightly alarmist analysis recognized the Zapatistas' use of human rights and posited that the uprising aroused a multitude of civil-society activists associated with human-rights, indigenous-rights, and other types of nongovernmental organizations (NGOs) to swarm—electronically as well as physically—from the United States, Canada, and elsewhere into Mexico City and Chiapas. There, they linked with Mexican NGOs to voice solidarity with the EZLN's demands and to press for nonviolent change. Thus, what began as a violent insurgency in an isolated region mutated into a nonviolent though no less disruptive social netwar that engaged the attention of activists from far and wide and had nationwide and foreign repercussions for Mexico.

Their argument that in the "information revolution" the danger exists that "small, previously isolated groups can communicate, link up, and conduct coordinated joint actions as never before" had resonance with many in Chiapas who did not see the uprising as a positive occurrence.

Whether or not one agrees that the Zapatista movement represents a "netwar" involving "swarming" activists, networks have been vital and many of the Zapatistas' networks hinge on human rights. In this polarized context, many who opposed the Zapatista movement considered human rights a tool of war and the networks of actors associated with human rights work their enemies in that war. Because the discourse of human rights strengthens the struggle to renegotiate the unequal relations of power in which certain people are subordinated and oppressed, those who stand to lose authority, legitimacy, control, and political power in this renegotiation view the mobilization of human rights discourse and practice in a very negative light: as an attack against them, and as something they must combat. For groups as diverse as the *Ladino* elite of San Cristóbal de Las Casas and Chol Indians from the Northern Zone associated with the paramilitary group *Paz y Justicia*, "human rights" represents a threat to the status quo from which they have benefited (though on very different scales) and which they understand to be the right way to live. Their interpretation is not ahistorical; it emerges from the particular context of relationships in which the discourse was introduced into the state, particularly through the Diocese of San Cristóbal, and the ways it has been mobilized to their disadvantage in recent years.

The *Coletos* of San Cristóbal de Las Casas

San Cristóbal de Las Casas, formerly Ciudad Real, is a colonial city founded in 1528 by the Spanish conquistador Diego de Mazariegos. Originally a Spanish stronghold against the surrounding Indian communities, it was eventually re-named in honor of Fray Bartolomé de Las Casas, the famous defender of the In-dians. The city experienced several Indian rebellions in the course of its history, leading its elite, nonindigenous residents (both European-born Spaniards and later, Chiapas-born *Ladinos*) to develop a deeply ingrained fear of Indian inva-sion. After independence, it was the state capital until 1892 and was the conserva-tive political rival of the liberal Tuxtla Gutiérrez, today's capital (Benjamin 1989).[8]

The relationship between the indigenous communities of the Chiapas High-lands to the city of San Cristóbal de Las Casas has been the focus of anthropolog-ical attention for many decades (e.g., Aguirre Beltrán 1953, 1957; de la Fuente 1968; Favre 1973; McQuown and Pitt-Rivers 1970; Pitt-Rivers 1973; Pozas 1958). The extreme nature of the relations of economic exploitation and the social divi-sion and racism between the *Ladino* residents of San Cristóbal and the Indians of the communities that surround it made this area a "laboratory for the study of interethnic relations"; one major research project in the 1950s cited among its ra-tionales for the study site its "notoriously retrograde *mestizo* elite" (discussed in Hewlitt de Alcántara 1984). Possibly, what the anthropologists found "retro-grade" was not only the town's colonial social relations but also the elite popula-tion's resistance to the modern national discourse of *mestizaje*. While in much of the rest of the country people had come to understand themselves as part of a *mestizo* nation (note the anthropologists refer to the elite as *mestizo*), in much of Chiapas *criollo* or *Ladino* have long been and remain the most relevant social cat-egory. Distinct from *mestizo*, which implies racial mixing, *Ladino* is posited against the category of Indian, the purpose of which is to fix social categories of power and domination (Paris Pombo 2000). As recently as the 1950s, San Cristóbal prided itself on being a *criollo* city, meaning one of direct Spanish her-itage and descent (Paris Pombo 2000). Nevertheless, by the 1950s there was a growing, if unacknowledged, *mestizo* population in the city, mostly a result of sexual relations—often rape—between *Ladino* (*criollo*) men and Indian women.

However, the identities and ethnic relations established during the colonial era have not remained static. As Paris Pombo (2000) argues, several significant social processes contributed to transforming San Cristóbal demographically, spatially, and in terms of identity since the 1950s. One was the migration of In-dians from the surrounding communities into San Cristóbal. Demographic pressures on the land, and more importantly religious-political conflicts in highlands communities, contributed to a dramatic influx of tens of thousands of Tzotziles and Tzeltales, who established neighborhoods on the peripheries of the city (CNDH 1995; Kovic 2005). This influx of indigenous people altered both the demographics and territorial division of the city and Indians began walking on the sidewalks, through the central park, and in other areas previously reserved for *Ladino* elites (Paris Pombo 2000). By the 1980s, the flow of indigenous people into the city had increased even more. Rus and Collier (2003) estimate that in the two decades between 1980 and 2000, the population of the city more than doubled, growing from 60,000 to 130,000, and that Indians represented half of that growth. The establishment of offices of the National Indigenist Institute (INI) in San Cristóbal in the late 1950s contributed to the emergence of an Indian elite composed largely of INI-trained bilingual teachers, who were able to acquire land and properties in the city during this period (Paris Pombo 2000). Newly arrived Indians in the 1980s and 1990s began to establish new neighborhoods in the city and new sets of social networks and relations and to appropriate specific sectors of the economy, such as taxi-driving (Cruz Burguete and Robledo 1989).

Also from the 1950s onward, tourism began to play a significant role in the economy of the city. By the 1970s, large numbers of foreign tourists visited the city each year, and a growing number of foreigners took up residence in the town. Many of these foreigners came to the area because they were interested in local Indian culture—what Van Den Berghe (1994) refers to as "ethnic tourism"—tourism motivated by an active search for the "ethnically exotic." Some *Ladinos* in San Cristóbal increasingly found themselves catering to, and eventually depending on, tourists' thirst for Indian culture and products. Eventually, many of those who were not engaged in the tourist industry also came to associate foreigners with Indians in some manner.

The changing demographic and spatial makeup of the city created the conditions for the emergence of an elite *Coleto* identity which, no longer based in the geography of the city, now asserted at times even more strongly than the *Ladinos* had, a neocolonial identity. *Coletos* adopted the identity traits of the old *criollo* families, asserting their Spanish heritage and reviving the myths of "conquistador ancestors." *Coleto*, literally "ponytail," refers to the braided hairstyle favored by Spanish and *criollo* men in this period. Faced with the influx of foreigners and Indians, *Coletos* developed a conservative, xenophobic discourse which posited outsiders as "invaders," "criminals," and, particularly Indians, as "savages" (Paris Pombo 2000).

This understanding of the socially subversive nature of Indians was exacerbated by the conflation, after the Zapatista uprising began in 1994, of foreigners (both from other countries and other parts of Mexico)[9] and Indians with political opposition. The Zapatistas' incursion into San Cristóbal and the taking of the municipal government building by armed indigenous people stimulated long-held fears of Indian invasion, illegality, and loss of control. One of the first things I noticed when I arrived in San Cristóbal in 1995 were small hand-lettered signs in the windows of some shops, and even one banner spread above the main tourist strip Real de Guadalupe, that called for a return to *el estado de derecho* (rule of law). While tourism dropped to near zero levels that year, the influx of national and international solidarity and human rights activists after the uprising linked foreigners to political opposition and fueled xenophobic sentiments. *Coletos*, looking for someone to blame for social instability and challenges to their dominance, had traditionally defined enemies at hand: Indians and foreigners. Some felt that Indians were incapable of planning and launching a rebellion of this scale and believed that foreigners were behind the revolt. The woman who rented an apartment to me for a short time in 1995, and who understood herself to be "a friend of the Indians," told me the following: "I don't blame the *Inditos* for what has happened; they were manipulated. But it is they who will have to pay the consequences, not the outsiders who tricked them."[10]

One of the "outsiders" conservative *Coletos* blamed for the uprising was the bishop of San Cristóbal. Perhaps not surprisingly, conservative *Coletos* had had tensions with Bishop Ruíz for some time. They did not identify with his approach of liberation theology and *teología india*, and his close relationship to indigenous communities were interpreted as betrayal of their values. One *Coleta* woman told me, "The bishop is close to many families in San Cristóbal, but there are people who say he is more interested in the Indians than in us."[11] When the Zapatista uprising took place, many *Coletos*, shocked at this challenge to established relations of power by Indians they regarded as uncontrolled and incompetent, accused Bishop Ruíz of having fomented the uprising. Not long after the uprising, a group of *Coletos* formed the "Civic Front of San Cristóbal." Calling themselves *Auténtico Coletos*, they strove to reassert their place of privilege in the city and organized protests against the indigenous rebels, international solidarity to the Zapatistas, and Bishop Ruíz.

I happened across one of these protests one day while passing the plaza in front of the Municipal President's building, adjacent to the cathedral in the center of town. I came upon a group of people burning an effigy, and to my surprise, when I got closer I discovered the effigy was of the bishop. I asked a woman near me why they were doing this. Her face showed visible annoyance at my question, and she responded, "What you *foreigners* can't understand is that these *Indians* you love so much are silly and ignorant. They can't even pull themselves out of the dirt, so how could they have planned all this [presumably, the uprising]? Everybody knows it was the work of 'the Red Bishop.' "[12]

When the Fray Bartolomé Human Rights Center began to coordinate the work of many national and international human rights observers through its program of civilian peace camps, to those inclined to view human rights workers as leftist agitators it constituted further evidence of the intimate connections between human rights advocacy, the Diocese of San Cristóbal, and indigenous rebellion. Human rights, which had become synonymous with the work of the diocese and of foreign activists in defense of indigenous people, provided *Coletos* another outlet for their defensive anger.

Of course, the *Auténtico Coletos* were correct in their belief that most of the human rights observers who came to Chiapas were sympathetic to the Zapatistas. While some, myself included, were interested in engaging in human rights work in Chiapas because we saw it as a means to support a movement we agreed with on many issues, others who saw their role in a more neutral way nevertheless argued that it was very clear whose rights were being violated and who was in need of human rights "defense."[13]

The visits of high-profile foreign diplomatic representatives often resulted in similar conclusions. For example, following the Acteal Massacre in December 1997, Chiapas was visited by three representatives of the United Nations: Asma Jahangir, special envoy on Extrajudicial Executions; Mary Robinson, High Commissioner on Human Rights; and Erika Daes, President of the Special Working Group on Indigenous Peoples. While the Mexican government stated publicly that the U.N. representatives were welcome and that the government was disposed to work on human rights issues, the reports by these representatives highlighted the discrepancy between the government's rhetoric and its actions, suggesting serious violations of the human rights of indigenous people, especially those living in the conflict zones (Burguete and Leyva 2000).

In an intensely polarized climate, with the governmental belief in a Zapatista netwar, dramatic support for the Zapatistas from abroad, and criticisms even from distinguished diplomatic sources, all foreigners in Chiapas became the objects of suspicion by government officials, *Coletos*, and local authorities of the ruling party in indigenous communities. Particularly after the governmental campaign against foreigners began in earnest following the events at

Acteal, virtually all foreigners were associated with human rights work and thus with Zapatista support (Global Exchange et al. 1999).

Thus, many *Coletos'* understanding of human rights as something partial, biased, and threatening to their interests and their notion of how social relations should be organized emerged from their history and their political subjectivity in the context of the conflict period. It is not my intention to justify their position, but to understand the social dynamics at work in relation to human rights. I do wish to suggest that *Coletos'* understandings are products of the globalization of the discourse of human rights, filtered through particular local understandings and political subjectivities.

"Derechos Humanos, Asesinos": *Paz y Justicia* and the Pro–Ruling Party Paramilitaries

In another part of the state, a very different set of social actors with a vastly different history and subjectivity came to a similar set of interpretations (minus the racialized overtones inherent in *Coleto* discourse) of human rights, the Church, and foreign human rights workers. In the Northern Zone, predominantly Chol Maya, pro–ruling party sectors of politically divided communities feared challenges to the legitimacy of their local power, which they long held as authorities of the ruling party. Beginning in 1995, pro-government paramilitary groups began to surge. This happened mainly in places that were long-standing PRI strongholds, but where PRI supporters have recently become the minority in relation to members of the PRD/Zapatista supporters (in some areas these were synonymous) and so felt threatened. The first groups appeared in the Northern Zone—the *Chinchulines* and *Desarrollo, Paz y Justicia* (generally called simply *Paz y Justicia*). Paramilitarization spread to the Highlands and later to the jungle with groups like *Máscara Roja* (Red Mask) and *Movimiento Indígena Revolucionario Anti-Zapatista* (Anti-Zapatista Indigenous Revolutionary Movement–MIRA), respectively. By 1997, there were as many as twenty-five paramilitary groups reported to be operating in Chiapas.

Because of the shadowy nature of the groups, it is difficult to document their relationship with the government and the military. However, there is in some cases clear evidence of links between the landed families, the state and federal governments, the military, and the paramilitary organizations. For example, it was a local congressperson, Samuel Sánchez Sánchez, who openly formed and directed *Paz y Justicia*. Though it was widely known that *Paz y Justicia* was a paramilitary group, it was given legitimacy and credibility by the

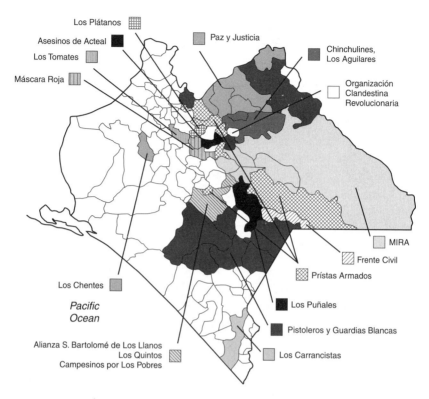

Los Plátanos
Asesinos de Acteal
Los Tomates
Máscara Roja
Paz y Justicia
Chinchulines,
Los Aguilares
Organización
Clandestina
Revolucionaria
MIRA
Frente Civil
Prístas Armados
Los Chentes
Pacific
Ocean
Los Puñales
Pistoleros y Guardias Blancas
Alianza S. Bartolomé de Los Llanos
Los Quintos
Campesinos por Los Pobres
Los Carrancistas

Map 3.1 Areas of paramilitary influence.

federal government in the form of status as an *Asociación Civil* (similar to non-profit organization status).[14] This status facilitated the channeling of funds to *Paz y Justicia*, for example through the state agency SEDESOL (Secretary of Social Development), which signed a *convenio* (agreement of collaboration) with *Paz y Justicia*. Notably, this *convenio* was sponsored by General Mario Renán Castillo, the commander of the Seventh Military Region (which covered the entire conflict zone).[15] Others have suggested that the State Security Council was also used to channel money and training to paramilitary groups (Ramírez Cuevas 1997). In May of 1998, the national magazine *Proceso* reported:

> The Attorney General has confirmed the participation of the previous attorney general and former president of the State Security Council, Jorge Enrique Hernandez Aguilar, as well as the former under-secretary of Government, Uriel Jarquin, in the violent activities of paramilitary groups. (Corro 1998)

Paramilitarization is argued to be part of a campaign of low-intensity warfare, a divide-and-conquer strategy designed to exhaust and terrify the rebellious population into submission (Global Exchange et al. 1998; López Astraín 1996; Olivera 1998). It was clearly part of military and governmental strategy to engage in exacerbating already tense situations in a number of areas, since this ultimately both diverted energy in these communities for engaging in open rebellion and justified increased state presence as necessary for maintaining control. This became public knowledge with the publication of the military's Plan Chiapas (Marín 1998).

Paramilitary violence pitted brother against brother within communities and had devastating local effects, including hundreds of deaths of members of both pro- and antigovernment groups and the generation of hundreds of political prisoners and tens of thousands of internal refugees (CDHFBC 1996). This violence reached its peak in the December 1997 massacre at Acteal. In this incident, paramilitaries in the highlands municipality of Chenalhó attacked members of Las Abejas, a group associated with the Diocese of San Cristóbal and committed to nonviolent resistance. Forty-five people, mostly women and children, were

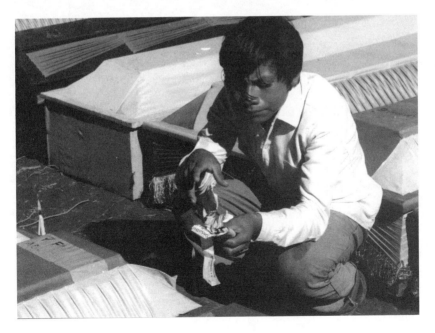

Figure 3.3 A young man in Acteal crouches among the coffins of the massacre victims. Jutta Meier Wiedenbach.

slaughtered with machine guns and machetes (Echohawk 1998; Hernández Castillo, 1995; Tavanti 2002). That the attack was directed against Las Abejas, who were open about their disagreement with the Zapatistas' methods of armed struggle, is in part due to the linkage made by the paramilitaries between the diocese and the Zapatistas. The Abejas were close to the diocese, the diocese is tied to the Zapatistas, and therefore the Abejas are understood to be the enemy.

In the Chol communities of the Northern Zone where paramilitary violence first surged, human rights was becoming an important political discourse by mid-1996, when I first entered the region as part of the *Estación Norte*. The Northern Zone was not part of the area designated as a conflict zone in the first months of the Zapatista uprising. Nevertheless, as support for the EZLN grew there throughout 1994 and 1995, the region grew increasingly tense. The dynamic of the conflict in the Northern Zone differed from those in the Cañadas of the Lacandón and the Highlands, which at that time in large part consisted of battles between the EZLN and Mexican security forces. In the Northern Zone, the conflicts were intracommunity—indigenous people against indigenous people, brother against brother—and very violent. Throughout 1996 and into 1997, the Northern Zone, though outside the official conflict zone, was the true conflict zone of the state.

On my first visit to the Northern Zone, I met exclusively with EZLN supporters and people associated with the Catholic Church. I heard a very positive interpretation of human rights. One young man said: "If human rights didn't come in here, we would be alone. Nobody would defend us." Several days later, a woman who had been violently expelled with dozens of others from her community by members of *Paz y Justicia* told me, "Today our hearts are full of sorrow. Human rights are our hope for tomorrow."

This contrasts sharply with the discourse of *Paz y Justicia*, whose popular slogan was "*Derechos humanos, asesinos*" or "Human rights, murderers." This dramatically divergent understanding and usage of the term (and I emphasize that this is their understanding of it, not just a political manipulation of the term) have to do with their particular history, the configuration of their relationships to the state and the Church, and the dynamics of local power relations.

Even a cursory sketch of their history tells us a lot about this process. During the colonial period, Chols suffered forced relocation to accessible areas and forced payment of tribute to the Crown (Carton de Grammont and Flores 1982). In the early years of independence, they also suffered domination by non-Indian elites who resided in the municipal seats. In 1891, Chol lands were privatized, opening them up to German and American companies that quickly began exploiting the region for coffee production (Benjamin 1995 [1989]). For the next fifty years, they suffered a period of near slavery to the foreign companies, known in Chol oral history as *el mosojüntel* or "the time when we were servants" (Alejos García 1988). The harsh treatment they received from foreigners and *Ladinos* from colonial times into the mid-twentieth century, but particularly during the *mosojüntel*, inculcated a strong aversion to all non-Chols (CDHFBC 1996). Alejos García (1988) argues that they developed a binary understanding of the world, in which Chols were equated with good, and Kaxlanes, or non-Chols, with evil. Their oral history—and certainly their current political discourse—reflect this binary understanding, frequently evoking images of evil Kaxlanes and good or saintly Chols.

During the 1930s, the regime of Lázaro Cárdenas carried out agrarian reform in Chiapas. Part of a larger postrevolutionary project of national consolidation, the Cardenista agrarian ideology posited the integration of all campesinos into the nation-state through land reform (Benjamin 1996 [1989]). The Northern Zone benefited, receiving large tracts of communally held farmland known as *ejidos*. The Cardenistas were a little surprised when the Chols, rather than integrating themselves into the national economy through coffee production, took their land and immediately withdrew, returning to subsistence agriculture based on corn production. Nevertheless, the agrarian reform embedded the state in the Chol imagination as an ally against exploitative Kaxlanes, and they remained strongly affiliated with the ruling party, the PRI, for the next several decades (CDHFBC 1996).[16]

In the 1970s, the liberation theology message of the Diocese of San Cristóbal began to have an impact in the region. Franciscans had been active in the zone since the 1950s, training a small number of educated bilingual Chol teachers as catechists. The liberation evangelizing propagated throughout the region by the pastoral agents of the diocese gave Chol communities both a group of trained leaders and a discourse that justified and organized community mobilization against marginalization and exploitation (CDHFBC 1996). By the mid-1980s, the diocese had developed its own human rights message (see Kovic 2005). When the diocese formed the Fray Bartolomé Human Rights Center, human rights became broadly associated with the Diocese of San Cristóbal: its bishop, its pastoral agents, and its catechists.

Also in the 1970s, the boom in the world coffee market motivated Chols to begin growing coffee again. However, because the agro-industrial processing, as well as the financing and marketing of the coffee industry, was in the hands of Kaxlanes, others reaped the benefits of their labor, and they ultimately ended up with social conditions starkly similar to those of the *mosojüntel* (Alejos García 1988).

In an attempt to strengthen the communities against outside exploitation, the coffee producers of the region participated in a cooperative credit union, Pajal Yakatik, formed in 1982 by advisor Adolfo Orive (Benjamin 1996 [1989]; N. Harvey 1998). The split in Pajal some years later would establish the lines along which the radical, violent conflicts of the 1990s were drawn. Pajal was the indirect product of the 1970s Maoist intellectual movement *Política Popular*, in which Orive was a leader (CHFBLC 1996). One of the most criticized tenets of the *Política Popular* was their *política de dos caras*, or two-faced policy of taking advantage of government programs for campesinos while organizing oppositionally, generally around agrarian issues (N. Harvey 1998). The credit union was formed with 25 million pesos from the National Banking Commission, and Pajal simultaneously engaged in campesino base organizing and worked with INMECAFE, a state organization that promoted monocultivation of coffee for export. The dependency on coffee cultivation and on INMECAFE left campesinos in the Northern Zone destitute when coffee markets fell in the 1980s (N. Harvey 1998).

Pajal went into crisis, and the communities of the Northern Zone divided into two camps, which pertained to the two faces of the organization: those who organized oppositionally and those who organized to benefit from alliance with the government. Orive was heavily criticized for being too pro-government (*gobiernista*) and for failing to protest government actions when necessary (N. Harvey 1998). Though Pajal continued to function until 1991, the split had serious implications for many Chols in the Northern Zone. In one community, I was told that the experience of Pajal radically altered their vision of the state from potential ally to oppressor. This faction again withdrew, engaging in passive resistance such as refusing to pay taxes or electric bills. Within a few years, these communities would emerge as bastions of the opposition PRD and as EZLN base supporters (PRD was virtually synonymous with EZLN support in the Northern Zone at that time). Notably, they were often communities that had strong leaders trained as catechists by the Diocese of San Cristóbal. A number of the communities that maintained a strong alliance with the government later emerged as participants in paramilitary organizations.

The political division exploded after the Zapatista uprising in 1994, as support for the EZLN increased in the region, and PRI militants increasingly became a minority and faced losing their hold on regional power.

When I talked to people in the Northern Zone, it became clear to me that their history and recent political experience strongly shaped their understanding and utilization of the discourse of human rights. For those who were pro-government, human rights were interpreted very negatively. I talked to relatively few of them, because my own position as an activist and a foreigner made this impossible, but I was able to talk to some people in PRI communities, and I have also relied on their own version of their perspective on human rights as elaborated in the underground publication *Ni Derechos, Ni Humanos* (Neither Rights nor Humans).[17] From these sources, it seems clear that *Paz y Justicia*'s understanding of human rights as "murderous" was based on their perception that human rights were associated with (a) foreigners/Kaxlanes (i.e., evil); (b) the Fray Bartolomé de Las Casas Human Rights Center, and thus directly linked to the diocese and Bishop Ruíz, and the catechists who were the

Figure 3.4 Thousands displaced from their home communities by paramilitary violence lived in appalling conditions in refugee camps, such as this one in the cold, damp Highlands. Shelters are made from sticks, leaves, and pieces of plastic tarp.

leaders of the communities they were fighting with; and (c) the EZLN, which was effectively mobilizing human rights to strengthen its position. For the Zapatistas "human rights" was the discourse and the embodiment of "the enemy." Communities who joined the EZLN had a similar set of understandings of human rights, though they interpreted them differently. The fact that they emerged from Pajal with an anti-government attitude, that their leaders were often trained catechists with strong links to the diocese, and their involvement with the EZLN all brought them to very different conclusions about human rights.

It was thus that two men from the same small, intensely conflicted community could make the diametrically opposed statements about human rights described at the start of this chapter. Both seemed to assert that theirs was the "true" Chol subject position. One expressed reliance on and trust in human rights, while the other associated human rights with meddlesome outsiders "butting in" to community business.[18] These diametrically opposed views on human rights cannot be understood as simply the rhetoric of opposing sides in a political conflict. Though these distinct interpretations are being deployed in support of each side's goals, they are more than strategic utilizations. They are local appropriations and interpretations based on the history and experience of the social actors involved.

Further Engagements: The State Government and Human Rights

In 1998, anthropologist Jane Collier attended a meeting in the highlands community of Zinacantán that had been called to debate the new state law on Indigenous Rights and Culture being introduced by the interim governor Albores Guillen.[19] Some in the community were concerned about a portion of the law that contained language limiting indigenous authorities' ability to apply customary norms and sanctions, stating that they can do so only when these are compatible with "constitutional guarantees, national laws, and internationally recognized human rights" (State Government of Chiapas 1999). During the discussion, a judge from the indigenous court stated his view that it would be impossible for the indigenous judges to apply their customary norms and sanctions if the clause that invoked human rights remained in the law, because "when we sentence someone to two weeks of community service, 'human rights' comes along and frees him" (analyzed in Speed and Collier 2000a).[20]

In Zinacantán, where at that time the indigenous authorities pertained to the ruling party (PRI), they enjoyed a good deal of local autonomy in conflict resolution and community governance. What the judge was referring to by "human rights" were human rights organizations (probably specifically the Fray Bart), considered by the Zinacanteco authorities to be external agents who might impede their exercise of their own indigenous traditions, which for decades were the basis of the clientelistic networks of the PRI (Rus 1994b). The Zinacantecos' reluctance to have such restrictions inscribed in law was not entirely unjustified, as the state did in fact utilize such a discourse to constrain forms of indigenous autonomy that it found unacceptable, particularly Zapatista autonomy.

Like other social actors in the Chiapas conflict, the state and federal governments have mobilized human rights in an attempt to strengthen their own position in that conflict. Human rights have regularly been utilized as the barrier setting the limits of indigenous autonomy. The kind of limiting language embedded in the state law is in fact the norm in indigenous rights legislation and is found in international legislation as well. Even the San Andrés Accords stipulated that the indigenous municipalities might "obtain the recognition of their internal normative systems of regulation and sanction, to the degree that they do not violate constitutional guarantees and human rights" (Ce Acatl 1996). There are important reasons for this language, and one can think of many instances in which the tension between individual human rights and collective indigenous rights might come into conflict in circumstances which necessitate the assertion of individual rights (see Chapter 5). Nevertheless, in the context of the Chiapas conflict, this privileging of individual rights over collective ones provided more than a safeguard for individuals; it also served as an important tool of the state for limiting indigenous resistance.

For example, the government utilized the discourse of individual human rights to justify its campaign of dismantling Zapatista autonomous municipalities. In one case, that of the community of Nicolás Ruiz, on the day prior to the massive raid involving hundreds of police and military troops in June 1998, interim Governor Albores set the justification up by declaring:

A group of radicals has once again disrupted normal life in Nicolás Ruiz with a highly primitive approach of *usos y costumbres*. But these cannot exist in opposition to the elemental laws and norms of human coexistence, [nor can they] trample individual rights. . . . We will not permit illegality, in Nicolás Ruiz or any other part of Chiapas. We will make the rule of law prevail and restore constitutionality. (*Cuarto Poder*, June 2, 1998)[21]

As we will see in the following chapter, which treats the conflict in Nicolás Ruiz, this raid had at least as much to do with challenging Zapatista municipal governments as it did with protecting the individual rights of the pro–ruling party minority (who were themselves utilizing a discourse of collective land rights). Similarly, accusations that the authorities of the Zapatista autonomous municipality of Tierra y Libertad had violated the individual rights of two men who had been detained in relation to a land dispute justified the detention of fifty-three indigenous people from that community in a raid involving more than a thousand soldiers, police, and immigration agents.[22] A closer look at the case demonstrates the dynamic appropriation of human rights discourse by the state government.

On May 1, 1998, approximately one thousand state police, federal police, soldiers, and immigration agents entered the town of Amparo Aguatinta, the municipal seat of Tierra y Libertad. The reason for the massive raid, according to state officials, was to arrest six persons for whom warrants had been issued and, notably, to reestablish the "rule of law."[23] Fifty-three persons were detained, only two of whom had been named in the arrest warrants. Three days after their arrest, forty-five of the detainees were released without explanation. Among those who remained in custody were the Municipal President, the Secretary of Agrarian Affairs, and the Vice-Minister of Justice of the Autonomous Council.[24] They were accused of having violated the individual rights of two brothers by illegally detaining them.

The conflict that gave rise to the police raid began as a simple matter. Two brothers of Guatemalan origin, Pascual and Pedro Gómez Domingo, were accused by people from Rancho Villa las Rosas of illegal woodcutting. When summoned by the authorities of the autonomous municipality, the brothers failed to appear. The President of the Autonomous Council, the Justice Minister, and the Vice-Minister then signed an order for their detention. On April 22, Pascual was detained and brought to the municipal jail in Amparo Aguatinta. He was held for one week while the authorities tried to negotiate a settlement between him and his accusers, though he steadfastly denied responsibility and refused to pay reparations. The autonomous authorities, following their regular procedure in cases involving Guatemalan refugees, contacted the offices of the U.N. High Commission on Refugees (ACNUR) and requested their participation in resolving the problem. On the seventh day of Pascual's deten-

tion, his brother Pedro turned himself in to the authorities in Amparo Aguatinta and, as is common practice, was "exchanged" for Pascual, who was then
released. On the third day of Pedro's detention, the same day that officials from
ACNUR proposed to travel to Amparo Aguatinta to help negotiate a settlement,[25] the joint army-police-immigration raid took place.

There is a legal argument that the autonomous authorities of Tierra y Libertad violated the brothers' constitutional right not to be arbitrarily detained by
keeping them in jail for longer than the thirty-six hours allowed by the Mexican
Constitution.[26] Although there are written laws against cutting wood, the authorities were less interested in finding out if a recognized law had been broken
than in negotiating a conciliatory solution based on repairing the damage. At
first, the authorities used jailing as a means of persuading the brothers to pay for
the damage. In Tierra y Libertad, people apparently believe it is important for
delinquents to replace or repair what they have stolen or harmed, not just to
compensate victims but also because delinquents must be convinced to "live
like other people."[27] Later, after the authorities had failed to negotiate a solution,
they continued to hold the brothers as "punishment." Because many inhabitants
of Tierra y Libertad do not have sufficient funds to pay reparations, people may
treat jail time as an alternative, referring to both as *multas*.[28] In fact, detentions
for periods longer than thirty-six hours take place on a regular basis in indigenous communities and rarely draw the attention of Mexican authorities.

There is also an argument to be made that state officials used the jailing of
the Gómez Domingo brothers as their justification for arresting the autonomous authorities of Tierra y Libertad and dismantling the municipal seat.
Several aspects of the events support the idea that the government's grievance
with the autonomous authorities had less to do with their detention of the
Gómez Domingo brothers than with the community's assertion of political autonomy and its affiliation with the EZLN.

First, this raid took place in the context of raids on several other Zapatista autonomous municipal seats, all within a period of a few months. The autonomous
authorities of Tierra y Libertad were charged with kidnapping, along with
"usurping the functions" of legitimate municipal authorities. Thus the "crimes"
allegedly committed by the autonomous authorities were directly related to their
performance of their duties as authorities of the autonomous municipality. The
autonomous authorities admitted having detained the Gómez Domingo brothers but emphatically denied having kidnapped anyone. Detentions of seven to
ten days, they said, are a standard practice in the region. In their interpretation,

they were acting on the authority vested in them by the people who had elected them to enforce the law while respecting *usos y costumbres*.[29] This is clearly the point of divergence in interpretation between Tierra y Libertad and the Mexican officials and thus the charge of having "usurped functions." They asserted the legitimacy of their posts in the Autonomous Council, noting that they had been properly elected by customary procedures, which involved consensus decisions taken in community assemblies.[30] One of the Gómez Domingo brothers even signed a declaration stating that he had not been kidnapped but had turned himself in to the autonomous authorities in Amparo Aguatinta because he believed that they were the competent body to resolve the dispute.[31] Further, as part of the campaign leading up to the 2000 presidential and gubernatorial elections, a key Zapatista demand—the release of Zapatista political prisoners—was met. Some of the accused from Tierra y Libertad were among the first released—after having spent one year and four months in state prison. Many observers understood their release in this context as an admission that the autonomous authorities had been detained for political reasons—namely, their affiliation with the EZLN—rather than for having broken the law or violated an individual's rights.

There is thus good reason to believe that the arrest and imprisonment of the Tierra y Libertad authorities was a political act undertaken by the state government, in coordination with the federal government, as part of a systematic effort to eliminate autonomous municipalities in rebellion. By camouflaging this act in a discourse of human rights, the government shifted a political conflict onto judicial terrain,[32] thereby obscuring its political motivation. At the same time, the state bolstered its role as the purveyor of stability, protector of rights, and guardian of the rule of law.

Conclusions

The globalization of the discourse of human rights has shaped the way many social actors involved in the Chiapas conflict express their positions and engage in political actions. Most are utilizing a discourse of human rights in one form or another to defend their actions and pursue their political goals. This is true of people who are struggling for social change, such as the Zapatistas and their allies, for whom the framing of their demands in a discourse of human rights allows them to mobilize support from broad networks of actors and organizations and thus strengthen their position vis-à-vis the state. The state and federal governments recognize this and, in the face of new strategies and new pressures exerted by this conjunction of global and local forces, seek new ways to defend their power. The discourse of human rights provides the state with a justification for its actions that is difficult to contest. Meanwhile, local groups as dissimilar as *Auténtico Coletos* and Chol paramilitaries redeploy the discourse of human rights in their struggle to maintain the status quo. The discourse of "rule of law" also plays a role in the Chiapas conflict, justifying state military intervention and providing an alternative legal discourse for social actors loath to mobilize human rights discourse because of its particular associations in the local context.

Human rights in Chiapas has been primarily associated with the efforts of the Catholic Church and NGOs to improve the lot of poor and indigenous peoples at the expense of current power-holders associated with Mexico's longtime ruling party, the PRI. In many parts of the state, "human rights" is understood to mean the Fray Bartolomé Human Rights Center of the Catholic diocese, with whatever positive or negative connotations this might have for the people in question. The term is also associated with foreign supporters of the Zapatista rebellion, whether such foreigners are regarded as protectors preventing a bloodbath or as meddling outsiders. In Chiapas, as elsewhere in the world, the discourse of human rights does not play a neutral role. Rather, the discourse of human rights takes on the meanings ascribed to it by social actors involved in particular political struggles. Close scrutiny reveals that there is not *one* discourse of human rights, but a multiplicity of discourses. The ascribed meanings the discourse holds for different groups are not simply political or rhetorical strategies, but rather reflect the distinct subject positions of the actors involved. The particular histories and relations of power in which the groups involved are enmeshed are reflected in their distinct utilizations of the discourse of human rights.

This argument is not intended as a complex re-elaboration of the relativist position that there are many different concepts of human rights in different cultural contexts. It is not that indigenous people or others in Chiapas have their own notions of human rights, separate and distinct from Western ones. Rather, there is a dialogic process in which differing interpretations of human rights emerge precisely from the intense interactions among globalized discourses, transnational actors, agents of the nation-state, and various local groups. In other words, the varying discourses of human rights which emerged during the Chiapas conflict were not a straightforward product of the imposition of Western ideas or of specifically indigenous or local concepts; rather, they were social constructions forged in dialogic interactions on a highly politicized terrain where all had much at stake.

This does have implications for the long-standing debate about cultural relativism and universalism and especially the issue of whether, in the context of globalization, human rights has become "imperialism with a global reach" (discussed in Merry 1992). To categorize indigenous people as passive receivers of "imperializing" or "globalizing" discourses eliminates their history and their agency. As the examples explored in this chapter demonstrate, the various understandings and cultural norms of these distinct social actors are historically constructed—products of an ongoing dialogue with the nonlocal. This is a process in which they actively take part: rearticulating and redeploying the discourse of human rights based on their own complex and dialogically constructed histories and political positionalities. This suggests something about the more threatening potentialities of globalization for local cultures and identities: that they are unlikely to be erased, homogenized, or eliminated. Local cultures will continue to be what they have always been: historical and social constructions, created by the local social actors in dialogic interaction with others. In the chapters that follow, we will see how such processes have played out in terms of one community's identity, gender norms, and forms of social struggle.

One further point is worth noting before moving on. As I have noted, it is easy to fall into viewing globalization (and resultant homogenization) as the bad or negative process, and therefore to keep local diversity as an innocent figure; to celebrate locality as a site of resistance through diversity and diversity as an inherently positive form of resistance to globalization. In part this chapter has been intended to demonstrate not only that there is local diversity but also that the local is itself quite complicated. It is difficult to view the diversity of ideas in the Northern Zone, for example, as inherently positive; local diversity there has been a product of violent conflict with bitter repercussions few would celebrate. Thus, both the global and the local need to remain constantly problematized categories. It is clear that which discourses get globalized is a result of specific relations of power and that once globalized, these discourses do shape the possibilities for how local people can formulate their identities and forms of resistance. However, I have tried here to emphasize local peoples' agency in that formulation in whatever spaces they find available and useful. Thus, local identities and positionalities are actively and continually reinvented in a dialogue of resistance and accommodation to a wider, ultimately global, social field.

4 Dialogisms, or, On Being and Becoming Indigenous in Nicolás Ruiz

> Our land struggle to recover the communal territory possessed by our Tzeltal ancestors has been long and even bloody. In this struggle we have suffered repression, assassinations, and imprisonment by previous PRI governments. . . . [A]s a *pueblo*, with a long history of struggle, at times we feel that our patience is running out.
>
> *Authorities of* **Bienes Comunales, Nicolás Ruiz**[1]

UNDER THE LAMINA ROOF in the midday sun, the large assembly hall was like an oven. The six hundred–plus *comuneros* of Nicolás Ruiz gathered for the monthly community assembly meeting had just shouted out a resounding "*Sí!*" to the proposal that they participate in a complaint before the International Labor Organization. "Wait!" a man on the left side of the platform called out. "I want to know if everyone realizes this means we are declaring ourselves a '*pueblo indígena.*' Is everyone in agreement that we declare ourselves a *pueblo indígena*?" There was a momentary pause as everyone drew in their breath, and six hundred voices filled the hall: "*Sí!*"[2]

In the previous chapter, we saw that there is nothing homogeneous about the interpretations and uses of the discourse of human rights in Chiapas. Local actors are engaging with human rights based on their own local histories and subjectivities, and they are reframing the discourse and its significations in the process. But human rights as a concept and a set of practices—regardless of the interpretation—do not get appropriated and reformulated in a vacuum. Processes of appropriation and resignification also have effects on those who are engaged in them. In the dialogic interaction between the local and the nonlocal, both are reshaped and redefined. In this chapter, I will examine more closely how this process plays out on the local terrain, looking at the effects of engagement with nonlocal social actors and discourses on one community's identity and resistance. I will analyze the manner in which community identity—including ethnic identity—emerges dialogically, and how the global-ized discourse of human rights has played into that dialogism in the Chiapas conflict.

The community of Nicolás Ruiz (previously San Diego de la Reforma) was founded by Tzeltal Indians, but it has been identified for the last several decades as "campesino" (i.e., nonindigenous). The community has recently been undergoing a process of recovering its indigenous identity, as the scene described above, in which the men in the community vote to declare the town indigenous, indicates. It is a process that, for a variety of reasons discussed in this chapter, many "for-mer" indigenous communities in Mexico may experience in the years ahead.

Nicolás Ruiz, now both a town and a municipality, is a notably understud-ied community in the state of Chiapas, where historical, anthropological, and sociological studies of the Highlands, the Lacandón, and even the Northern Zone abound. Its neighbor in the central region of the state, the municipality of Venustiano Carranza (San Bartolomé de los Llanos), has been the subject of much study, including articles, theses, and books (e.g., Díaz de Salas 1995; Molina 1976; Moncada 1983; Morales Avendaño 1974, 1977, 1985; Renard 1998; Salovesh 1972; Verduzco 1976). Histories of the state of Chiapas rarely mention Nicolás Ruiz, and very little has been written specifically about the town or mu-nicipality from the perspective of any discipline.[3]

However, in recent years Nicolás Ruiz has been one of the municipalities most often mentioned in news articles and reports on the Chiapas conflict. This notoriety is because of the serious and often violent intracommunity conflict Nicolás Ruiz has suffered since 1996. This "local" conflict is inseparable from the broader conflict and counterinsurgency campaign, which as we saw in Chapter 3 left many communities divided and, not infrequently, armed. The conflict in Nicolás Ruiz produced a death toll of over one hundred people between 1996 and 2000, leading one journalist to refer to the municipality as Tierra Sin Ley (Land Without Law) (Gurguha 2000). Yet while such extreme internal discord is a new phenomenon for the community, conflict is not new to Nicolás Ruiz; its history has been one of ongoing struggles over land, struggles that have shaped the understandings and identities of its inhabitants in particular ways.

When looking at the Chiapas conflict from the community level, what quickly becomes apparent is the seemingly endless local complexity of the con-flict and the incredible diversity of the communities involved. From region to region, often even from community to community, quite distinct local histo-ries and experiences mark the particular insertions of each community into the larger conflict. A study of virtually any community from any region involved would likely tell us a fascinating story about identity and resistance.

One of the things that is most interesting about Nicolás Ruiz is its dissimilarities from other regions involved in the conflict: it is outside the officially defined "conflict zone"; it was not part of the original uprising, becoming a Zapatista base area in 1996; and it has not been defined (either officially or by residents until very recently) as an indigenous community for many decades. But its similarities with other conflicted communities are also interesting: the community's relationship to official discourses of the state, agrarian reform and agrarian struggle, and more recently to state multiculturalism, the EZLN, "civil society," and the national and international human rights community. Most importantly, I am here concerned with how the community's dialogic interactions with all of these have shaped their political subjectivities and community identity over time.

In this chapter, I want to show a particular trajectory of community identity formation that begins with indigenous identity, then moves into a campesino identity in large part through the community's relationship with the state agrarian and *indigenista* policies, then a radicalization of campesino identity as community members grow frustrated in their interactions with the state, and finally a radicalized indigenous identity as they engage with new social actors in the context of the Zapatista uprising and the larger social conflict in the state. In order to explore these questions, I will begin with a brief description of Nicolás Ruiz, then turn to its history and consider how its identifications have shifted over time in relation to changing historical dynamics and community circumstances.

Nicolás Ruiz Today

Nicolás Ruiz is the third smallest municipality (of 118) in the state of Chiapas.[4] The municipal seat (also called Nicolás Ruiz) is its only town, and 98 percent of the inhabitants reside there. With a population of only 3,276 people, Nicolás Ruiz does not reach the category of "urban" and thus is considered a totally rural municipality (INEGI 2000).[5]

At seven hundred meters above sea level, the town is surrounded by rugged hills and fertile fields. The town itself is situated on a rise and is made up of eight blocks by eleven blocks of paved streets. Homes are constructed mainly of adobe or cinderblock walls, dirt or cement floors, and roofs of tile or lamina. The streets are neat and the town has a well-ordered feeling to it, despite the horses and occasional livestock which roam freely about. Towering over the town to the north is the notable landmark La Lanza, a high-peaked hill. In the words of one resident, "La Lanza protects us, takes care of us." There is a legend that the spirit of La Lanza appears during battles as a man riding a white horse, to defend the men of Nicolás Ruiz. La Lanza is the town's trademark, even appearing on the letterhead of the municipal government.

Nicolás Ruiz is an agricultural town and virtually all men are farmers, growing corn and beans, as well as raising cattle, horses, and sheep. The majority of the corn harvest is sold to the state company, Maseca. Only a small portion is retained for family consumption. While many people raise chickens, turkeys, or pigs in their yards, all other products are brought in from outside the municipality. There are a few men engaged in construction work, furniture making, and brick and roof tile production. As a general rule, agricultural work and skilled labor are undertaken only by men, and census statistics list only 2.4 percent of women as being economically active. Nevertheless, women do raise animals for family consumption and engage in small commerce, meaning that they run a small store in a front room of their home where they sell soft drinks, snacks, and small canned and dry goods. The two small pharmacies and the town's only public telephone *caseta* (public phone service) are owned and operated by women.

Figure 4.1 The *Presidencia Municipal* of Nicolás Ruiz (left), with La Lanza in the background. Shannon Speed.

Nicolás Ruiz's "state of marginalization" was considered "medium" on a scale of low to very high in 1997 (CIACH et al. 1997). In a state where marginalization is marked in many communities, the category of "medium" suggests that the inhabitants of Nicolás Ruiz do not confront as many challenges to their livelihoods as some others in the region. Nevertheless, life in Nicolás Ruiz is made difficult by the lack of resources and infrastructure. For example, although Nicolás Ruiz has one secondary and two primary schools, the majority of the population has less than a sixth-grade education because children need to begin contributing to the family income from a very early age. In 1990, only 17.3 percent of the population had completed primary school or higher and 30.5 percent of the population reported having no education whatsoever (INEGI 1990). The majority of the homes have running water and electricity, though fewer than half are connected to the town's sewerage system. There is a state-run rural medical clinic of the *Instituto Mexicano de Seguridad Social* (IMSS) in Nicolás Ruiz; however, it is staffed by a physician only sporadically and must serve the entire population. Although Nicolás Ruiz is the seat of a municipal government and is relatively close to the state capital, Tuxtla Gutiérrez (about 80 kilometers away), until 2002 there was no paved road reaching the town. Travel in and out of Nicolás Ruiz can be difficult, especially in the rainy season. Dirt roads with paved segments connect it to Teopisca to the north and Venustiano Carranza to the southeast. There are two telephones in Nicolás Ruiz, one in the *Presidencia Municipal* (office of the municipal president) and one in a private home, which operates as a *caseta*. Only the *caseta* has a phone line; the *Presidencia* must make due with a satellite connection. Both are frequently out of service, making communications sporadic and unreliable.

Ninety percent of the land in Nicolás Ruiz is held communally and is distributed in parcels to individuals. All decisions about land administration are made by the authorities of *Bienes Comunales* (loosely, "Communal Properties"). Men become *comuneros*, meaning that they are entitled to work a parcel of the communal land and have a corresponding responsibility to participate in the community assembly when they marry or become the head of household through a death. Decisions about virtually every aspect of community political life are made by consensus decision in the community assembly of *Bienes Comunales*, in which all of the more than 700 *comuneros* participate. While there is significant variation throughout the state, this is the predominant mode of decision making in indigenous communities in Chiapas. Even where many indigenous communities were once governed through civil-religious hierarchies (cargo systems), the assembly is today the principal space, and consensus decision making the principal form, of local governance.[6] In Nicolás Ruiz, this means that the *comuneros*—usually not all of them, unless it is a highly important or contentious issue—meet and publicly debate decisions that must be made, until reaching a point at which either everyone is convinced or at least no one is willing to continue to express dissent. At that point, "consensus" has been reached. The decision may be raised and challenged again in a later assembly meeting, though the challenger would probably first informally make sure he had sufficient support from others to do so.

"Community" consensus is in fact the consensus of the adult men. Women do not participate in the assembly unless invited to address a special issue. Nevertheless, the women of Nicolás Ruiz are notably well organized and have a history of "women's organization" that goes back several decades. Since 1996, there have been two women's committees: a "health committee" that specializes in herbal medicine and a "resistance committee" that specializes in political support work. There has also been a "women's assembly" that held monthly meetings similar to those of the general assembly, though recent divisions among the organized women have caused the women's assembly to be discontinued.[7]

While the community makes its decisions through *Bienes Comunales* and in the assembly, there is also a constitutionally elected municipal government, which has been of the center-left PRD since 1996. Often, decisions are made in the assembly and then implemented through the *Presidencia Municipal*. This decision-making process holds even in the selection of candidates for offices in the municipal government, who are chosen in a consensus decision in the assembly, then elected in the official election. Because they are chosen by consensus, meaning that presumably everyone has agreed, it is expected that everyone will vote for the candidate when elections are held. In other words, leaders are chosen through the traditional practices of the community, then ratified—and legitimized for the purposes of interaction with the state—through the official electoral process.[8] A recent public statement by the *comuneros* affirmed:

> We elect our representatives—communal and municipal—in general assemblies of the community. And, if in the election for municipal president we vote for the PRD, it is because due to the laws that are in force, we find ourselves obligated to register the will of the people through that political party, after we have already chosen our municipal president in the assembly.

Figure 4.2 The *comuneros* of Nicolás Ruiz in the community assembly. Shannon Speed.

Elected officials are not conceptualized as having the authority to make decisions on behalf of the public, but rather are understood to be responsible for carrying out the collective will, as manifested in consensus decisions made in the assembly.

Many of these aspects of community political life—collective landholding, the rights and responsibilities corresponding to the status of *comunero*, consensus decision making, and authorities that are beholden to the collective—are what people in Nicolás Ruiz consider their *usos y costumbres*: traditional customs and practices that distinguish community life from that of the national culture. These *usos y costumbres* are very similar to those that exist in other rural communities throughout the state and often in recent years have formed the basis of claims about indigenous identity and indigenous rights. While these and other *usos y costumbres* do set them apart from the larger society, they are not vestiges of pre-Conquest cultures, but rather historically constructed forms that have been forged in relationships with the state and other social actors in the contexts of specific relations of power. In the following section, I want to consider in a little more depth those historical contexts and the dialogic engagements that have shaped Nicolás Ruiz's identity and forms of struggle over time.

San Diego de la Reforma: Nicolás Ruiz of Yesterday

The community of San Diego was founded in 1734 by Tzeltales from Villa de Teopisca, which is about thirty miles south of the colonial capital Ciudad Real (later renamed San Cristóbal de Las Casas). The *títulos primordiales* to the land and the record of the sale are still in existence.[9] They show that the land that made up the Haciendas San Diego and San Lazaro was purchased by the *naturales* (Indians) of Teopisca from the Coutiño family, Spanish landholders in the region. The land of the Hacienda San Lazaro had been measured and purchased in the name of Doña Catalina de Ballinas from the Spanish Crown in 1656. The Coutiño family had come into possession of the land through the marriage of Diego Coutiño to Francisca Ysidro de Trujillo, granddaughter of Catalina de Ballinas, who inherited the land of both San Diego and San Lazaro.[10]

It is unclear whether the land was occupied by indigenous peoples at the time it was purchased from the Crown or during the period it was owned by the Coutiño family. Lisbona Guillén (1992) makes reference to the Coutiños' establishment of the haciendas on the land of the "extinct" Indians of Ostuta,[11] though the Ostutans' continued existence seems to be indicated by documents relating to the purchase of a piece of land called El Agua Caliente by the Teopiscans "from the people of Ostuta" between 1699 and 1701.[12] Renard (1998), following Morales Avendaño (1977), claims that Ostuta still had inhabitants through 1767 but that the Spanish Crown began measuring and selling off their lands by 1655—the first of these was apparently the sale of San Lazaro to Catalina de Ballinas and her husband Alonso Orduñez de Villaquixan in 1656.

In any case, the Teopiscan Indians (Tzeltales) did occupy land bordering the hacienda properties, and on several occasions in 1699, 1702, and 1707 they requested *amparos* (essentially stays or injunctions) from the colonial authorities against the Coutiños, who were seeking entitlement to further tracts of lands to expand the haciendas. For example, in 1702, Pedro de Coutiño (Diego de Coutiño's son) received title to twenty *caballerías*, which were occupied by the Teopiscans.[13] The Indians filed and eventually received an *amparo* against this entitlement in November of 1707.[14]

In 1734, the community of Teopisca purchased the Hacienda San Diego and Hacienda San Lazaro from Pedro de Coutiño's widow, Doña Ana de Paz y Quiñones, and her children. The total sum of the purchase was 1,680 pesos.[15] This tract of land was quite large—the original titles speak of it reaching from Acala in the west to San Bartolomé in the east and south to Teopisca and Amatenango in the north. Twenty-five Tzeltal families from Villa de Teopisca occupied the land and formed a rural community called Hacienda San Diego, or simply San Diego.

Over the course of the nineteenth century, San Diego lost significant portions of its land to regional *caciques*,[16] as in the case of Ixpeb (later known as "El Gran Poder"), San Juan, La Mesilla, Santa Lucia, and La Lanza. Most were taken from the community through deception or fraud. Oral histories abound. One story I heard many times was that regional *caciques* invited seven community elders to discuss some sort of deal regarding certain lands. The elders went, carrying the titles to the parcels of land. The *caciques* proceeded to get the elders drunk, and when they passed out they took the documents from their pockets. What is clear in the historical record is that the cattle ranchers of the region used a variety of dishonest tactics to usurp the lands of the Tzeltales of Teopisca, including requesting title to tracts of land with the claim that they were *baldios* (unoccupied, lying fallow) and the manipulative redrawing of boundaries to increase their holdings. Much of the community's history into and through the twentieth century has been forged in the struggle to regain its lost territory.

The first large-scale loss of community lands took place in 1856. That year, the Reform Laws or *Leyes Lerdos* (after liberal finance minister Miguel Lerdo de Tejada, who issued the law) were passed. These laws included the *Ley de Desamortización de Fincas Rústicas y Urbanas Propiedad de Corporaciones Civiles y Eclesiásticas*, a measure designed to facilitate the conversion of national and Church property into private property (Mallon 1994). In Chiapas, the laws gave landholders an opportunity to acquire lands belonging to indigenous communities (García de León 1985; Renard 1998). Because many indigenous communities did not have title to the lands they had traditionally occupied, *criollo* landholders were often able to gain title to them. Power relations being unfavorable to indigenous communities, even in extraordinary cases where the community held title to their land—as was the case in San Diego—the *criollo* landholders often gained title anyway.

The *cacique* Jose Antonio Larrainzar was apparently able to acquire the title to the Finca San Diego through these laws. In a letter to the parish priest of Teopisca in 1857, Larrainzar declared: "As a consequence of the law of June 25, 1856, the finca called San Diego, communal lands pertaining to the *Naturales* of la Villa de Teopisca, was auctioned off in my favor."[17] In this letter, Larrainzar petitioned the Church to have it reassigned to the Parish of San Bartolomé for his own convenience, arguing that it was closer and that it had pertained to Teopisca "for the sole reason that Teopisca was the parish of its owners (the Indians)."[18] The Teopiscans apparently managed to recover the land within a few years, because in October of 1862 the Parish of Teopisca requested that San Diego be returned to its domain, due to the fact that "it has returned to its previous owners, the Indians."[19] Though this land was recovered quickly, it is a good example of how easy and accepted it was for landholders to gain control of Indian lands.[20]

Many other lost tracts of land were more difficult to recover, and some remain to this day contested and contentious. One of the most important in the history of the community (because of the conflict it would cause) is that of Ixpeb / El Gran Poder. In the 1890s, San Diego de la Reforma was fighting to recover Ixpeb from cattle rancher Lauro Castro. In a clear case of deceit and fraud, Castro, to end the ongoing legal battle over the division between his finca and the communal lands of San Diego de la Reforma, signed an agreement in 1898, ostensibly ceding part of the lands he held to the San Diegans. He requested that the engineer Silviano Chacón remeasure and redraw the boundaries. Sixteen years later, when another engineer measured these lines, with the titles to both landholdings in hand, he confirmed that the lands belonged to San Diego and revealed Lauro Castro's treachery. Not only had Castro failed to cede any lands to San Diego in 1898, but, in fact, Chacón had redrawn the lines to increase the territory of El Gran Poder.[21]

This remeasuring of the community boundaries was a result of the Revolution, which for a brief time put power on the side of the community, rather than the large landholders. In September of 1914, General Jesús Agustín Castro assumed all executive, judicial, and legislative power in the region (Benjamin 1996 [1989]). A *Carrancista*[22] and a member of the "radical wing" of the Constitutionalist movement, General Castro was "hostile to tradition and privilege, both secular and clerical" (Knight 1986:239, cited in Benjamin 1996 [1989]:120). He proclaimed, "If the privileged robbed the poor, the Revolution will return to them their rights; if there was one justice for the rich and another for the poor, the Revolution will impose equality before the law."[23] Only two months after Castro's arrival, the *Jefe Político y Comandante Militar* of the Department of La Libertad (in which San Diego—now the municipality of San Diego de la Reforma—was located) received orders from the general to place all the lands taken illegally by the neighboring ranchers under the control of the municipal president of San Diego de la Reforma, Damián Adulfo López.[24] Lauro Castro (the owner of El Gran Poder) was specifically ordered to remove, at his own expense, the wire fencing he had placed on San Diego's land.[25]

The definitive measurement of the lands in 1914 redrew the boundaries of the community to be in accord with the *títulos primordiales*. The landholders protested the redrawing of the boundaries and proclaimed their ownership, but not to the satisfaction of General Castro, who ratified the measurements, stating that their protests were not "well-founded, nor did they prove in any way the right upon which their request was based." The general's formal ratification is worth quoting, because it reflects clearly the relationship of the redrawing of the boundaries of San Diego with his revolutionary vision:

The Municipal Government of San Diego de la Reforma, has proven sufficiently with all the documents it has exhibited that the lands that were unjustly occupied by Señores Castro, Franco, and Bermudez respectively, belong to the community of said peoples, which has been ratified and proven by the mathematical operations carried out by Engineer Solís. . . . It is the mind of this Government to impart full justice to he who is right, so as not to disturb nor to distort one of the great ideals the Revolution pursues, and to avoid, on the other hand, allowing two or three persons, accustomed to the arbitrary practices of other Governments, to benefit on a whim while notably jeopardizing a collectivity, such as a "pueblo." This Government holding to the most strict and healthy Justice, would approve as in effect APPROVES, the measurements, verified on the lands of San Diego de la Reforma, by el Señor Ingeniero Lic. Herminio M. Solís.[26]

Thus, the Revolution resulted in the recognition of San Diego's *títulos primordiales* and the official demand that their lands be returned to them. This recognition was the one good to come of the Revolution for San Diego and it was a crucial recognition of their claims, though it had limited effect on the recovery of their lands.[27] Not surprisingly, the landholders targeted by General Castro and his revolutionary government refused to give up the disputed land. The residents of San Diego de la Reforma continued to petition the government, pointing to the new measurements that reaffirmed their rights to the land, but to no avail.[28]

Apparently, the shifting tides of revolutionary and post-revolutionary politics worked against them. Several years later, the government of Venustiano Carranza issued *certificados de inafectabilidad,* which made the lands held by large landholders untouchable. Ironically, it was during the actual agrarian reform of the 1930s—when some communities in Chiapas were finally finding some hope of justice through land redistribution—that the authorities of Nicolás Ruiz were informed by government officials that their *títulos primordiales* would no longer be considered valid. The officials of the agrarian reform intended to title several large sections of Nicolás Ruiz's land to others as *ejidos*.[29]

Over the next several decades, inhabitants of Nicolás Ruiz continued to fight to regain their lands. The transformation of social relations brought about by the Revolution and the corporatist state that emerged in the post-revolutionary period led the community to see the state as its primary inter-locutor in these struggles, which were waged for the most part within the pa-rameters of state agrarian policy and agencies. This fact contributed strongly to shaping the relationship of the community to the state and its ruling party, the PRI, which they supported up through the mid-1990s. The correlation of the land struggles of Nicolás Ruiz to its relationship with the state and the ruling party, and the community identity that emerged from this relationship, are ex-plored in the following section.

Being and Becoming Campesino in Nicolás Ruiz

Indigenous identity waned in Nicolás Ruiz in the mid-twentieth century. By 1960, the external markers of Indian identity had disappeared: traditional dress was no longer worn, and fewer and fewer people spoke the Tzeltal language. As early as 1900, census records state that there were no speakers of Tzeltal in Nicolás Ruiz, though these data are strongly contradicted by the testimonies of inhabitants. (It is worth noting that in Mexico, the primary identifier of an in-digenous person is language.) Many older adults told me in the late 1990s that their parents had spoken Tzeltal, and these people would clearly have been alive after 1900. As recently as 1998, there were still several very elderly Tzeltal speakers, though by 2001 they were no longer alive. Interestingly, until 1941, the last year in which race was noted as a category by the *Registro Civil* in records of deaths, almost all those who died were registered as "*raza indígena*" (those clas-sified as "*mestizo*" or "white" [in one case] were from nearby ranches and not from the town of Nicolás Ruiz). Similarly, the majority of births were regis-tered as *raza indígena*.[30] Regardless of how the census characterized the inhabitants of Nicolás Ruiz, they clearly identified as indigenous into the mid-twentieth century.

The decline in indigenous identity in Nicolás Ruiz was the result of the com-munity's interaction with nonlocal discourses, particularly that of the state. One elderly man told me, "It's that our parents believed we should speak Spanish and wear these clothes in order to be like other Chiapanecos. They believed we would not get ahead as Indians." This was not a surprising interpretation on their part. Indians had suffered tremendous discrimination and oppression since the beginning of colonial rule. In the liberal period, with its push to "modernize" the country, Indians were seen as anachronistic. Emilio Rabasa, liberal governor of Chiapas from 1891 to 1894, sustained that Chiapas's indigenous people were completely disconnected from their pre-Conquest ancestors, "morally and intellectually inferior," and capable of education and achievement only when immersed in the society of "the superior classes" (cited in Montemayor 1997).

In the period following the Revolution, the "forging of the nation" would require the creation of a unified and homogeneous populace (Gamio 1916). The Revolution had ended the Porfiriato, and with it the existing alliances between landed elites, the state, and foreign capital (Alonso 2004). As Alonso notes, ten years of warfare and the breakdown of old social structures left a populace "sharply divided along ethnoracial and class lines and fragmented by competing sovereignties of regional strongmen and local communities" (Alonso 2004:462). Vasconcelos's concept of *la raza cósmica* or "the cosmic race," a blend of different races into a new civilization, became popularized as the blend of Spaniard and Indian into one *mestizo* people, an idea that formed the cornerstone of Mexican national consciousness and was nearly hegemonic until changes in the national project developed in the late 1980s and early 1990s. The "new Revolutionary mythohistory" of *mestizaje* simultaneously constructed the Indian as a part of the past, posited the ideal subject/citizen of the new nation as *mestizo*, and supported assimilationism in the pursuit of the ideal homogeneous populace (Alonso 2004:462).

In the post-revolutionary period, the discourse of the Indian as part of a "glorious Mexican past" had concrete manifestations in state policies of education and resource distribution.[31] These were designed, often literally, to make the Indians a part of the past. Luis Cabrera, a close collaborator of Venustiano Carranza, supported a program for the elimination of indigenous languages, and Montemayor claims that up through the 1930s, "the majority of leaders in educational policy prohibited the Indian from using his maternal language" (Montemayor 1997:110).

The census data, which erased indigenous presence in Nicolás Ruiz, may be understood in this context. It is possible that people, when asked, did not identify themselves as indigenous, given the racism and governmental policies directed against them. However, that is inconsistent with the registration of deaths and births in the civil registry, where people continued to identify themselves as indigenous. More likely, perhaps, is that the census was used as part of the policies designed to "eliminate" the indigenous population by defining them out of existence. Censuses are clearly one component of governance strategies. As Corrigan and Sayer (1986) argue, the control and systematization of information not only constitute a powerful tool for defining reality in agreement with certain interests and to benefit the structure of domination, but also are a form by which people identify themselves and define their place in the world.[32] From the perspective of those in power, a homogeneous, modern Mexican population was required. The disappearance of indigenous peoples through the manipulation of census data was but one means to achieve that end.

Public policies of the early post-Revolutionary governments also sought to consolidate the nation, in part through cultural homogenization. In Chiapas, the Department of Social Action, Culture, and Indigenous Protection (DPI) was created in 1934. Programs and policies discouraging Indian dress and the use of Indian languages were developed throughout the 1930s through this agency, and a number of harsh practices designed to force indigenous people to relinquish their indigenous identity were carried out in some regions. Hernández Castillo (2001a) recounts that in one instance in a Mam community in the Sierra Maestra of the state, an elderly man was forced to remove his traditional dress and allow state agents to burn it in public, under the threat that if he did not do so, they would burn it with him inside. These policies did not affect the Central Zone directly, and to my knowledge they were not imposed upon Nicolás Ruiz. Nevertheless, these stories give us a sense of the climate in the state for indigenous people. Similar programs were executed through the public education system, to eliminate indigenous languages.

Another important component of the integrationism of the post-revolutionary state was a policy of integration through land reform. From 1934 on, President Cardenas incorporated the popular discourses of the Revolution, especially those references to the land, and applied a policy of land reform that benefited many rural dwellers. Nevertheless, it is important to understand these agrarian discourses and policies as part of the post-Revolutionary state-building process: agrarian reform was to integrate campesinos and indigenous people into the state project. Armando Bartra (1991) has characterized agrarianism as the route through which the new state can create a solid base among the masses. Thus, these policies formed part of broader processes of the hegemonic construction of the Mexican state and the ruling party. If, as Roseberry

(1994) argues, hegemony is not complete agreement or ideological acceptance but rather the establishment of a common discursive framework, for the rural population of Mexico in much of the twentiety century, *agrarismo/campesinismo* formed that framework.

Specific state practices utilizing agrarian support were put into practice to draw in potentially rebellious sectors of the rural population. Radical campesino organizations that had existed in the 1920s were repressed or coopted by the conservative wing of the state-level *Partido Nacional Revolucionario* (PNR) (later the PRI) (Rus 1994b:273). This cooptation reached new heights in the 1930s as conservatives and Cardenista reformists struggled for control. Rus (1994b) documents how, in 1934, the governor—from the conservative wing of the PNR—offered campesino leaders the promise of economic/agrarian support from the government in exchange for their political royalty. This model was widespread during much of the twentieth century, although it took different forms in different localities. In the Northern Zone, as we saw in Chapter 3, Chol communities were able to take the land and withdraw, keeping some distance from the state-making practices. However, in many highlands communities during the latter part of the 1930s and early 1940s, the *Cardenistas*, through Erastro Urbina, a native of San Cristóbal who spoke several indigenous languages, developed a process of "subversion of native government" (Rus 1994b). Urbina, as head of the Department of Social Action, Culture, and Protection of Indigenous Peoples and the Union of Indian Workers (STI), formed agrarian committees that were then tied to the state-level organ of the *Confederación Nacional Campesina* (CNC, the PRI-affiliated peasant union). Urbina formed local leaders who functioned as intermediaries to the ruling party, enjoying the benefits of a privileged relationship while ensuring support for the ruling party within the community. The authority structures of some highlands communities were appropriated and adapted to the hegemonic project of the state and its ruling party through these agrarian committees (N. Harvey 1998; Rus 1994b). In other areas, such as in Nicolás Ruiz, community structures were also penetrated by the state and became closely tied to the ruling party through agrarian policies, though it had an opposite effect on their community identity, as we shall see below. Cardenista policies and practices, particularly through the DPI and agrarian reform, worked to assimilate some indigenous communities and to accommodate others to the hegemonic state project. Although the administrations that followed Cardenas at the federal level did not continue his commitment to land reform and had a much more limited discourse in relation to reform of the rural economy, they did continue to engage the rural population through agrarian policies and agencies in a variety of ways.

The other instrument for the incorporation of the rural population into the state project was the *Instituto Nacional Indigenista* (INI). The INI opened an office in San Cristóbal de Las Casas in 1951 and established the program for regional development, *El Centro Coordinador Tzeltal-Tzotzil*. This program worked in tandem with the programs of the DPI and the STI, creating bilingual intermediaries to facilitate state penetration and appropriation of the community structures. However, the program was focused on the Highlands and had little effect in other parts of the state, including Nicolás Ruiz.[33] For Nicolás Ruiz, the state's agrarian discourse, which echoed its own unflagging land struggle, became and remained the most important discourse framing their interaction with the state for decades to come.

Thus, the campesino identity encouraged by these policies, at the same time indigenousness was increasingly discouraged and even prohibited, soon began to replace indigenous identity in many areas of Chiapas, including Nicolás Ruiz. While in the Northern Zone Chols took their land and withdrew (and thus maintained their indigenous identifications) and in the Highlands indigenous structures became linked to the ruling party, Nicolás Ruiz (like many other communities) engaged with the state principally through agrarian reform and agrarian support, which made sense in terms of its community history of struggle to regain its lands.

As campesinos, they organized to defend their land rights and established a relationship with the ruling party, PRI, which characterized their interactions with the state for decades to come. Like many other indigenous communities throughout the state, Nicolás Ruiz was a staunchly PRI community up through the 1980s. This relationship allowed them access to agrarian credits and subsidies, as well as a hope of resolving their land claims. While the multiple requests and demands made by the community to various state agencies, particularly the agrarian reform agency, are too numerous to discuss here, it is worth noting that they did have some successes, even if these were limited in important ways.

For example, the administration of President López Portillo emitted a *Resolución Presidencial de Reconocimiento y Titulación de Bienes Comunales* (a presidential resolution of recognition and titling of communal properties) on behalf of Nicolás Ruiz on August 5, 1980.[34] This resolution defined 4,722–63–99 hectares for 313 *comuneros* (which represented all the *comuneros* with land rights at the time).[35] However, the resolution also stated that 10 percent of the land under the resolution was already held as private property, specifically the *predios* of Monterrey, Bella Vista, El Ciprés, La Mesilla, Candelaria, El Potrero, La Lanza, San Juanito, Tzintuli, Las Mercedes, La Providencia, and El Nacimiento.[36] These remained in the hands of landowners. The *comuneros* protested this to no avail. Thus in spite of having achieved the presidential resolution, the *comuneros'* struggle to recover all their lost lands continued.

While being a PRI community did not mean that all of their land claims were resolved, had they belonged to an opposition party there would not have been even a shadow of a hope of resolving them. Their relationship with the PRI meant that the *comuneros* had, if not an open door to the state government, at least not a closed and locked one.

Changing Relationship with the State: Local Conflicts and Their Impact

The illusion of the open door began to fade after decades of attempts to get the government to intercede on the *comuneros'* behalf. Key events, in particular the land struggles over San Juanito and El Gran Poder discussed below, left them feeling that the government was engaged in deceptive tactics and eventually that the strategy of allegiance to the ruling party was not working. The two cases are complex and the details are not necessary to our discussion here, but it is worth mentioning the cases because of their importance in the collective memory and the shifting political subjectivities in Nicolás Ruiz.[37]

The *predio* San Juanito formed part of the original land title of Nicolás Ruiz. It had been held by the Coello family, large landowners in the region, since prior to the Revolution, and recently had been sold by Vicente Coello in three sections to different landholders.[38] In July of 1981, the *predio*, which Nicolás Ruiz continued to claim, was invaded by residents of a neighboring *ejido*, Flores Magón. For the *comuneros* of Nicolás Ruiz, this changed the situation dramatically, because there was a serious risk that once the *ejidatarios* (members of the *ejido*) occupied the land and made a claim to it, they could gain recognition of it as part of their *ejido*.[39] The *comuneros* did not wish to fight other campesinos, which they perceived as a very different undertaking than struggling with a large landholder. On July 15, the *comuneros* attempted to forcibly remove the *magonenses* (the *ejidatarios* of Flores Magón) from the land, but they were unable to do so. They petitioned for help from the state and even had at least one of the landowners on their side, because he preferred to have the land in the hands of the pro–ruling party *comuneros* than in the hands of the *magonenses*, who were affiliated with the leftist campesino organization the *Casa del Pueblo* in the neighboring municipality of Venustiano Carranza.

Betting on their relationship with the PRI, the *comuneros* entered into negotiations with the state government of Juan Sabines, who offered to buy the lands from the landowners for Nicolás Ruiz and get other lands to expand the *ejido* Flores Magón. Such purchases of private lands were not an uncommon practice during Sabines's administration (1979–82) as a form of alleviating the pressure of land conflicts and invasions (Villafuerte Solís et al. 1999). Nicolás Ruiz agreed to this, but while awaiting its realization, the *comuneros* discovered an engineer measuring the lands on behalf of Flores Magón for its petition to the lands, which was apparently proceeding before the Agrarian Reform. The *comuneros* felt they had been tricked by the government, and they detained the engineer. When a government official and another engineer came looking for him, they were also detained by the *comuneros*. One *comunero* described the events:

> We saw how deceitful (*mentiroso*) the government was. They placated us yesterday saying that the Agrarian Reform wouldn't act until the Governor returned from [a trip to] Mexico City, and there they are today measuring.[40]

This perceived deception, and the frustration of the failed attempt to negotiate the problem through the government, brought the efficacy of the relationship with the ruling party into doubt and justified other forms of struggle. Another *comunero* said:

> This is the trickery (*transa*) that we have always faced, always. We never get beyond it. This is the sadness that has been imposed on the *pueblo*, which we have had to confront with blood. As the saying goes, *al que le toque, de a puro riesgones.* It isn't a question of choice.[41]

Further, although the *magonenses* were engaged in a petition before the *Secretaría de la Reforma Agraria* to increase their *ejidal* lands (to include San Juanito), they were reluctant to enter direct negotiations with the government. In April of 1982, according to the *comuneros*, an agreement was reached in direct negotiations (between Nicolás Ruiz and Flores Magón, not through the government) to divide the land in half. However, the *magonenses*, who were still in possession of the land, had little motivation to give up half of what they had. Feeling there was little hope of rectifying the problem through either government negotiations or direct negotiations, the *comuneros* decided to retake San Juanito by force on July 7, 1982. There was an open battle, and fifty *ejidatarios*—men and women—were detained by the *comuneros*. They were later freed after the intervention of state police and a leader from the CNC. But the violence was not over; on August 23, the *magonenses* attempted to retake the land from the *comuneros*. This battle lasted eight hours, resulting in the death of one *magonense* and several from Nicolás Ruiz injured with bullet wounds. When it was over, Nicolás Ruiz retained the land.

The violence of the conflict over San Juanito motivated the new government of General Absolón Castellanos Domínguez (1982–88) to address Nicolás Ruiz's land claims against landholders of numerous tracts lining the southern side of the municipality. Through a program called *Programa de Rehabilitación Agraria* (Program for Agrarian Rehabilitation, PRA), Castellanos Domínguez attempted to address the remarkable number of land invasions (209 at the start of his administration) in the state and tried to bring campesino discontent under control (Villafuerte et al. 1999). Notably, 84 percent of the beneficiaries of this program, which lasted several years, were from the ranks of the CNC, as were the *comuneros* of Nicolás Ruiz (Villafuerte et al. 1999). Through this program, in 1984 the state government purchased San Juanito, as well as the lands known as El Cipres, Bellavista, Monterrey, El Nacimiento, and La Providencia, from the landholders on behalf of Nicolás Ruiz. This purchase of 385 hectares constituted a "restitution" of communal lands, not a *dotación ejidal* (as many PRA purchases were defined).[42]

But even in this act there was deception. The landowners sold the parcels to the government, but the agrarian reform had already designated eighty-four hectares of El Nacimiento and La Providencia to the neighboring *ejido*, Guadalupe Victoria. The state government wanted Nicolás Ruiz to sign an act renouncing the eighty-four hectares in exchange for regularizing the other lands, but the community refused. Thus the lands of these *predios* are in Nicolás Ruiz's possession, but the official titles have never been resolved. The *comuneros* viewed this as an open attempt by the government of Castellanos Domínguez to trick them into ceding part of the lands that rightly belonged to them.

Their negative encounter with Absolón Castellanos likely had to do with shifting alliances and factions within the PRI and the state. The change from Governor Sabines to Castellanos Domínguez had a significant impact on campesino organizations, even those within the official CNC and PRI. Sabines had a strong alliance with Germán Jiménez, the CNC leader, during a high-spending period of the *Sistema Alimentaria Mexicana* (SAM), through which oil money was used to subsidize basic grain production (N. Harvey 1998). This program functioned, of course, to support the PRI and CNC members. After 1982, the oil money was no longer available, SAM dried up, and a national security agenda took over, due to the war in Guatemala and the Central American revolutions. This national security concern led the PRI, in alliance with a conservative faction of the landholding class, to propose a general to succeed Sabines. Opposition surged from within the ranks of the state-level PRI, led by Germán Jiménez and supported by significant numbers of campesinos who had benefited from SAM and the Sabines administration (N. Harvey 1998). Nicolás Ruiz was aligned with this faction, and this resulted in some loss of favor for the *comuneros* of Nicolás Ruiz.

Nicolás Ruiz's land struggles continued. Demonstrating the multiple and ongoing land disputes in which Nicolás Ruiz was embroiled, an official document from 1987 reported *eighteen* different *predios* invaded by the *comuneros* of Nicolás Ruiz. Among them were El Gran Poder, Bellavista, and El Nacimiento,[43] the latter two ostensibly having been purchased in the PRA deal several years earlier. El Gran Poder was another matter and would become one of the most important factors motivating the *comuneros* to break with the government.

In the PRA purchase of lands to be returned to Nicolás Ruiz, there was one landholder who refused to sell his lands to the state government—the lands of Ixpeb / El Gran Poder. The authorities of Nicolás Ruiz continued to demand legalization of their land holdings and the *ampliación* (increase) of their recognized lands to include El Gran Poder, a piece of land of significant size that fell well within the borders of their original titles. In 1986, they invaded the land and were forcibly removed by the government of Absolón Castellanos. The *comuneros* felt angry and betrayed by the violent government attack and, already distrustful of the government's position, they now openly distrusted it.

This violent response to the *comuneros*' invasion of El Gran Poder was not inconsistent with Castellanos's approach. Repression was a key characteristic of his administration, making him one of the most hated governors among large sectors of the peasantry. This repression was particularly directed to movements associated with the other faction of the PRI, such as the corn growers' union led by Germán Jiménez. It was also during his administration that the state was increasingly militarized, ostensibly to guard against guerrillas in neighboring Guatemala, but Neil Harvey reports complaints about soldiers intimidating campesinos, especially in areas where independent organizing was strong (N. Harvey 1998). So disliked was Castellanos Domínguez that he was detained by Zapatista forces during the uprising and a trial was held. In a communiqué on January 13, 1994, the Clandestine Indigenous Revolutionary Committee (CCRI), the highest authority body of the EZLN, wrote that Castellanos Domínguez was accused of

> having repressed, kidnapped, jailed, tortured, raped, and assassinated members of the Chiapaneco Indigenous populations who fought legally and peacefully for their just rights, before, during, and after the period in which he occupied the office of State Executive in Chiapas.[44]

It was during Castellanos's *sexenio* (six-year period in office) that the *comuneros* began to reach a point of serious questioning of their alliance with the PRI. The illusion of the open door provided by their relationship with the PRI was fading. Key events such as the slippery business of San Juanito, in which their membership in the CNC and loyalty to the PRI did not result in a resolution of their land conflicts, the perceived deceit involved in the PRA purchases, and the violent removal from El Gran Poder contributed to shifting loyalties in Nicolás Ruiz. Notably, people cite 1986, after the forced eviction from El Gran Poder, as the first moment in which they began to think about leaving the PRI. However, the context was still not right for such a move. While their frustration made them angry enough to consider a party shift, such a move in 1986 or 1987 would have gotten them nowhere in terms of their goals.

The year 1988 brought in a new president, Carlos Salinas de Gortari, and a new governor in Chiapas, Patrocinio González Garrido. At the state level, there was hope that González Garrido would be less repressive than his predecessor, but in the first months of his administration several important leaders of independent campesino organizations were murdered (N. Harvey 1998). It was in this context that the Fray Bartolomé Human Rights Center was formed by the Diocese of San Cristóbal. The *comuneros* of Nicolás Ruiz negotiated with the González Garrido government, but to only minimal result.

The Salinista reforms, particularly the agrarian reforms discussed in Chapter

2, had a devastating effect on the peasantry in Chiapas, and particularly on small grain producers (Villafuerte and García Aguilar 1998). The Agrarian Law of 1992 gave a strong push to land privatization and signaled that the state was no longer committed to agrarian reform, while the reforms that came with NAFTA were even more detrimental. These reforms entailed the reduction of state investment in agricultural production, the gradual elimination of price supports for corn and of trade tariffs and import quotas for grains. Given the much higher agricultural productivity in the United States and Canada, their low-priced corn exports to Mexico would out-compete the more expensive Chiapas corn (N. Harvey 1998). The discontent felt by many corn producers throughout the state was shared by the *comuneros* in Nicolás Ruiz and gave further impetus to their distrust of the PRI.

President Salinas's anti-poverty program, Solidaridad, added to their frustration. This program was designed to cushion the negative effects of NAFTA and other agricultural reforms. But the national program of Solidaridad dealt primarily with problems of unemployment, malnutrition, illiteracy, and overcrowded housing, not the marketing and production needs of agricultural producers (N. Harvey 1998). In Chiapas, Solidaridad's limited funds were disbursed largely by the governor, local political bosses, and municipal presidents loyal to the PRI. Nicolás Ruiz was at that time a pro-PRI municipal presidency, and the community did receive Solidaridad loans, though they found them difficult to repay and were generally frustrated with the ineffectiveness of the program in alleviating the problems being wrought by the agrarian reforms.

The Zapatista Uprising: Political Change in Nicolás Ruiz

However, nearly a decade later, the *comuneros* had begun to look for alternatives. In 1993, by consensus decision in the assembly, they left the PRI. There was much debate at the time, but eventually the *comuneros* decided to remain independent rather than joining the ranks of another political party. For a short time, they affiliated with the *Partido Frente Cardenista*, which had appeared offering to resolve their land conflicts. But the relationship did not last long because less than a year later, the Zapatista uprising began, changing the political landscape dramatically.

The uprising challenged the PRI's hegemonic power and presented alternatives for political organization and struggle. Given the community's discontent with the government and the continued centrality of land struggle in their collective identity, and their political tendencies and affiliations, it is perhaps not suprising that the Zapatistas' discourse would be alluring to them. "Juan," currently the regional authority of the EZLN, has "walked with the organization since '94."[45] He explains the process in the community after the uprising in the following way:

> I paid attention to the radio, the television, and to the newspapers that published a broader perspective, and learned that this was an armed uprising so that the voice of the poor could be heard. . . . This made people interested in taking this path, because of our own need, because of the land issue. . . . It woke us up, the declaration of this armed group; we began to hear that they were fighting for twelve points, among them, land. So we began to analyze and see that it was important for us to join the organization and the community, through the assembly, decided that the authorities should seek out someone who could advise us about this.

The *comuneros* of Nicolás Ruiz experienced the uprising at a moment when they were highly disillusioned with the state and the ruling party. When information about the Zapatista uprising and its goals began to reach Nicolás Ruiz, people there—already searching since 1993 for a new path for the resolution of the land claims—became interested in the movement. They were open to the Zapatista discourse, especially as it related to land rights.

In 1994, following the Zapatista uprising, land occupations surged in a number of areas of the state, as indigenous campesinos took back lands they felt they were entitled to. Between January and August 1994, an estimated 60,000 hectares were invaded in the conflict zone and another 36,925 outside the conflict zone (Villafuerte et al. 1999). In this context, the *comuneros* again invaded El Gran Poder in March of 1994.

The following year, the *comuneros* shifted their loyalty to the center-left PRD by consensus decision in the community assembly. In most areas at that time, affiliation with the PRD was synonymous with Zapatista support, not because the state-level PRD was pro-Zapatista, but because at a local community level it was the only political option for expressing dissent against the PRI. Although Nicolás Ruiz had not yet declared itself Zapatista, the PRI government was undoubtedly displeased with the community's new political affiliation.

El Gran Poder: Renewed Conflict

In 1996, government forces attacked the *comuneros* occupying El Gran Poder in an attempt to force them off the lands. The *comuneros* fought back, and the battle that ensued at El Gran Poder left three *comuneros* dead and two others with gunshot wounds.[46] Despite these losses and being heavily out-gunned, the *comuneros* fought off the military and police forces and re-mained in possession of El Gran Poder. They continued to hold these lands in 2005, though their right to the land demonstrated both in their *títulos pri-mordiales* and in the measurements of 1915 that specifically reiterated their ownership of this land has never been officially recognized. The events at El Gran Poder had a strong impact on the mindsets of those in Nicolás Ruiz, who now viewed the government as an enemy. Following the violent en-counter at El Gran Poder, Nicolás Ruiz elected the first PRD municipal pres-ident and declared itself a "community in rebellion," an open declaration of Zapatista affiliation.

"Como si fuéramos un pueblo guerrero": Local Conflict in Nicolás Ruiz (?)[47]

In 1996, as the community took a new direction toward Zapatismo and the PRD, the *comuneros* of Nicolás Ruiz were still able to make consensus decisions and avoid visible or open dissent. However, given the political context in the state and the dramatic nature of change in Nicolás Ruiz, it is perhaps not sur-prising that this was difficult to maintain. In 1997, twenty-three families led by Abel Lopez Zuñiga officially returned to the PRI. Though I was never able to interview members of this group, the *comuneros* believe that *priístas* (members of the PRI) from the state government encouraged them to return to the PRI, promising support and assistance if they did so. I do not have evidence of this, though it would be consistent with the PRI's actions in other parts of the state where these dynamics are better documented (see the discussion of paramilita-rization and low-intensity warfare in Chapter 3).

The majority group felt that this dissent was an intolerable violation of the community norm of consensus. As one resident expressed it, "We were in agreement for 264 years, and this changed everything."[48] While this comment undoubtedly glosses over considerable disagreement over the two and a half centuries since the community was formed, the men around him nevertheless all nodded their agreement with his observation. This is because they hold a collective notion of consensus that does not mean everyone agrees all the time, but rather that even if one disagrees, that person should not take actions that directly challenge the decisions of the collective (such as changing political parties and running an opposition candidate). Individuals, as we shall consider in further depth in the next chapter, are expected to act in accord with the collective. In any event, what is very clear is that this level of dissent was unprecedented in the community.

It is this division and the ensuing conflicts that have kept Nicolás Ruiz in the newspapers off and on for a decade. In the assembly on March 29, 1998, the *comuneros* decided to revoke the land rights of the 108 dissenting community members who were no longer fulfilling their corresponding responsibility to participate in the assembly. This revocation resulted in a massive raid by the army, state and federal police, and immigration officials on June 3, 1998. The raid was a clear sign that the state government was going to back the small *priísta* minority by force. Men believed to be *priísta* community members, wearing masks on their faces, accompanied the police through the town and pointed out houses of community leaders. Masked men and public security forces entered the private home where the important documents of *Bienes Comunales* were stored and removed the *títulos primordiales*, among other vital records. These documents have never been recovered by the community. One hundred sixty-four people were arrested in the raid, sixteen of whom were charged and six of whom spent the next five months in prison.[49]

The intercommunity conflict in Nicolás Ruiz, and the army/police raid that was a part of it, while they have their unique local characteristics, also bear a marked resemblance to dynamics in other parts of the state where there was a Zapatista presence. In fact, community fractionalization and internal violence were prevalent throughout the zones of Zapatista support and were understood by many to be part of a government divide-and-conquer strategy characteristic of low-intensity warfare. However, while these conflicts may have been fomented or supported by state agents, it was often the case that they spiraled out of the control of those who had fostered them. By 1998, there were numerous paramilitary groups (most born of this type of intracommunity divide) in operation throughout the state, seemingly outside anyone's control. This type of approach served several purposes in the context of low-intensity warfare: it kept people in the affected communities occupied with their internal conflict, making it difficult for them to actively participate in the larger resistance movement; it exhausted their energy and their resources; and it justified military and police intervention and occupation. In some cases the support from official channels was more obvious than in others; in Nicolás Ruiz there was little doubt in the *comuneros'* minds that the state-level ruling party had made promises to this group in exchange for their loyalty to the PRI. The quick and violent response of the government in the June 3 raid supports that interpretation. Following the raid, state security police set up a roadblock outside the community that remained there for two years.

Local elections were held on October 4, 1998, and the *priístas* ran a candidate for municipal president, Narciso López Díaz, son of Abel López Zuñiga, the leader of the dissenting group. Not surprisingly, the PRD candidate was elected. A month later, López Díaz was found dead outside the town. The *priístas* accused the *perredistas* (members of the PRD) of the crime, and Armando Jímenez Pérez was jailed and charged with the crime. He proclaimed his innocence and accused the state of holding him as a political prisoner. Two years later, charges against him were dropped and he was released along with nearly 100 Zapatista political prisoners after the PRI lost power in 2000. Conflicts between the *perredista* majority and *priísta* minority have been ongoing since 1998. Interestingly, the affected *priístas* have deemed themselves *desplazados* (displaced people) and many people regard them as such, although they still live in the community. This shows how critically important the twin right and responsibility of working a piece of land and participating in the assembly are in Nicolás Ruiz. One who does not is "outside" the community, even while living within it. The *comuneros* continue to defend their right to internal cohesion and to remove rights of *comuneros* who do not fulfill their responsibilities to the community.

In sum, while it was the expectation of resolution of their land disputes that brought them to support the PRI, it was precisely around land issues that the community began to become disillusioned with that party. It was around the retaking and subsequent forced eviction of El Gran Poder that the *comuneros* first began to realize that their PRI affiliation was not going to get them their land back and did not assure them of government allegiance. And it was the battle against government forces at El Gran Poder that gave impetus to their shift in party affiliation to the PRD, and ultimately toward base support for the EZLN. In the words of one *comunero*: "In '94 we still spoke of ourselves as *priístas*, but then the curiosity aroused by the uprising combined with the ugly way the government treated us." (*"En el '94 todavía se hablaba de priísta, pero en el '94 se fue juntando la curiosidad del levantamiento y lo feo que nos trataba el gobierno."*)[50] The uprising, along with the increasingly conflictive relationship with the state government over land issues, brought them to declare Nicolás

Ruiz a "community in resistance." Their affiliation with the EZLN set them on a new path, one that not only drastically altered their relationship with the ruling party but also reconfigured local political relations.

Being and Becoming Indigenous in Nicolás Ruiz

But shifting political subjectivities were not the only effects of the new political terrain. These changes, and the new types of dialogic interactions they brought the community into, affected their understandings of themselves and their community in profound ways.

In 1998, when I first talked with people from Nicolás Ruiz, I was told, "In Nicolás Ruiz, we are not indigenous people, but we struggle because we are campesinos." The documents in the archive of the municipal presidency reflect this: they often portray themselves in their communications with the state government as campesinos, using language like "we, the campesinos who work the land, request . . ." Their evocation of such identity categories in interactions with the state government suggests that it had some value as cultural capital, that it helped them to gain leverage in their negotiations for greater concessions from the state.

By mid-1999, there was something notably different about their response to questions about their identity. I was now told in response to the question, "What is the ethnicity of people in Nicolás Ruiz?" that they *used to be* Tzeltales. "Unfortunately," I was repeatedly told, "*perdimos nuestros usos y costumbres,*" "we lost our customs and traditions." This loss happened, I was told again and again, because "being Indian caused our grandparents shame."

A year later, in mid-2000, several people told me they (meaning the community) were hoping to "recover" their Tzeltal culture, at least the language. One young man, "Ricardo," even told me, "The truth is, we are Tzeltales. Look at us: we have the faces of indigenous people. We lost our customs and traditions, but we are in the struggle with indigenous people. We want to declare this an autonomous municipality."

The shift in self-identification from nonindigenous in 1997 to ex-indigenous in 1999, and then to potentially future Tzeltales (or even "truly Tzeltales") in 2000 may not seem dramatic, but the fact is that in a very short period of time, people in Nicolás Ruiz had begun to change the way they experienced, understood, and presented their ethnicity.

This process is tied to changes in the discourses of the social actors with whom Nicolás Ruiz has been engaged over the last decade. There has been a process in which, as the discourse of human rights and particularly indigenous rights became more widespread in Chiapas, there is a reassertion of local indigenous identities, even in places where such identities had been superseded by others, such as "campesino." Just as the "loss" of their indigenous identity had to do with a dialogic interaction with other social actors, especially the state, their recent reencounter with their indigenousness emerges from their interactions in a variety of social fields. Certainly, the shifting discourse of the state—Nicolás Ruiz's principal interlocutor prior to the uprising—must be considered. As we have seen, there was a marked shift, even a turnaround, in state discourse regarding its indigenous populations as the state began to neoliberalize. This shift was manifested in the constitutional reforms of 1992, which recognized Mexico's pluricultural composition. While this does not mean that the state is embracing indigenous people, it is a significant change from previous discourses of *la raza cósmica* and the *mestizo* Mexican nation. At the same time, Mexico ended agrarian reform, signaling the end of campesinist agrarian policies of the past. Given this shift in state discourse, now de-emphasizing campesino identity and struggle and at least legalizing indigenous ones, it is not surprising that some communities might alter the aspects of their history and identity that they choose to emphasize and assert. Note, for example, that in the context of asserting that they are, in fact, Tzeltales, "Ricardo" pointed to their aspirations for declaring autonomy, an option viable only to indigenous communities based on their cultural difference.

This does not mean, of course, that everything suddenly changed and the government at all levels was determined to establish rights for indigenous people. The state government, in fact, seemed unable to manage the shifts and the potential they opened up for Nicolás Ruiz. On one hand the interim governor Albores justified the raid of 1998 by arguing that the authorities were utilizing "primitive *usos y costumbres*," harking back to the assimilationist/modernizing discourse of the Indian as primitive and the state as the modernizer (and recognizing Nicolás Ruiz as indigenous while doing so).[51] Yet a short time later in 1999, Secretario de Gobierno Rodolfo Soto Monzón told them in no uncertain terms that if they wanted to be considered indigenous, they would have to provide *proof* that they still spoke Tzeltal. Nevertheless, at a broader discursive level, indigenous people had been recognized, and a message had been sent about the new frame for indigenous-state interactions.

Also of key importance has been their participation in a social movement that has increasingly adopted a discourse of indigenous rights. This is reflected in "Ricardo's" comment in 2000. His assertion that they are "in truth" indigenous is linked to their involvement in a struggle with other indigenous people. Even the language of *usos y costumbres* is part of the current discourse of indigenous rights. It is strongly associated with the Zapatista autonomy project, and it is a recent terminology for most indigenous communities to describe their cultures and traditions.

People in Nicolás Ruiz point to the 1994 uprising as key to shifts in their consciousness. One man told me, "It was in '94 that we began to get oriented" (*"Ya en el '94 nos empezamos a orientar"*),[52] and a woman explained, "After 1994, people began to gain [political] consciousness" (*"Después del '94 a la gente les fue entrando la conciencia"*).[53] They regularly mentioned the land struggle as the aspect of Zapatista discourse that drew them in 1994. But as we saw in Chapter 2, Zapatista discourse, which in 1994 had a strong campesino component, became over the following years a predominantly indigenous rights discourse and movement. The shift began to be apparent from the time of the negotiations of the San Andrés Accords (signed in February 1996) and was reflected even more strongly throughout 1996 and 1997, becoming a movement predominantly understood as one for indigenous rights and autonomy. When people in Nicolás Ruiz became interested in the Zapatista movement, it was because of its campesino element. A movement for indigenous rights likely would not have had the same resonance in the community that the discourse of land rights did in 1994. But once involved with the organization (and the larger dynamics it set in motion), the shifting discourse became part of their own experience. Given the prominence of the discourse of indigenous rights in the movement and in the state more broadly by the late 1990s, it would have been remarkable if it had not affected their understanding and interpretation of their own history and their place in the world.

Also significant, no doubt, has been their increased interaction with activists and other nonlocal actors who valorize indigenousness. Precisely because Nicolás Ruiz defined itself as "in resistance" and because it suffered severe and violent conflict from 1996 to 2001, the people of the community had a good deal of interaction with human rights and other "civil society" organizations. These actors brought Nicolás Ruiz into interaction with the discourse of human and indigenous rights. Nicolás Ruiz has ongoing interaction with several organizations, and these interactions undoubtedly shape ideas and understandings in the community in new ways. One of these organizations was *Red de Defensores Comunitarios por los Derechos Humanos*.[54] The *Red de*

Defensores has had a relationship with Nicolás Ruiz since 1997, when the community was invited by attorney Miguel Angel de los Santos[55] to name two *defensores* (defenders) to be trained in human rights legal defense. Further, the organization had as one of its principal goals contributing to autonomous processes in indigenous communities by preparing indigenous defenders to do their own human rights work, eliminating reliance on NGOs and other organizations. Over the course of the last several years, the work of these defenders has clearly brought the community into contact with the discourse and practice of human and indigenous rights. This is but one example; there are multiple organizations and their distinct versions of human rights discourse all have interactions with community members.

Of course, we can assume with so much engaged dialogue between some community members and nonlocal actors and discourses of rights that this had an influence on community thinking. But a closer look at one such interaction helps us to see such processes at work. In June 2001, I and two other members of the *Red de Defensores* advisory team approached the authorities of *Bienes Comunales* regarding the possibility of including Nicolás Ruiz in a "representation" to the ILO regarding violations of the ILO 169 Convention by the Mexican government.[56] We explained our view that the community had a claim to indigenous lands under this convention both for recovering lands and for restitution for unrecoverable lands that the Mexican government had been complicit in diminishing by reducing their titles through the discriminate use of land censuses and agrarian reform, a violation of ILO 169 Land Articles 13, 14, and 16.[57] We also suggested the possibility of arguing that the government was violating Article 1, Section 2 on self-identification by claiming that the members of Nicolás Ruiz can no longer be considered indigenous because they have lost the use of their language.

Nicolás Ruiz would need to first establish its right to define itself as indigenous. As a *pueblo indígena* (indigenous people) the community could fight for its land claims as territory, rather than private property. Further, the community authorities would have the right to make internal decisions about punishment of its members (such as revoking land rights) based on its internal customs. The right of the state to intervene on behalf of the dissenting members it favors would be limited, because, as an indigenous community, Nicolás Ruiz has the right to autonomy in local decision-making processes. The ILO case presented a new strategy for pursuing their goals and their self-defense: a strategy that is dependent on this reemergent indigenous identity.

The response from the *comuneros* was positive. They were clearly interested in making a claim for lands they had lost over the years, as well as in defending themselves against further violent invasions by state forces. Notably, they were particularly interested in the potential for asserting their identity as an indigenous community and establishing their right to define themselves in this way. In the words of one, "I think this is very important, to be able to say to the government, 'We are not *Zona Centro* [a region defined as nonindigenous]; we are Tzeltales; we feel that we are part of the *pueblos indígenas*.' " Another said, "This is what is most important [about participating in the ILO representation], that they recognize who we are. We are Tzeltales." Two weeks later in the community assembly, hundreds of *comuneros* voted unanimously to "declare themselves as indigenous people" as part of the ILO representation.

This does not mean that everyone in Nicolás Ruiz woke up the next day "feeling indigenous." Even today, despite a very prominent public discourse of indigenous community identification, there are people in Nicolás Ruiz who would not self-identify as indigenous (though all would readily agree that their grandparents were). Indeed, significantly, it is those with the most contact with "outsiders"—those closely involved in the EZLN or with human rights work or those in the land struggle in positions of authority with *Bienes Comunales* or the Municipal Presidency—who were most likely to do so. Yet there was little debate about the issue in the assembly that day. There were questions about how the case would function, what a case before the ILO really meant, but not about either the validity or the value of reasserting their identity as an indigenous community. In fact for many, like the man quoted above, the act of defining themselves as indigenous was not just a necessity of the case in a strategic sense, but rather a claim that was equal in importance to the land claim. If there was anyone present who disliked the proposal, they did not dislike it enough to raise their voice. And that is consensus in Nicolás Ruiz.

Conclusions

Nicolás Ruiz, formerly San Diego de la Reforma, formerly Haciendas San Diego and San Lazaro, is a community about which little has been said by those who study Chiapas. But Nicolás Ruiz is also a protagonist in the current history of Chiapas, which is unfolding daily before our eyes. This chapter represents an effort to place Nicolás Ruiz within the current context and consider the ways in which both its past and its present contribute to the future of Chiapas, Mexico, and beyond.

In large part, the history of Nicolás Ruiz has been one of the community's struggle to recover its lands. From at least 1699, when they first filed an *amparo* against Diego de Coutiño, the Tzeltales of Teopisca were struggling against incursion onto their lands. In 2001, they were still struggling to recover Ixpeb / El Gran Poder.

These struggles, and their enemies and allies in them, have defined the community's identity over time. Identity in Nicolás Ruiz, once and potentially again a Tzeltal community, is historically and continuously constructed in relation to other social groups and through the ongoing struggles over land and territory. During the period in which land struggles were waged via the state through agrarian reform and "campesinist" policies, Nicolás Ruiz's community identity became "campesino." That is, indigenous identity gave way to campesino identity as state discourse and state policies engaged land struggles through agrarian reform and agrarian assistance to the campesino population.

The year 1992 was a key turning point in state discourse and policy. Although the constitutional reform has been played down in terms of its importance for indigenous people because it does not establish any concrete juridical rights, the recognition of the nation's pluriethnic composition and the simultaneous end to the state's commitment to land redistribution through agrarian reform signaled an important shift in the state's approach to its rural indigenous population.

The second key turning point was, of course, 1994. The Zapatista uprising and the national indigenous movement it helped to consolidate became major interlocutors, and, over the last seven years, many land conflicts have shifted onto the terrain of "indigenous issues." Now, land struggles are tied to issues of territory and to land rights, which transcend the state's designation or nondesignation of lands to certain populations.

In Nicolás Ruiz, this shift was reflected in their changing discourse of identity. The campesino identity which emerged in a dialogic relationship with the state, their principal interlocutor in their ongoing land struggles, ceded to a reemergent indigenous identity as the state failed in this role and new interlocutors—principally the EZLN, but also the other civil society actors which followed—emerged. Identity is still based around their land struggles, but these struggles themselves have moved out of the realm of the "agrarian" and into the "ethnic" struggle.

The ILO 169 case highlights these dynamics, but also the dynamics of dialogic interactions between local and nonlocal actors, and between local concerns and global regimes. The *Red de Defensores* is an organization with an explicit objective of creating a space for indigenous peoples to engage with the globalized discourse of human rights (as manifested in both Mexican law and international law). The *Red* team that worked on the case consisted of nonlocal actors, along with the two *defensores* from the community, who brought our nonlocal understandings to bear on the situation in Nicolás Ruiz. This included not only our knowledge of the existence of a legal regime and a Convention on the Rights of Indigenous People (ILO 169), but an understanding of what an indigenous person is, how indigenousness is defined, as it has been inscribed in those legal regimes. This understanding was quite distinct from the one the Mexican government held (and in fact, the conceptual linkage of language and identity enjoys broad currency in Mexico, including in indigenous communities). In our understanding, indigenousness was based on descent, self-identification, and group recognition. Being of Native American descent myself, I found these criteria to be part of my own experience in sorting out identification in a context where great intermixing and migration had taken place. In Mexico, as we have seen, language and secondarily traditional dress or rural dwelling were the principal criteria. I recognized that these criteria, if applied in the United States, would have a devastating impact on the numbers of Native Americans living today. Further, the members of the *Red* understood that these definitions had been hammered out through long negotiations and enjoyed broad acceptance. We brought these ideas to Nicolás Ruiz, and there they were accepted. They made sense to the *comuneros* and of course served their purposes. They responded to us and saw both strategic value of "being indigenous" for their land claim and for autonomy in political practices, but they also saw a chance to strengthen their emergent re-identification. Inevitably, our interaction had effects on their understandings of themselves and their struggle, which was recast in a distinct light. But those effects were products not of unidirectional flow from us to them, but rather of our interaction, as they took what was useful to them, reinterpreted it through their own understandings, and made use of it for their own objectives.

While I am suggesting that in some cases there may be a reemergence of cultural identities as part of a process of appropriation by local peoples of global discourses to their own goals, I do not mean to say that such identities are simply strategic, and therefore not authentic or legitimate. What I want to suggest is that culture, identity, and tradition are all continuously being constructed and reconstructed in light of the experience at any particular historical moment. The *usos y costumbres* upon which people from Nicolás Ruiz base their cultural identity claims are, like all traditions, "invented," in Hobsbawm's sense, in that they are "responses to novel situations which take the form of reference to old situations" (Hobsbawm and Ranger, 1983:1f.), and their indigenous identity "strategic" in the sense that it "suits a situation" for the purposes of struggle (Spivak 1988). But in responding to novel situations in ways that make sense for them at a particular historical moment, people's experience of the world and their place in it also changes. Nicolás Ruiz is notable because it is not the case, as in some communities (Hernández Castillo 2001a), that residents maintained their indigenous identity even after they lost the external markers of indigenousness. Rather, they maintained a land struggle and certain practices of social organization that, as they increasingly adopted a discourse of cultural rights, they have begun to reinterpret and identify as indigenous practices. That is, in the process of mobilizing globalized discourses to their own ends, they also reinterpreted their history and their practices in ways that altered their own understanding of their community and their place in the world. If we understand identity as inherently "unstable and unfixed" (Lowe 1991), in a constant process of construction and reconstruction, strategic versus authentic is simply not a relevant distinction. Both are part of the same process, one in which no identity is more or less legitimate than others.

In Nicolás Ruiz, community identity and tradition are constructed and reconstructed in dialogue with other social groups: the state, the EZLN, and other "civil society" actors. Importantly, this process is not unique to Nicolás Ruiz. As the state has shifted from a corporatist approach of cooptation of struggle through "assistance programs" and land reform to one of "government of business, by business, for business,"[58] indigenous rights has become one of the principal terrains of struggle, and we will likely see a shift in the aspects of their identity that many rural communities forefront. In this chapter, I have used the case of Nicolás Ruiz, its ethnohistory and its "ethnopresent," to highlight the historical process of identity construction and reconstruction in ongoing dialogue with various actors and discourses. I did so in order to suggest that in the current global context in which rights are the dominant discourse both of the state and of resistance, rights discourses are shaping how local communities construct their identities and their struggles. However, this is a process in which they actively participate, bringing their own histories and understandings to bear. Further, these dialogic interactions are not something new, but part of an ongoing process of identity construction and of struggle in dialogue with other social actors that began, in the case of Nicolás Ruiz, even before the community itself was formed, as they engaged in struggle with landholders through the legal system by requesting *amparos* to prevent encroachment on their lands. The globalization of rights has simply created the discursive space within which the people of Nicolás Ruiz—once and again self-defined as indigenous—construct themselves and their resistance. In the following chapter, I will narrow the focus, turning the lens on one incident within the community as a starting point for a discussion of how meanings of rights are negotiated and struggled over within the context of the community itself.

5 Gendered Intersections: Collective and Individual Rights in Indigenous Women's Experience

THE WOMEN SAT IN THE DARK FRONT ROOM of a house in Nicolás Ruiz. They had gathered to discuss with me their experience with social movement participation, as base supporters or as *milicianas* (militia members) of the Zapatista National Liberation Army (EZLN). The talk wound through various topics before finally making its way to the conflict among women in the community that had surged the previous year. I was worried about the topic. "What happened?" I asked uneasily. The talk became suddenly animated, leaving behind the reserved decorum of our earlier discussion. The women talked over each other, anxious to add details or elaborate their perspectives. Finally, one woman's voice rose above the others, who fell silent. "*Lo que pasa,*" she said with emphasis, "is that in this community, we don't want *protagonistas* [those who assert themselves forcefully in a certain situation, usually for personal gain of prestige or power]." "We women want to organize for our rights," she said, "but we want to do it collectively."[1]

"Rosalina's" words spoke directly to the theoretical questions I had been struggling with as a feminist, an activist, and a researcher, regarding the presumed contradiction between indigenous communities' collective rights to maintain their culture and the rights of individual community members (in particular, women) that might be violated by those cultural norms and practices. Taking the women's conflict in Nicolás Ruiz as a starting point, in this chapter I examine the tension between individual and collective human rights and the specific issues raised by gender and ethnicity in that tension. I argue that resolving this tension is not possible and that focusing our analytic efforts on establishing whether individual or collective rights should have primacy is

unproductive and obscures as much as it clarifies. In fact, the conceptual dichotomy individual/collective often serves to deny many women's—especially
indigenous women's—lived experience of oppression and resistance. Further,
I suggest that indigenous women's gender demands, constructed in active engagement with discourses at the intersection of individual and collective rights,
contributes to an alternative way of thinking about rights that is consistent
with local understandings and underpins local forms of resistance.

The Individual and the Collective: Theory and Practice in the Neoliberal Context

> That is the Mexico we Zapatistas want . . . one where respect for difference
> is balanced with respect for what makes us equals.
>
> *Comandanta Esther (2001)*

As we have seen, the Zapatista uprising began at a key moment in Mexico's history in which relations between the state and civil society were shifting dramatically as the corporatist state gave way to the neoliberal multicultural
model. This shift had been set in motion two years earlier with the changes to
the Mexican Constitution that ended agrarian reform and other nationalist and
corporatist policies while simultaneously recognizing its population for the
first time as "pluriethnic."

This process was not unique to Mexico but was under way in a number of
Latin American countries in the 1990s. Legal and constitutional reforms implemented to "neoliberalize" states—shrinking state functions and giving priority
to ensuring stability and the free market—were regularly accompanied by legal
recognition of indigenous populations and, to differing degrees, their rights
(Assies, van der Haar, and Hoekema 2000; Postero and Zamosc 2004; Van Cott
2000; Yashar 2005). In the "neoliberal multiculturalism" (C. R. Hale 2002)
model, recognition is a part of the new logics of governance that predominate in
the neoliberal state.

However, it was not the reforms but the Zapatista uprising that put indigenous rights on the national radar screen and in the process drew out the tensions
and contradictions with which this shift was fraught. The reform of Article 4
had acknowledged Mexico's multicultural makeup, but it did not recognize indigenous peoples as "peoples," nor did it provide indigenous groups with any
specific rights. Such a move would have implied a more dramatic break with
the past, as Mexico's Constitution of 1917 is founded on liberal concepts of the

equality of each individual Mexican before the law. However, Mexico might have gone forward with a broader recognition of collective rights, as did countries such as Colombia, Bolivia, and Ecuador, were it not for the uprising and the emergent national indigenous movement, which called into question the terms of such reform. The Zapatistas did so in several important and interrelated ways; they are the subject of this and the following chapters. Here, I want to highlight one: a refusal to accept either modern liberal individual rights or state-defined multicultural recognition of collective rights as the unitary model for the exercise of their rights. This has been particularly clear in the case of indigenous women.

The tension between collective and individual rights was a thorny one both for the state and for the Zapatistas. With the uprising, it was not just indigenous people who stepped onto the national stage to assert their rights but also, quite prominently, indigenous women. From the start, the EZLN highlighted the presence of women in their leadership and elaborated a strong rhetoric of indigenous women's rights. Women constituted 30 percent of the Zapatista Army. Karen Kampwirth (2002) notes this is similar to the percentage of women involved in the Central American guerrilla movements of the 1980s, but the fact that the women participating in the Chiapas uprising were almost exclusively indigenous made this level of participation notable and distinct, because the subordinated position of women in indigenous communities and the hardship of their lives were well-known. For example, women in indigenous communities disproportionately suffer illiteracy, lack adequate access to medical care, have a life expectancy two years shorter than their male counterparts, and experience the highest maternal death rate in Mexico (Kovic and Eber 2003). Their personal autonomy, including the ability to choose when and whom to marry and when to bear children, the ability to travel freely outside the community, and the ability to inherit property and participate in political decisions concerning the community are frequently limited by community norms (Kovic and Eber 2003; Rovira 1996). The Revolutionary Women's Law, made public immediately after the uprising, represented a clear and systematic elaboration of the movement's support for "women's just demands of equality." These included the right to choose their partners, decide the number of children they will have, hold positions of authority in the community, and be free from rape and violence.[2]

Some feminists criticized what they viewed as the Zapatistas' "masculinist" approach to resistance. For example, Rojas (1995) and other contributors to her edited volume questioned, from their own feminist perspectives, Zapatismo's libratory effects for women. In particular, Bedregal (1994) argues that women are inherently more peaceful than men and that by taking up arms and inserting themselves into male hierarchical structures (such as that of an army) women concede too much from the start. These same authors also suggested that the women's laws were limited and did not constitute feminist demands because they did not contain a critique of patriarchal social relations. In the terms of the feminist debates of the day, they were seen as "practical" demands for bettering women's lives rather than "strategic" ones for challenging and altering unequal relations of power between men and women (Molyneux 1985; and see Stephen 1997 for a discussion of this debate). Others feminists, even while noting that in many communities little had changed for women on the ground, nevertheless argued that the Zapatista movement contributed to creating a cultural climate in which gender relations could be renegotiated and opened spaces in which new forms of women's participatory citizenship could flourish (Eber and Kovic 2003; Garza Caligarís 2002; Hernández Castillo 1998a; Olivera Bustamante 1995). What the Zapatistas have made clear is that the presence of women in their ranks and the demands put forward by the movement are the result of women's active struggle within the movement for a position equal to that of men. Undeniably, this remains an ongoing struggle within Zapatista communities, which has had uneven results from community to community and region to region (Speed, Hernández Castillo, and Stephen 2006). Comandanta Yolanda highlighted this ongoing process in a speech on International Women's Day in 2003:

> The men are struggling to totally understand what we are asking for as women. We are asking to have rights and for the men to give us liberty, and for them to understand that we have to fight for that along with them. For them to learn to not take our participating here badly, because, before, we never went to meetings. Now there's just a few of us who go, but the path is opening up in all ways. There's more freedom. The men now take our words into consideration, and they understand that we, as women, have a place where we can present everything we feel and everything we are suffering.[3]

Few would deny that in the decade since the uprising, Zapatista women have made a vital contribution to the advancement of the indigenous women's movement (Hernández Castillo 2006). They have made it clear to all that while the Mexican Constitution established equality, including women's equality, in legal practice and everyday life, some people—like indigenous people and women—enjoy "real" equality considerably less than others. In Comandanta Esther's words:

> I would like to explain to you the situation of the indigenous women who are living in our communities, considering that respect for women is supposedly guaranteed in the Constitution. The situation is very hard.[4]

Comandanta Esther's speech, made in the context of the legislature's consideration of the Law on Indigenous Rights and Culture, reiterated two important points that organized indigenous women had been making for some time. The first is the inseparability of indigenous women's experience as women and as indigenous people, an inseparability ignored by many in the debates about women's individual rights. Another point was made by her lament of the futility of rights established in law, such as the right to equality that could not in fact be exercised.

The tension between individual and collective rights, rendered highly visible and contentious by the Zapatista uprising, was one that Mexico, like other neoliberalizing states, had to grapple with. Theorists of multicultural recognition such as Kymlicka (1996) suggest that states must grapple with the antagonism between the concept of individual equality and collective claims in the interests of doing justice to the individuals who make up those groups (though individual rights trump collective ones in the final instance). But as we have seen, other theorists have suggested that the increasing prevalence of a state recognition model and associated multicultural reforms is a trend that signals a shift away from democratic states' focus on the pursuit of democracy per se and in fact may serve to manage and limit the force of collective indigenous demands (Gustafson 2002; C. R. Hale 2002; Postero 2001). In other words, in the recent Latin American context, in implementing multicultural policies the state is engineering a program that entails much more than trying to be fair to all its citizens. The limited recognition of collective rights for particular groups is an integral part of neoliberal subject formation and the construction of neoliberal rule.

The flourishing of demands for indigenous community autonomy and women's personal autonomy combined with the shifting terrain of governance and public policy to generate a national debate about collective and individual rights, about equality and cultural difference. The demand for autonomy in

Mexico—as elsewhere in Latin America—has been built on the concept of *usos y costumbres*. *Usos y costumbres* usually refers to consensus decision making, local administration of justice, and the election of authorities through traditional means, but it can also encompass virtually anything a community or its leaders define as "tradition." In the autonomy debate, government officials, as well as some prominent jurists and intellectuals, argued that indigenous peoples' *usos y costumbres* served to justify local power relations and that collective norms frequently violated individuals' rights. Some argued that the state should not allow indigenous people any measure of autonomy based on their *usos y costumbres* because they had antidemocratic tendencies and would almost certainly violate the basic human rights of individuals in the community (R. Bartra 1997; Krauze 1999). One prominent jurist went so far as to express his concern that respecting indigenous peoples' *usos y costumbres* could lead to accepting "some ethnic groups that engage in the human sacrifice of babies."[5]

This is a thorny issue because, of course, there are many instances in which the individual's ability to act autonomously is subordinated to collective norms in the community context. The specter of extreme cases that resulted in violence, such as the expulsion of politico-religious dissenters in the highlands community of San Juan Chamula (CNDH 1995; Kovic 2005), was often raised in the public debate. Yet in many cases the arguments made relied on essentialized and static notions of indigenous *usos y costumbres*, suggesting the Indians were inherently antidemocratic and that this was an unchanging and unchangeable part of their culture. Such ideas were relatively easy to "sell" to the public, since the assimilationist national discourse had long cast Indians as culturally backward, in need of modernization and integration to the national culture.

These perspectives were manifested in government policies and actions. This often went beyond the state's defense of liberal individual rights, reflecting a more utilitarian use by the state of individual rights protections as a tool to limit indigenous rights (see Speed and Collier 1999). I have already mentioned some cases of this, such as use of individual rights as limiting language in agreements on indigenous autonomy, such as the Chiapas state law on indigenous rights, which in Article 10 states that "uses, customs, and traditions will be applied within the limits of their habitat, as long as they do not constitute violations of human rights." This dynamic was further evident in the rhetorical strategies of the government in justifying its attacks against autonomous municipalities, as in Interim Governor Albores's declaration prior to the raid on Nicolás Ruiz that tied "radical" and "primitive" to *usos y costumbres*, then suggested that they "trample individual rights."[6] So widespread was this brandishing of individual rights to limit collective ones that indigenous people in many areas—even those who supported the ruling party—began to understand human rights as a potential limit to their local autonomy (Speed and Collier 1999).

It was not infrequent in the public debate to hear women's rights serve as primary examples of the dangers of the collective violating the rights of individuals. *Usos y costumbres* such as arranged marriage, exclusion of women from political participation, and male-line inheritance were cited as examples of practices that violated women's rights to personal autonomy, civic participation, and economic sustenance. The legislators who drafted the COCOPA law, for example, included the following limiting language regarding the enjoyment of indigenous autonomy: "respecting individual constitutional guarantees, human rights and, *in particular, the dignity and integrity of women*" (emphasis mine). While few would debate the importance of respect for women's dignity and integrity, the inclusion of this phrase both reflects the prevalence of and perpetuates the notion that indigenous culture, when not restrained by the protective state, will violate individual rights and that women are in need of special protection.

These arguments echoed debates in the literature on gender and human rights, which has, as a recent article stated, a "central concern" regarding the struggle for cultural rights "when respect for customary law or traditional customs and practices violates the individual rights of women" (Deere and Leon De Leal 2002:76; see also Okin 1999). In the theoretical realm, such debates are between cultural relativists who believe that "culture is the principal source of validity of right and rule" and feminists concerned that such a position requires accepting the subordination of women and negating indigenous women's individual human rights (Deere and Leon De Leal 2002:76; Okin 1999). In this framing, given the direct contradiction between collective claims to culture and women's individual human rights, one is forced to side with one position or the other. Thus cultural rights are positioned against gender rights in the many academic writings and in public discourse.

In Mexico, such arguments were made by a broad range of people, from feminists to conservative constitutionalists. Some critiques were made by people with a long-established commitment to women's rights. Others highlighted certain gender practices only to substantiate their claims about the authoritarian and undemocratic nature of indigenous communities. But while the actors making these arguments are diverse, they are nevertheless united by an underlying adherence to notions of liberal individualism inscribed in both the Mexican constitution and popular consciousness of much of Mexico: that the rights and equality of individuals should always have primacy and that these rights are always inherently put at risk by the collective.

This position, while consistent with liberal principles of individual equality that underpin human rights and women's rights claims, nevertheless runs the risk of paternalism and ethnocentricity. No matter how that argument is made, it is difficult to escape the implicit notion that indigenous communities (that is, the individuals within them) are in need of external protection from the civilized Mexican state to keep the "collective" from running amok.[7] The state, in this view, is posited as the legitimate enforcer of liberal discipline on illiberal cultures. Further, while often mobilized to limit the struggle for indigenous rights, this is far from being an anti-multicultural position. It is in fact consistent with classic liberal multicultural "politics of recognition" (see, for example, Kymlicka's 1996 position on the need for "external protections" by the state over "internal restrictions" on individual liberties imposed by the collective). I'll return to these issues later in this analysis, but what I want to suggest here is that what we can see in the Mexican case, and especially in the debate at the intersection of gender and ethnic rights, is the manner in which during the neoliberal moment, the hegemonic premises of liberal individualism get mobilized to limit any collective rights that might be implied by an ascendant multiculturalism.

But indigenous women, rather than accepting the designation of individual rights–bearer in need of protection from the liberal (or neoliberal) state against the illiberal collective, have instead constructed a distinct position for themselves, which articulates both the collective and the individual aspects of their experience into their social struggle on various terrains: in the community, in their organizations, and with the state. Drawing in part on the arguments of indigenous women themselves, some recent writings have argued that culture is continually changing and that indigenous groups are capable of both defending their culture and transforming it from within (toward better gender equality). This position rejects the dichotomy between relativism and women's rights and interrogates the definition of culture that underlies both the relativism and universalism stances (Engle 2005; Hernández Castillo 2002; Kapur 2002; Merry 2006; Sierra 2001). Below, I explore these questions in the context of one community's experience, focusing my discussion on the difficulties of separating out distinct realms of individual and collective experience for many women and the implications of their integration into a unified struggle for women's rights that are not formulated, arbitrated, and enforced exclusively by the state.

Nicolás Ruiz: The Multiplicity of Local Experience

As we saw in the preceding chapter, the community of Nicolás Ruiz has lived the effects of the recent social dynamics in the state. Today in Nicolás Ruiz there is some reassertion of indigenous identity and the community's right to govern itself based on its *usos y costumbres*. Like many other communities in rural Mexico, Nicolás Ruiz went from identifying as "Indian" to identifying primarily as "peasant," and more recently authorities have begun to more strongly forefront the community's indigenous identity.

These shifting subjectivities reflect the fact that community identity is a fundamentally relational concept, historically constructed in dialogue with external social actors and groups. During the period in which the state's relationship to rural peoples was formulated through agrarian reform and "campesinist" assistance policies, Nicolás Ruiz's Tzeltal identity gave way to campesino identity. As the Chiapas conflict brought Nicolás Ruiz into dialogue with new interlocutors, giving them increased interaction with the discourse of human and indigenous rights, and as the discourses of the state shifted from agrarian corporatism and toward the indigenous as a basis for rights claims, people in Nicolás Ruiz reinterpreted their history and their practices in ways that altered their community identity.

We also saw that Nicolás Ruiz does have traditional customs and practices, whether or not they have been defined in the recent past as indigenous. Since the community's formation, land has been held communally. Decisions about community political life are made in the community assembly by consensus, in which all *comuneros* participate. Leaders, even municipal officials, are chosen through the *usos y costumbres* of the community and then ratified through the official electoral process. Those who are elected are expected to carry out—not to make—the decisions that affect the community. That is, decisions are made in the assembly, then implemented through the elected officials. Consensus is crucial to the community's understanding of itself.

Violation of these *usos y costumbres* is considered serious enough that community members are quickly punished. One example is the revocation of the land rights of the *priísta* community members, that is, those in support of the PRI, who were refusing to participate in the assembly. Those arrested in the subsequent military-police raid in defense of the ruling-party loyalists articu-

lated a legal defense similar to that of authorities in several other Zapatista autonomous municipalities that were raided in the same period. They argued that
they were acting based on their *usos y costumbres*, which they had a right to do.
By "*usos y costumbres*," they were referring to their traditional practice of decision by consensus and the concomitant responsibility to participate in the assembly, both of which had been violated by the dissenting members.[8]

It is worth noting that in Nicolás Ruiz, as in most rural communities in
Chiapas, there is some internal differentiation—in class position (this is limited in Nicolás Ruiz and is more evident in some highlands communities,
where *caciques* have enriched themselves, creating greater social divides), in
political and religious stances, and, of course, along gender lines. In situations
of internal discord, all sides are likely to legitimate their actions based on "customs and traditions," rendering the debate, in many cases, one over which
"traditions" are the legitimate ones. In Nicolás Ruiz, the dissenters argued that
the community tradition was to be *priísta*.

Las Mujeres: Life at the Intersection

In Nicolás Ruiz, as in many communities, consensus means consensus of the
men. Women do not hold land and therefore do not participate in the community assembly. Nevertheless, women in Nicolás Ruiz have a history of organizing that predates the Zapatista uprising. This has been especially notable in
times of conflict, when women organized to support the men, but also on occasion to wrest benefits from the state, such as a corn mill that reduced the
labor involved in producing tortillas.[9]

After the community became Zapatista, women began to have new types of
interactions with people from outside the community. Some became involved
directly in "the organization" as *milicianas*, actively training with and responding
to Zapatista leadership. Others became involved with "civil society" activists—
generally pro-Zapatista but not tied directly to the organization. Several of these
activists were feminists with long histories of activism in the region.

The work of women with civil society groups had a high profile, whereas
that of the women with the organization was of necessity more clandestine.
The women formed two committees: a health committee that studied and
practiced herbal medicine and a "political committee" that did political support
work, such as providing a presence at political events in other communities.
A prominent figure among these women was "Doña Matilde," coordinator of
the health committee. Over the course of several years, "Doña Matilde" became

something of a spokesperson for the community and was often seen at rallies with a microphone or megaphone. An ode to "Doña Matilde's" strength and courage circulated on the Internet.

Not surprisingly, as women became increasingly organized and had increased interaction with outside actors with a women's rights orientation, some began to question and challenge their lack of political voice in the community. A women's assembly was formed, parallel to the men's assembly. Though they did not have the power to make decisions affecting the community as a whole, they could address the men's assembly on certain issues and try to sway opinion there. The women I spoke with at the time expressed their preference for a women's assembly over joining the men's assembly. In the words of one woman, "We have too much work to do to sit in there day and night," referring to the notoriously long assembly meetings. "We have little ones to take care of."[10] "Yes," agreed another woman, "It's better to have our own meetings, in agreement with our own schedules."[11] Whether all agreed with their position, I don't know. In the course of my work in the community, I did not find women who expressed interest in participating regularly in the men's assembly. But women from both the organization and civil society groups participated in the assembly, and it seemed a big step forward in women's right to political participation. "Doña Matilde" was the president of the women's assembly.

After being away for a period of several months, I returned to the community to find that the women's assembly had been officially dissolved, the committees were no longer meeting, and "Doña Matilde" was all but censured by community authorities. I was shocked by this turn of events, and it took me some time to piece together a picture of what had happened from the various and distinct versions. There had been a split among the women, along lines that could be divided roughly into those affiliated with "civil society" and those affiliated with the Zapatistas. A variety of reasons were mentioned for the rift. One that was raised often by the Zapatista-affiliated women was their resentment over "Doña Matilde's" insistence that women who did not attend the assembly pay a fine. This practice mirrored that of the men's assembly, where rules state that a fine can be levied against *comuneros* who fail to participate without good reason. But the Zapatista-aligned women complained that they had family and organizational commitments that made occasional absences necessary. They resented the fines and felt that "Doña Matilde" was wielding power over them. Tensions grew into open rupture, and the issue was brought into the general assembly. During a very tense session, "Matilde" addressed the assembly. She defended herself and in anger pointed out members of the assembly and accused them of being Zapatistas. In the context of the open conflict with the *priístas* in the community and of low-intensity warfare in general, this act was perceived by some as a threat to denounce them to the authorities. At the petition of the Zapatista-aligned women, the male authorities of the community voted to discontinue the women's assembly.

This was clearly an unhappy episode for the women involved—one that affected women's solidarity and their advances in political participation within the community. As an activist and individual involved in the social dynamics, I was personally affected by some of the fallout associated with this conflict. Nevertheless, I deeply respect women in both camps, including "Doña Matilde," and owe all a debt of gratitude for the time they spent answering my questions, telling me about their own lives and that of the community. There were many conflicting versions of events and it would be fruitless to attempt to establish whose account was right and whose was wrong. The outline constructed above is a portrayal that all (more or less) agree upon, though interpretations of the events differ. For the purposes of this analysis, it is more important to examine how the issues were perceived and interpreted by the different actors and why.

Both the male authorities and the Zapatista-aligned women accused "Matilde" of *protagonismo*—of asserting her own agenda, wielding power over others, and flaunting the community's norms and collective will. For her part, "Doña Matilde" and her supporters felt that the other women were jealous of her strong position, that the male authorities were threatened by her, and that the community's response was little more than an attempt to keep an assertive and capable woman "in her place."

One can clearly see the outlines of a classic collective culture versus individual gender rights debate in this conflict. A fairly straightforward argument could be made—and in fact was made quite cogently by a feminist sociologist close to "Doña Matilde"—about the violation of an individual's rights based on claims to the collective. The reassertion of indigenous identity and the mobilization of a discourse of *usos y costumbres* in Nicolás Ruiz was, from this perspective, functioning to maintain relations of power within the community, especially gendered relations of power.

I felt uncomfortable with the interpretation, as I often do with the form *usos y costumbres* critiques take, and this is why I was so worried about the subject of the conflict when it came up in the conversation with the Zapatista women. It was not that I doubted that the male authorities of Nicolás Ruiz are capable of exerting their power to maintain patriarchal relations, and in fact they do this to differing degrees in a myriad of ways on a daily basis. Yet I kept returning to the fact that the conflict erupted between women, and to the intuitively illogical fact that it was the Zapatista-aligned women who requested that the male authorities cancel the women's assembly. Were the Zapatista women caught in the all-too-familiar bind of subverting their own gender demands to the greater struggle of the community (organization, movement)? I gingerly tried to broach this with the women and got little response. But the question continued to gnaw at me: had my query been too vague, or had they purposefully avoided it? I decided to be more direct. Had it ever been suggested to them—by men in the organization or in the community—that they put aside or on hold their own struggle for gender equality because it might be divisive at a time when a unified front was needed in the struggle? The three women with whom I was talking looked thoughtful. After a few moments of reflection, one of them said, "I think the opposite is true. It was through the organization that we began to organize, that we began to become conscious of our rights as women."[12] The others agreed. But, I asked, what about the male authorities of the community? They thought about that for a few more moments, and then another woman spoke. "Some men are more *consciente* (enlightened) than others," she said, "but they also know that a community, to advance, must work as a collective, both men and women. That's why they supported us."[13] Undoubtedly, other women would have had a different interpretation. But I found it interesting that, again, the Zapatista women framed the issue as one of individual versus collective.

Nicolás Ruiz's particular insertion into the dynamics of social conflict in Chiapas had a variety of results. One was the separation of the women of the community into distinct groups: one aligned with civil society and one aligned with the organization (and a third, for that matter, aligned with the PRI, as I discussed in the preceding chapter). The division between these groups is not insignificant, since it brought them into engagement with somewhat distinct discourses regarding women's rights: the civil society version, which, while diverse itself, was strongly influenced by feminist individualism; and the Zapatista version, also uneven across various terrains, but in which women's rights were tied continuously to the collective. The latter perspective, I believe, resonated more strongly with notions of collectivity and consensus that prevailed in Nicolás Ruiz prior to the events narrated here. This was notable in the fact that, at least in my discussions with community members, it was more often women than men who raised the issue of community norms of non-*protagonismo* being violated, in their view, by "Matilde's" increasingly public activism. In other words, it was not a straightforward matter of men mobilizing this discourse in order to subvert women's organizing. Women, of course, also participate in reproducing oppressive gender roles. But the fact that it was Zapatista women who were potentially playing this role seemed counterintuitive. In any case, given the community's historical privileging of the consensus model, particularly its heightened sensitivity to the issue in light of the current conflict between pro-Zapatistas and *priístas*, it is perhaps not surprising that the view prevailed that individuals need to conform to community consensus and community norms. The stakes were high, and "Matilde's" pointing to Zapatistas in the assembly brought the women's conflict into the context of the larger conflict in the minds of those present, who felt she had gone too far and was acting without regard for "the common good."[14] In this context, the individual women's rights perspective was more easily discredited, marked by many men and women as an "outsider" perspective.

Rethinking Women's Oppression and Resistance: Toward an Embrace of the Intersection

> We resist hegemonic dominance of feminist thought by insisting that it is a theory in the making, that we must necessarily criticize, question, re-examine and explore new possibilities. . . . The formation of a libratory feminist theory and praxis is a collective responsibility, one that must be shared.
>
> *(hooks 1984:5)*

U.S. Third World feminists have long warned us of the dangers of essentializing all women as a homogeneous group, pointing out that women in different cultural contexts have distinct experiences and understandings of gender (Anzaldúa 1987; Bhavnani 2000; hooks 1984; Lorde 1984; Moraga and Anzaldúa 2002 [1989]). It should be clear that even in the localized context of one community, women's experience differed, and for that reason they had differences of opinion and took distinct positions regarding gender rights. "Rosalina's" statement about wanting to struggle for women's rights collectively suggests that liberal notions of individual rights are not necessarily usefully applied to all women and are not inevitably the principal element of all struggles for women's rights. Overcoming the "feminist ethnocentrism" inherent in applying liberal individual feminist notions of rights to all women and reconceptualizing women's rights in ways that encompass other experiences, such as collective identities, is critically necessary at this juncture.[15]

Feminist legal scholars and other analysts have developed the notion of intersectionality in order to theorize precisely that multiple and multiply constituted experience. Intersectionality theorists argue that race, class, and gender work together as "interlocking axes" to create an "overarching structure of domination" that is distinct from the subordination suffered on any of these axes alone (Collins 1991:222). They suggest that efforts to study just one of these axes at a time can only result in inadequate understandings of the way that that social hierarchy is created and maintained and of the way inequality and oppression are experienced (Carbado 1999; Collins 1991; Crenshaw 1991; Wing 2000). Intersectionality works as more than description of women's reality—it is a theoretical tool to understand multiple oppressions and discuss rights through them. From this perspective, it becomes vital to approach women's experience of oppression and resistance to that oppression from a complex place where they are not first individual women, then members of an indigenous community, or first indigenous, then women. Prioritizing one over the other in seeking to strengthen women's rights does unintended violence to all women's struggles by imposing the notion that one aspect of our identity is more significant than others, and by undermining our ability to understand and resist oppression by sectioning it off into fragments of experience that are not individually comprehensible.

This does not mean that one must be resigned to women's oppression in cultural contexts in which the collective is a significant aspect of women's experience (see Merry 2003). Such arguments are based on notions of culture as static and bounded: collective norms are "traditional" and therefore unchanging. But collectively held norms, like individually held ideas, are in a state of continual change forged in dialogue both with external social actors and between members of the community who challenge hegemonic configurations of power. As we saw in the preceding chapter, Nicolás Ruiz's culture and identity are constantly being reshaped in relation to changing social forces, and there is no particular reason to think that gender norms and relations cannot be altered as part of that process. Looking at the multiple axes of oppression indigenous women suffer might move us beyond blaming local culture as the culprit and open a panorama in which we can understand how gendered power in the collectivity is articulated with gendered power in a broader context to create and reproduce women's and indigenous peoples' oppression in one process.

Though it seemed counterintuitive at the time, I have come to understand

that it makes sense that it was the Zapatista women in Nicolás Ruiz who emphasized the need to struggle for women's rights in the collective context of the
community. They have been vocal in drawing attention to the multiple oppressions suffered by indigenous women—typified by Comandanta Esther's
statement, "We have to struggle more, because we are triply looked down on:
because we are indigenous, because we are women, and because we are poor"
(Comandanta Esther 2001).[16] Zapatista women have been among the leading
voices expressing rejection of arguments that would make them—indigenous
women—the reason their communities are denied autonomy. This is not a position unique to the Zapatistas. Women in many indigenous communities are
facing the challenges of renegotiating gender relations in the context of the
movement that they support and in the communities they call home. These
women struggle to change gendered relations of power in the cultural context
of their communities while simultaneously defending the right of the community to define for itself what that cultural context is and will be (see Hernández
Castillo 2006).

Binaries such as individual / collective rights or cultural rights / women's
rights, while they exist on a conceptual and definitional level, are not always so
clearly defined in women's lived experience. Focusing instead on how women
in a particular social context understand their rights, variously and differen-
tially, may be the best way to think about women's rights and how to gain them.
This does not mean, necessarily, accepting all practices and traditions of a culture as valid. We can disagree with some practices without calling the entire
culture into question (Merry 2003). And we can, as many indigenous women
in Mexico now are doing, call on the male authorities of indigenous communities to alter their cultural understandings and community norms to include
women's rights. But those of us who are elaborating a discourse of women's
rights from outside the community also need to adjust our own historically and
culturally specific notions of the individual nature of those rights, so that we
may encompass the experience of women throughout the world who understand themselves and their rights as existing and being defined largely in a collective context.

Challenges at the Intersection: Neoliberalism, Zapatismo, and Indigenous Women

Avoiding theoretical binaries is crucial, not just because it should be our goal to
fairly represent the women involved in such struggles and not entrap them in

dichotomies foreign to their experience, but also because it may be in this assertion of such multiple and intersecting experiences that resistance may be located. Gender provides us with a key site for exploring the challenges presented
by the Zapatista uprising to the neoliberal state. Some analysts have argued that
indigenous women's demands, at the intersection of gender and ethnicity, are
fundamental to the imagining and the mapping of a multicultural Mexico
(Hernández Castillo, Paz, and Sierra 2004). While this useful perspective coun-
ters the assertion of indigenous women as a barrier to indigenous rights, I want
to suggest something different here—that they actually present a challenge to
state multiculturalism. That is, to the extent that Zapatista indigenous women
are imagining or positing a multicultural Mexico, it is a very distinct one from
the "politics of recognition" model pursued, in sporadic and limited fashion,
by the Mexican state.

The neoliberalizing Mexican state has not effectively harnessed multiculturalism to the project of rule. The initial "multicultural moves" gave way to a
serious government reticence to institute multicultural policies, notably in its
refusal to implement the San Andrés Accords on Indigenous Rights and Culture signed in 1996 by the EZLN and the government and in the failed Law of
Indigenous Rights and Culture of 2001. This law (discussed at greater length in
Chapter 7) was originally proposed as the implementing legislation of the San
Andrés Accords. The version approved by the Congress actually set indigenous
rights back by limiting indigenous jurisdiction, by denying rights to territory
and to natural resources, and by passing the definition of indigenous peoples
and what rights pertain to them on to the individual state-level governments.
While multiculturalist rhetoric predominates, it is nevertheless clear that the
Mexican government is not prepared to cede rights to indigenous peoples to
the extent that some other Latin American countries have.

One important reason for the Mexican state's reticence is undoubtedly the
Zapatista uprising, which raised the stakes on indigenous rights substantially.
This was not simply because it generated fears of out-of-control primitive collectivities that made ceding indigenous rights and creating a multicultural state
seem too dangerous. The real risk posed by the Zapatista uprising was in their
refusal to accept the categories of neoliberal multiculturalism, including that of
the *indio permitido* (C. R. Hale 2004): the state-defined subject of multicultural
policies. I will discuss this idea further in the following chapters. One aspect of
it that I want to explore here is in indigenous women's refusal to accept formulations of rights that limit them to one aspect of their experience.

The line between individual and collective rights is one of the most difficult for neoliberalizing states to negotiate. After the Zapatista uprising, Mexico halted the process it had undertaken with the 1992 constitutional reforms toward a politics of recognition of collective rights and strongly reasserted the primacy of the individual. Perhaps the clearest and most evident response against the Zapatistas' autonomy project was waged, both by government officials and in public discourse, on the sanctified terrain of individual rights. While gender issues were not the only site where individual rights and collective ones were said to clash, it was certainly among the most prominent in public debates. Indigenous women, put forward as the standard bearers for the primacy of individual rights, refused this position and reaffirmed their commitment to collective goals and to maintaining the conjunction of the individual and the collective as central to their struggle.

Once again, I do not wish to suggest that "the collective" is always inherently progressive or contestatory. It is precisely at the intersection of gender and collective rights that the inaccuracy of such a claim is made clear, when "the collective" is marshaled to justify and defend practices that are harmful to specific members or groups within that collective. What I do want to suggest is that the Zapatistas' refusal to separate them makes the state, whose judicial system is premised on this separation, extremely uneasy.

Through their "double activism" (Hernández Castillo 2006) that refuses to conceptualize women's rights outside their collective context, women present a double challenge to oppressive relations of power. The first challenge is to men within their communities and organizations to recognize women's rights and change traditional gender norms; this challenge is strengthened because it is not a product of paternalistic external protections and because it cannot be discounted as the discourse of outsiders. The second challenge, which arises by their refusal to disarticulate their struggle for women's equality within their communities from their struggle for rights based on cultural difference, is to the multiculturalism of the neoliberal state in Mexico, drawing the contradictions to the fore and offering an alternative logic.

Mexico has not "multiculturalized" in the manner that some other Latin American countries have for a variety of reasons. One of them, I have suggested, is that indigenous challenges from within made the internal contradictions of such an undertaking too difficult to overcome. Zapatismo and the indigenous women's movement that has gained force since the Zapatista uprising are a part of that internal challenge. Indigenous women, due to their location at the juncture of multiple identities of race, class, and gender, may well be at the forefront of contributing to a new multicultural Mexico. However, the one they advocate is not only different from but also challenging to that of the neoliberal state.

Conclusions

In this discussion of women's rights in one community, we have seen that local appropriations, even in the context of one community, may be diverse, depending on the differing subjectivities of groups of actors within the community and the types of external actors and discourses with which they are in dialogue. In the context of this conflict in Nicolás Ruiz, it made a significant difference for the two groups of women whether they were interacting primarily with the Zapatistas, who as a movement were mobilizing a collective rights discourse, or with activists from civil society, who were more likely to have a Western feminist notion of women's rights. Though these are generalizations of both groups of actors, it is nevertheless clear that the perspectives of the women involved were influenced by the dialogues they were engaged in with their primary interlocutors. The women's different interpretations of gender rights forged in dialogic interaction with outsiders are then brought into dialogue inside the community, itself a complex space of interaction within which continual struggles over meaning, culture, and power are always present.

All of these dialogisms take place in the larger context of conflict, counterinsurgency, and the renegotiation of power relations with the state. It was the uprising and social struggle that brought these particular external actors and discourses through the porous boundaries of the community. This was also what created the cultural climate in which gender rights could be and were debated and new interpretations were forged.

In Nicolás Ruiz, as in many other communities, these interpretations are still being struggled over, among women and between women and men. But even on this uneven and shifting topography, there is more, I want to suggest, at the intersection of gender and ethnicity than the collision of individual and collective rights. By overcoming "feminist ethnocentrism" (Hernández Castillo 2006) and thinking beyond these binaries to their multiply constituted meanings, we may see many indigenous women fostering potentially powerful new ways of conceptualizing rights and of resisting oppressive power relations. In the chapter that follows I will turn to a different context, that of an indigenous organization called the *Red de Defensores Comunitarios por los Derechos Humanos*, in which rights are being appropriated and reconceptualized in similarly challenging ways.

6 "Assuming Our Own Defense": Rights, Resistance, and the Law in the *Red de Defensores Comunitarios*

Positive law is not our law; in our communities we have a different way. But it is very useful for us to understand it, in order to defend ourselves from the government.

"Juan" of the Red de Defensores[1]

Every tool is a weapon if you hold it right.

Ani DiFranco

THE *DEFENSORES* SAT CLUSTERED around a large set of tables configured in a rectangle. They were describing the *Red* to a group of visitors from a U.S. solidarity delegation. "Before," one *defensor* explained, "human rights was the work of NGOs, of the Fray Bart. But what we want is to defend our own rights. That's what we mean by 'assuming our own defense.' It is part of our *autogestión*.[2] If someone else is always defending our rights, that's fine, but we aren't living our autonomy."

Thus far in my exploration of the "social life of rights," I have suggested that they have multiple trajectories and divergent uses in Chiapas, and that these "local" engagements with rights have effects on both the individuals and groups involved. I suggested in the last chapter that appropriations of discourses of rights may in fact result in reformulations that challenge certain forms of power. In this chapter I return to the question of the implications of the origins and nature of global rights discourses for the forms of resistance that base themselves in these discourses. I ask whether such resistances are ultimately bound within hegemonic globalizing discourses, and if so, whether they are constrained to forms that reinscribe hegemony.

To examine this question, I focus on the experience of the *Red de Defensores Comunitarios por los Derechos Humanos* (called the "*Red*" from the Spanish for "network"). Exploring the work of the participants of the *Red* (*defensores*), I consider their dialogic engagement with human rights. How did human rights become relevant to them? To what extent and in what ways have they appropriated this discourse? In doing so, are they reproducing forms of power they intend to challenge?

In considering the *Red*'s work, I highlight the ways in which, through what they bring to that dialogue, they also reformulate rights discourses and potentially put them to the task of renegotiating relations of power. Specifically, I look at the way that the combination of distinct rights discourses merge in a particular form of resistance that utilizes law and rights as one of its principal tools and consider whether legal discourses and the legal system can function as effective tools of resistance. I argue that in this case, the linking of the *Red*'s work to a larger political process of indigenous autonomy might make the usage of dominant discourses and legal structures more subversive than they would seem.

Rights and Sovereign Power

To understand the role of rights-based resistance in the current era it is important to first consider what law is, where it is positioned in the architecture of power, and what its relationship to rights is.[3] It is insufficient to examine law as a system of signs or even as a cultural artifact; the law must be understood as a particular form for the exercise of power.

In Chapter 2, I discussed the two main trajectories of human rights in Chiapas up until the current period: one with a natural law orientation disseminated through the Catholic Church and one with a positive law orientation, framed in the Mexican legal system and propagated through the agencies of the state and NGOs. These are very broad generalizations, of course, for the many distinct philosophical lines that each encompasses. But for my purposes here, there is no need to review all subcategories of theorization. Rather, what I wish to do is point to the fundamental aspect of the lines of thought within each: the conceptual basis for and justification of the existence of human rights, one which views these rights as innate, natural, and prior to any judicial normativity; and one which posits that rights, human or otherwise, do not exist prior to their establishment in law. In both, rights are generated by a higher, sovereign power: that of God or of the state.

Throughout the history of Western juridical thought, law has regulated and supported the exercise of a sovereign power: the enforcement of a command-obedience relationship between ruler and ruled. This does not, however, mean that law is the naked use of force, but rather "a form of violence endowed with the legitimacy of formally constituted authority" (Merry 1992). It is an authority justified mainly through the fiction of the "social contract." This fiction posits that because of the fear of others, individuals in the state of nature will give up their unlimited number of rights to a sovereign. This sovereign, through the collection of these rights, holds absolute power within a society and is, in turn, charged with the task of mediating among competing individual interests with the goal of creating social unity and peace.

Within this contractarian philosophy, the rights that we exercise as subjects of a sovereign are the absolute limits beyond which the sovereign is not allowed to act. But how is it possible to limit the actions of a sovereign (i.e., of an absolute power)? That is the question that has vexed both natural and positivist legal philosophers, the great majority of whom have been unable to escape the philosophical hegemony of the contractarian theses within legal thought. The natural law solution to this puzzle has been to appeal for rights from a sovereign above and beyond that of the state (God), whereas the positivist legal solution has been to ask the sovereign itself to create a system of checks on its own power through the recognition and pronouncement of the rights of its subjects. Yet, both natural and positivist legal philosophies accept in whole the theses that all power within a state society emanates from the sovereign (Speed and Reyes 2002).

The power of the law is thus the power to produce and reproduce daily practices within society that continually reinforce the founding myth of sovereign power, the power to create subjects that act as if all power emanated from the state. This mystifying or "normalizing" power of the law, the unparalleled legitimacy it gives the state, and the command-obedience relationship it maintains with its citizens becomes particularly dangerous given our current global juncture.

In the neoliberal era, law has been mobilized in new ways. As we have already seen, rights struggles became the primary form of social struggle in the context of neoliberal globalization. Some have viewed this as the good side of globalization, a countermovement to that of out-of-control capitalist exploitation wrought by hyperfree markets (see Chapter 1 for discussion). This perspective, while tempting in its simplicity, does not take into account the power of the law, a basic component of rights struggles, which are waged on the legal terrain and with legal outcomes.

Neoliberalism, the extension of liberal ideas that emphasize and privilege the free market to the entire realm of social interaction, entails a variety of government policies and practices designed to ensure that the workings of economic markets and social relations are unfettered by state mediation. Neoliberalism differs from classic and modern liberalisms by the philosophy that essentially all human interactions—not just economic ones—should be regulated by market forces. States may increasingly recognize rights (human rights, indigenous rights), but no longer are states interpreted as the responsible party for ensuring those rights. This function is "privatized," passed from the state to industry and business (corporate social responsibility), communities and individuals, and especially civil society organizations such as NGOs (Deleuze 1994; Guehenno 1995; Hardt 1998). Thus, as the market is prioritized and the state is divested of responsibility for social welfare, relations between social groups are defined by market forces and mediated by civil society itself (Gill 2000).

In the state devolution of responsibility for mediating social relations to civil society, NGOs have a special place, replacing the state in its managerial role. NGOs also play a significant role in reproducing and disseminating these logics through training programs, workshops, and other projects which have at their root conceptions of rational, self-managing citizens (Feldman 1997; Joseph 2002; Postero 2001; see discussion in Chapter 1). Hardt and Negri (2000) suggest that NGOs do the work of missionaries for the civilizing project of Empire. Their description of the new global NGOs as working through a kind of "moral interventionism" analogous in form to the role of missionaries during classical imperialism seems particularly resonant in the case of human rights NGOs:

> NGOs conduct "just wars" without arms, without violence, without borders. Like the Dominicans in the late medieval period and the Jesuits at the dawn of modernity, these groups strive to identify universal needs and defend human rights. Through their language and their action they first define the enemy as privation . . . and then recognize the enemy as sin. . . . Within this logical framework it is not strange but rather all too natural that in their attempts to respond to privation, these NGOs are led to denounce publicly the sinners . . . nor is it strange that they leave it to the "secular wing" the task of actually addressing problems. In this way, moral intervention has become a frontline force of imperial intervention. (Hardt and Negri 2000:36)

That NGOs are playing a role in the neoliberal process is perhaps obvious. But NGOs not only take over for the state in its mediating role; they do so in a way that reinforces state power by pursuing their goals through a discourse of rights, and thus ultimately through the law.

Law may provide a privileged space for the state to engage in neoliberal subject making because of its inherent delimiting and regulating capacities. Gledhill has argued that it is risky to "settl[e] for the politics of rights alone under liberal political institutions which embody various kinds of regulatory power" (1997:71), while Brown argues that rights may become "a regulatory discourse, a means of obstructing or co-opting more radical political demands" (1995:98). Geared to narrow legal goals, rights struggles may actually reinforce structures and discourses of inequality, in part by "fixing" identities and delimiting culture in the law, subjugating them to a stable set of regulatory norms (Brown and Halley 2002:24). Similarly, Goodale has called rights the "foot soldiers of liberalism," arguing that they are "essential features of a particular disciplinary regime in which the grandeur of liberal legality is used to create loyalty to the wider project of liberalism within the consolidation of late capitalism" (2005:553). These theorists all emphasize the regulatory and disciplinary force of rights discourses and law in the current stage of capitalism. Importantly, this regulation is not only by the state, which holds the power to grant and take away rights, but also self-regulation on the part of those who seek to gain or retain them.

With the increasing abandonment by the state of its mediating role, it would seem that a critique of law and sovereign power would be the order of the day for disenfranchised groups in Mexico and elsewhere. Ironically, it is exactly at this juncture that most disenfranchised groups have adopted the language of rights and the practice of law, most often through NGOs, to further their struggles. Thus, at the moment that the state is capable of doing least to transform society in a positive fashion, its capacity for self-legitimation through the creation of "normalized" subjects and the dissemination of its legal discourse is at its highest point. This would seem to leave human rights and indigenous rights organizations in a contradictory position of reproducing and sustaining the very relations of power they are intended to keep in check or to change. Yet, as I will argue below, not all rights-based movements have the same relationship to the law.

The Red de Defensores Comunitarios: "Assuming Our Own Defense"

The defensor stood before the Ministerio Público (MP), attempting to ascertain the whereabouts of and charges against two men who had been detained earlier that day.[4] *The mestizo MP looked annoyed. "Are you a family member?" he asked. "No," replied the defensor, "I am a community human rights defender." The MP, surprised at this unexpected response, replied dismissively, "A public de-*

fender will be assigned." "I would like to know where the men are being detained," the defensor *continued. Looking disdainful, the MP shot back, "You have no right to that information!" The* defensor *paused before responding calmly, "I know what my rights are. In the community, we now know what our rights are. And I am here to claim them."*[5]

The *Red de Defensores Comunitarios* (Community Human Rights Defenders' Network) was formed in early 1999. I have worked with the *Red* since its inception in a variety of roles, including as a member of the advisory council and as a project coordinator. At the time of its formation, the goal was to bring together a group of young indigenous people from various conflicted regions of the state to train them in national and international human rights and law, as well as in the fundamental practice of legal defense in the Mexican justice system. A significant portion of the training over the following years was dedicated to national and international agreements on indigenous rights and the workings of the Inter-American Human Rights system. They received extensive training about human rights in the national framework, essentially constitutional law and the study of the "individual rights and guarantees" contained in the Mexican Constitution. They studied and practiced legal defense work within the Mexican legal system, which included criminal defense and the everyday practice of law in the jails, courts, and *Ministerio Públicos*. Training was also provided in the political practice of human rights defense, which included writing press releases and public denouncements and handling negotiations and other interaction with public officials. In addition, there was a significant portion of the workshops dedicated to technical training: in the use of video and still cameras for human rights documentation and in the use of computers, word processing programs, and other office technology.

This project parted significantly from the numerous existing projects for training human rights *promotores* (promoters) in the communities, because it sought to train *defensores*. In general, human rights *promotores* have been trained either to inform their fellows that they *had* human rights and what those were or to recognize and document human rights violations, then proceed to the nearest human rights organization (usually the one that provided them the training). From there, the NGO would take the information and make decisions about the appropriate course of action. Once the information has been taken, the *promotores* are often sent on their way, while the organization undertakes the work of preparing the complaints, contacting the *Ministerio Público* and government human rights agencies, as well as the press and/or the international community; preparing the documentation; and, when necessary, providing follow-up on the case. In essence, human rights NGOs take the case out of the hands of the indigenous people involved: in a classic middleman role, professionalized human rights activists interact with the state to "defend" indigenous people. In contrast, the *Red* was conceived and designed to prepare the *defensores* to make the decisions and proceed with the actions on their own, thereby eliminating dependence on attorneys and NGOs.

This is especially vital to communities pursuing autonomy processes. It has been documented that indigenous communities in Zapatista autonomous regions (as elsewhere, no doubt) have often substituted NGO support for the support previously received from the government (Van der Haar 2004). While NGOs have provided valuable assistance and reinforcement to communities pursuing autonomy, the problematic nature of the community-NGO–neoliberal state relationship renders this dependency even more problematic. At a minimum, shifting reliance on the government to reliance on NGOs still leaves the communities in a situation of dependency which can hinder their ability to act autonomously. Further, it entails a type of interaction in which state processes of subject making are occluded. One purpose of the *Red*, then, was to eliminate the NGO middlemen and allow the communities to "assume their own defense" (which is the slogan of the organization).

The participants are all from Zapatista base support regions and were chosen by their authorities through the particular *usos y costumbres* of their regions in response to letters of invitation sent to the five *Aguascalientes* (Zapatista regional points of public contact). After some initial dropouts and new recruits, the course took shape with fourteen participants: two from Nicolás Ruiz, two from San Miguel (Palenque), two from Cuauhtemoc Chancalá (Palenque), four from the Northern Zone municipality of Tila (Misopá Chinal, Emiliano Zapata, and Petalcingo), two from Morelia (Altamirano), one from San Jeronimo Tulijá (Chilón), and one Guatemalan refugee representing the communities of Frontera Comalapa. These representatives are from Tzeltal-, Chol-, Tojolobal-, and Mam-speaking zones. After an initial year and a half of training, the *Red de Defensores* became a formal organization, made up of the participants of the training workshops. Since that time, two new generations of *defensores* have been added, bringing the total to thirty-six men and women participants.

Initially, all of the regions covered by the *Red* were suffering different degrees of violent conflict. Because of the situation of microregionalization of conflict in Chiapas, the types of problems faced by the *defensores* in the different regions were varied. The primary concerns posited by the *defensores* at the start of the workshops were militarization, paramilitarization, occupation by state police forces, and the politically motivated imprisonment of community members. Since that time, some areas have seen considerable calming of tensions. The most recent group of *defensores* was recruited in late 2005 from regions suffering the effects of neoliberal economic policies and has had training specifically focused on economic, social, and cultural rights (DESC by the Spanish acronym).

The *defensores'* work thus entails a range of activities which vary according to the needs of their regions at any particular time. The *defensores* remain in and work from their communities, coming into San Cristóbal for monthly workshops which also serve as opportunities for information sharing among the *defensores*, interaction with other organizations, and press conferences or other events. Remaining in the community allows them to continue with other activities, such as maintaining a *milpa* (corn plot), caring for families, and engaging in community activities such as assemblies. Their principal activities as *defensores* are taking declarations and testimonies from victims and witnesses regarding rights abuses, videotaping and photographing for evidence, presenting complaints before the *Ministerio Público*, sending denunciations to the press and the human rights community at large, and seeking the release or pursuing the defense of people who have been unjustly detained. One of the most high-profile human rights cases they have been involved in is the case of the three Zapatista base supporters killed by the Mexican Army in Morelia in January 1994. The *Red* is working in collaboration with the *Comision Mexicana de Defensa y Promoción de los Derechos Humanos*, which has consultative status before the Interamerican Commission on Human Rights, to seek redress for the widows of the victims. Also, the *Red* has prepared two complaints presented to the ILO through the *Frente Amplio de Trabajo* (FAT), the first regarding violations by the Mexican government of Convention 169 in the 2001 passage of the federal legislation on Indigenous Rights and Culture (discussed in Chapter 7) and the second for violations of the articles on territory and self-ascription, on behalf of the community of Nicolás Ruiz (discussed in Chapter 4). At the time this writing was being finished in 2006, the *Red* was poised to launch a campaign on the right to electricity and water as basic DESC rights.[6]

Thus, the work of the *defensores* is varied, involves interactions with a variety of actors across social fields, and reflects a significant level of training. Prior to coming to the *Red*, some *defensores* had little or no experience with the concept of human rights. In the words of "Ricardo" from Nicolás Ruiz, "Before,

Figure 6.1 A *defensor* from the Community Human
Rights Defenders Network gathers documentary evidence about human rights violations by filming a
military activity. Rubén Moreno Méndez.

no one talked about 'human rights.' It had no meaning for us." "Miguel," from
the Northern Zone, notes the transition they have made as part of the *Red*: "We
indigenous people do not know what our rights are. They say we have rights,
but we don't know what those rights are, for example [in relation to] the taxes
imposed on us by the government through its institutions. Indigenous *priístas*
don't know their rights. The government helps them, in order to get their votes,
but they still don't know what their rights are. We as human rights *defensores*
are learning what our rights are, and we are reclaiming them."[7]

Some of the *defensores* had previous experience or training as *promotores*.
For example, "Manolo," from Altamirano, had been human rights *promotor*
and regional coordinator for three years before coming to the *Red*. Because of

this previous experience he was chosen by his community authorities to participate in the training and later in the *Red* when it became a formal organization: "When the invitation from Lic. Miguel Angel came, the authorities of my community told me, 'You should go because you already know something about law and you will quickly learn how to do this work.' " "Rafael" had also had several years of training as a *promotor* given through the local Catholic parish in Tila, which ended when the 1994 uprising began. He was clear about the difference between the training he received as a *promotor* and what he has received with the *Red*: "They taught us what human rights are . . . and if we saw violations, they told us, we should go to the Fray Bartolomé. With the *Red* it is more practical— we are learning how to handle the MP, write documents, defend rights with the Articles [of the Mexican Constitution], the penal codes, the ILO 169."

Learning to "handle the MP" and other people with whom they would interact in the course of their human rights defense work was one of the most difficult parts of the training for some of the *defensores*. They gained confidence as they confronted their own fears while facing the exclusionary structures of power and the racism of the *Ministerio Públicos* and others. Speaking of himself and his co-*defensor*, "Ricardo" of Nicolás Ruiz notes, "In the workshops of the *Red*, we have learned not to be afraid. When we began we were afraid to go before the judge, but now we feel more sure of what we are doing, and what we have learned." "David," a Chol speaker from Palenque, also noted that "because Spanish is not our first language, we were afraid that we would have difficulty expressing ourselves before a judge, and that the judge would not listen to us." This fear is not unfounded, as they have often run directly up against such discrimination. "Manolo" recalls one incident:

> I have accompanied *compañeros* who have problems when they go to meet with their public defenders. So I've seen what happens, the lawyers think they know everything, and they don't take into account what we [*defensores*] say. . . . They want us to pay them for their work! When this happened, I knew what their job was, and I told them: "It is your obligation to defend them, it's your job." That's what I said to that attorney. The next time we went, they told us that if we weren't willing to pay, they would not attend our case, that we had to wait until the indigenous public defender came. I told them again that it was their job to defend the case, that public defenders are not paid by those they defend. Those lawyers were surprised. They wanted to know how I knew all this. . . . I told them, "I am a human rights *defensor*. I know."[8]

By standing up to the public defenders who wanted to manipulate and exploit the indigenous defendants, "Manolo" was able to avert one more violation of their rights in the process of their detention.

"Manolo" pointed to some of the other reasons why having trained *defensores* is important in his region:

> In our communities, we don't have a lot of economic resources and we don't have any way to go quickly to San Cristóbal. Even if we [do], by the time we arrive in San Cristóbal and go to an organization to explain, it is too late to make the denunciation—those who committed the violations are long gone. The journalists and human rights observers also arrive to the community too late to gather information and make the denunciation. *We* are *in* our communities. That's why we are taking this course to learn how to take testimony and write a denunciation [a *denuncia* may be a complaint before an MP or a public statement denouncing a violation]. This is very important, because one never knows when [human rights violations] will happen. When the Federal Army comes or Federal Police or state police enter the communities, we are ready.

As "Manolo's" comments suggest, the ability to act directly from the community is important to the victims of rights violations and facilitates human rights work. For this reason, the *defensores* are based in their regions, rather than in San Cristóbal or another town. Another *defensor*, "Pablo," notes the value of coming from a shared language, culture, and experience: "An attorney from the city doesn't speak our language. We *defensores* understand more clearly what [victims and witnesses] are trying to say and express. This is much better because we think the same, talk the same, and we have suffered the same repressions. They trust us."

There are thus some clear practical reasons why *defensores* based in the community may work more effectively without intermediary NGOs. But beyond eliminating the "middle man," their effectiveness can also be understood as a result of strengthening autonomous practice in the nascent Zapatista autonomous municipalities, as I will discuss below.

Community at the Center

The defensores *seated around the meeting table in the San Cristóbal office smiled broadly when the topic of the recent workshop they had attended in Huehuetenango, Guatemala was raised. "Ricardo" spoke excitedly: "It went very well," he said.* "*Everyone was very impressed with the* Red. *There was an exercise in which they asked us to draw a picture of the structure of our organization, and when we showed ours with the three circles and the community in the center, everyone was silent for a minute, surprised, then they all started asking, 'Can you explain it again? How does it work?' They were very impressed.*"

After an initial two years of training, the *Red de Defensores* became a formal organization, made up of the participants of the training workshops. Its unique structure, which "Ricardo" refers to above, resembles conceptualizations of power relations in the communities of the *defensores* and is distinct from the structures often seen in NGOs. The latter have traditionally been conceived as pyramids with the officials at the top (coordinator, director, president, executive secretary, etc.), the attorneys, project directors, public relations and press coordinators, and fundraisers in the middle, and *promotores* from indigenous communities at the base. The *Red*, by contrast, is conceptualized in concentric circles, with the communities at the center, the *defensores* in the second ring, and an advisory council in the outer ring. Perhaps the obvious difference is in not having "outsiders" at the top and the elimination of the top-down mode of operation. This structure emphasizes the fact that the indigenous communities are the heart of the project.

The work of the *Red* begins with, is directed by, and is answerable to the communities themselves and the authorities of the Zapatista autonomous regions to which they pertain. The thirty-eight Zapatista autonomous regions established following the uprising had by 1997 become the heart of their strategy for resistance and for indigenous political participation. Regional councils administered the political and juridical processes in the regions, responding directly to Zapatista authority structures. These were essentially military structures of the Zapatista Army until 2003 when the civilian Good Governance Councils were formed (the subject of Chapter 7). The highest authority in the regions is the Clandestine Indigenous Revolutionary Committee (CCRI), the general command of the Zapatista Army. The autonomous municipalities have been actively engaged in developing their own systems of education, healthcare, and agriculture since at least 1997, often with impressive results. The Zapatista regions are governed according to the principle of *mandar obedeciendo*, a philosophy of governance in which authorities have the responsibility to carry collective consensus decisions, rather than to make decisions for the collective, and are directly accountable to the collective for their actions.

In Chapter 5 I noted that in Nicolás Ruiz authority is understood in this way, even that of elected officials. I learned how critical this concept was for the *comuneros* in an assembly meeting in late 2004. The special meeting had been called by the authorities of *Bienes Comunales* to discuss recent events in the ongoing conflict with the *priístas*. The *comisariado* (the head of *Bienes Comunales*) opened the meeting and the discussion. But the first *comunero* who took the floor to speak stated boldly that they were not interested in new proposals; they wanted to know what was being done by the authorities to carry out decisions already made by the assembly. Many voices rose to support him. "How can it be that you [the authorities of *Bienes Comunales*] are acting alone?" "Why haven't you done what was agreed upon in the assembly?" The surprised authorities tried to return the discussion to their proposal for dealing with the *priístas*, but the *comuneros* were not willing. As the authorities tried to give explanations, murmurs of "*Cárcel! Cárcel! Cárcel!*" ("Jail! Jail! Jail!") began to circulate. All the authorities of *Bienes Comunales* were removed from their posts that night, and they narrowly escaped jail time for their failure to carry out, directly and to the letter, the collective consensus decision of the assembly. One *defensor* who was with me in the meeting later smiled about the incident. "That's our way," he said. While forms of authority vary from region to region, and in some cases it is an ideal rather than a consistent practice, this is a fairly widespread conceptualization of authority in indigenous communities in Chiapas, and the Zapatista concept emerges from those communities. This fundamental principle underlies the work of the *defensores*, which is based in the community and is continually accountable to the autonomous communities. If the *defensores* do not carry out the word of the community, they can expect to have their designation as *defensor* summarily removed. The *Red*'s organizational structure, designed to keep the community as the center, reflects the *defensores*' understanding of their role as human rights "authorities" in relation to their communities.

Analyzing the *Red*

I came to the project of the *Red* with a critical analysis of rights and the law, one I held in tension with the day-to-day work of human rights defense and training. There were many things I thought interesting and new about the *Red*, from its structure to its elimination of the NGO middleman. I considered local empowerment to be significant, as the indigenous participants learned and expanded their activities in the legal realm, giving them both skills and connections that they could use toward their own goals. But at the same time, I considered the project in many ways a classic example of human rights globalization, as the bearers of the global concept "trained" the "locals" in its meaning and uses. The *Red* was founded and coordinated by *mestizo* attorney Miguel Angel de los Santos, and supported by a team of *mestizo* and international advisors (of which I was one). Its funding came from the same international NGOs and foundations dedicated to the spread of human rights practice and civil-society building that all other organizations' funding did. While it was by no means our goal, I expected that, as the project unfolded, we might inevitably produce professionalized human rights workers who would end up disengaged to some extent from their communities, stepping into the new role of being the middlemen between their communities and the state.

This was not, in fact, what happened. What I began to see over time was that in most cases, the *defensores* were "learning" the discourse of human rights, but in a detached fashion. While they have become intermediaries in a sense, moving easily between the legal structures of the community and those of the state, they have maintained a community focus as central to their work. In the course of seven years, several *defensores* have come and gone for personal reasons, usually commitments in the community that do not allow them to engage in the work of the *Red*. But only three *defensores*, two men and one woman, have left their communities, turning to NGO work in the city. They are no longer with the *Red*, precisely because they have lost their community's support or *aval*. Once a *defensor* has left his or her community, or for any reason has lost the community's support, that person is asked by the *defensores* to leave the organization. It became clear to me that the *defensores*, rather than becoming distanced from their communities through "the learning of human rights," instead maintained a critical distance from the perspectives of human rights activists whose community is constructed through international law.

"To Organize Ourselves in the Way That We Choose"

It was a sunny afternoon in June of 2000, when Abelardo Méndez Arcos made some casual comments that would later contribute to a shift in our thinking on the work of legal defense from the community in Chiapas. "It's simple," he said, "I began doing legal work to help the compañeros *[Zapatistas]. It is all part of the struggle, the struggle for autonomy." Méndez Arcos, a Chol from the Northern Zone of the state, was a Zapatista political prisoner from 1996 to 1997 and upon his release became the external representative of the political prisoners' group* La Voz de Cerro Hueco. *He was in a sense the proto-*defensor, *having worked with and learned from attorney De los Santos on the cases of dozens of prisoners over several years preceding the formation of the* Red. *Given to lengthy political monologues, he repeated the simple prem-*

ise several times in different ways before flashing a suddenly self-conscious smile and concluding: "That's what the Red *is for: to defend our rights, our autonomy."*[9]

At the time, Abelardo's comments seemed like straightforward political rhetoric about "the struggle." But in the course of dialogue with the *defensores*, I began to focus on this conceptual linkage of the *Red's* work in legal defense and the broader project of Zapatista autonomy of the communities that form its base. That is, there is more to "defense from the community" than simply eliminating the middleman or even creating local empowerment by appropriating the legal terrain of the state. Carrying out legal defense from the community is important, from the *defensores'* perspective, primarily because it allows community members to "defend their autonomy," as Méndez Arcos put it, and because it is in itself an extension of autonomous practices.

The opening quote of this chapter, "Positive law is not our law; in our communities we have a different way. But it is very useful for us to understand it, in order to defend ourselves from the government," suggests that the *defensores* recognize positive law, and the Mexican legal system specifically, as alien to their forms of organization and conflict resolution but nevertheless as an important tool to use precisely in defending their communities' ability to do things "their way." They understand the political nature of "rights" as a tool of power wielded by the government against them, and which they can use to fight back. In the words of one *defensor*:

> We, as human rights defenders, are getting to know what our rights are and we are demanding them. But the government is playing a political game. For example, for the government, "civil resistance" is a violation of the law, but they do not take into account all the laws that have already been established, the international laws which they themselves signed, [because] they don't want to recognize that we have the right to organize ourselves in the way that we choose. . . . We know how to defend ourselves with the law, because the government is not going to do it for us—it is not in their interest.

In statements such as this one, I began to see an alternative understanding of rights held by the *defensores*. For them, positive law was a tool, a means to defend their self-organization, their autonomy. Over time, I began to understand that they do not aim to protect or expand their own ability to present cases in courts or with state officials, even though this is the daily work in which they are engaged. That is, their end goal is not the search for a just, or even an adequate, state mediation of local problems. Rather, they tend to view their work as the subproject of a much larger undertaking, which the above-quoted *defensor* refers to as "civil resistance."

This resistance is practiced by utilizing the legal system to protect communities from general violations of law, including assassination, torture, disappearance, arbitrary detention, and military occupation. But the rights violated by these sorts of actions are not viewed as a priori rights; rather, they are viewed as derivative of a more central demand and "right": the right "to organize ourselves in the ways that we choose." Thus, the *defensores* not only recognize the political nature of law and the political motivations for the abuses directed against their communities, they also identify their source of strength in the larger social architecture of power and their ultimate political difference with the "law," which lies in their self-organization. Rather than adopting human rights discourse, the *defensores* have engaged it, taking from it what makes sense in terms of their own needs, goals, and understandings.

The autonomy and self-determination that the indigenous rights movement seeks will not be provided by organizations such as the *Red de Defensores*. However, legitimizing the internal decision-making structures of indigenous communities, eliminating dependence on intermediaries, and disseminating at a grassroots level useful tools for resisting state repression, the *Red* does contribute to their *autogestión*. This, in turn, strengthens those communities' ability to engage in autonomous practices, allowing them to accumulate the space necessary to further expand their internal projects, such as building schools, hospitals, and water systems, as well as forming a generation of health promoters, teachers, and community-trained engineers. Further, it thus improves their position in the national and global structure of power, making violations of human rights less likely and state mediation of local problems less and less necessary.

Zapatista communities and other indigenous groups in Mexico demand autonomy and self-determination, expressed not as the capacity to build another state under a new sovereign (as is the case with many nationalist ethnic minorities), but as the capacity to function unimpeded so as to affect the daily lives and future of their members. The San Andrés Accords reflected this by recognizing (1) the right of indigenous peoples to choose their authorities through their internal selection mechanisms; (2) the right of those authorities to exercise their power in order to make decisions affecting the future development of their communities, as well as the further divestiture of state political and economic power to the indigenous communities in question; and (3) the right to interact with the state in a relationship which functions on the principle of consensus decision making. All of these are concrete aspects of autonomy: the right to maintain and have recognition of an independent system of electing leaders and making decisions affecting the community. In Zapatista areas (as in many others throughout Mexico), this is based on logic of consensus decision making, which has its ultimate expression in the Zapatistas' *mandar obedeciendo*, in which leaders quite literally act on the consensus of the followers.[10] Another important aspect of Zapatista autonomy is precisely the fact that, in the absence of real constitutional reform based on the San Andrés Accords, the project of autonomy is being carried out unilaterally from the communities themselves. In doing so, Zapatista communities assert both the validity of rights regardless of the recognition of the state and the validity of a distinct structure and logic of rule, outside the laws of the state. In fact, the unilateral nature of their autonomy disengages them with both natural and positive law discourses of rights, because there is no longer recourse to the higher authority of either God / the Church or the sovereign/state.

Conclusions

Many rights-based movements and NGOs in Mexico and around the world are caught within the power of law. That is, they are trapped waiting for the sovereign to recognize their "rights" while leaving the power and myth of the sovereign unquestioned. Thus, the risks are great that movements will waste valuable energy and resources on actions that further legitimate institutions and empty forms that function to guarantee their ultimate subordination. In mobilizing discourses of power, they may reinscribe the very relations of power they are resisting. In this chapter, I have focused on the *Red de Defensores* because I believe that it can be interpreted as a form of political resistance through the use of identity-based rights claims and a direct exercise of local power that has implications for these questions. I offer the experience of the *Red de Defensores* as one example of potential alternatives that break with the normalizing characteristics of legal discourse and practice and offer us a glimpse of possible alternatives.

The *Red de Defensores*' appropriation of the concept and structures of law as a "site of contestation" (Hernández Castillo 2001b) or a "space of resistance" (Merry 1997) does not necessarily "reinforce the centrality of law as a mode of protest" (Merry 1997). The nature and power of the *Red* goes beyond the strategic use of rights discourses and the Mexican legal system, to the larger political project which this tool is wielded to defend. Its power is that of the Zapatista communities its defenders come from and respond to, and whose movement asserts the right to autonomy and self-determination—expressed as the capacity to control and affect their daily lives—that inevitably puts sovereignty (state or global) and its power of absolute command in question.

On the material terrain, this challenge comes through the assertion of parallel power structures. That is, indigenous communities function on the knowledge that "law" and its sovereignty are a myth, and their communiqués and anti-neoliberal rhetoric signal that they are well aware of the sclerotic nature of the current state. Their actions, the shape their political project has taken, exposes the myth of sovereign power and escapes the dangers of the normalizing force of the state by directing their resistance toward a project of self-organization: to enlivening a parallel power structure. This parallel power might engage with the state and even ask it to recognize a series of "rights," as is the case with the San Andrés Accords. But this engagement with state structures thrives on the knowledge that such rights and their protection arise as a result of a struggle of social forces in which they must engage, and not because of the will of the sovereign.

The *Red de Defensores* allows this powerful political understanding to be fully expressed because its purpose is to eliminate the need for intermediaries between the indigenous communities and the state. Besides participating in the strengthening of the communities' internal organization, the *Red de Defensores* allows indigenous people themselves to engage the state in order to halt repression, without having to give up their ultimate political goals. More than "local empowerment," the *Red de Defensores* signals the reemergence of a truly politicized legal defense. Without this kind of defense, the indigenous communities of Chiapas are left vulnerable to intermediaries that conceptualize rights in a different manner and inadvertently contribute to putting indigenous communities at the mercy of law and its myth of sovereign power.

Like other actors in the Chiapas conflict, in appropriating the discourse of human rights the *defensores* interpret it through their own political subjectivities, understandings, and goals. As part of a larger movement for autonomy, they view human rights law as a tool for the defense of the space in which their autonomy is realized. But in that strategic engagement, the meaning of human rights is redefined. In the next chapter, I will consider how that reshaping has worked in a related context: the Zapatistas' autonomy project and particularly the *Juntas de Buen Gobierno*.

7 "Improving the Paths of Resistance": The *Juntas de Buen Gobierno* and Rights in Their Exercise

Now, we have to exercise our rights ourselves. We don't need anyone's permission, especially that of politicians. . . . Forming our own autonomous municipalities, that's what we are doing in practice and we don't ask anyone's permission.

Comandanta Esther (August 2003)

Here we are once again in the same struggle, improving the paths of resistance.

Comandante Zebedeo (August 2003)

Indigenous peoples can live our rights, just as they are stated in the San Andrés Accords.

Comandante David (August 2003)

ON AN AUGUST DAY IN 2003, I huddled beneath a plastic tarp through a typical afternoon downpour in the Highlands community of Oventic, Chiapas. While the weather was not unusual, the day itself was far from typical: I stood, accompanied by several thousand others—indigenous people from throughout the state and activists from throughout the country and the world—listening to the speeches of Zapatista leaders. They spoke of the birth of the five *caracoles* (literally, shells, but indicating meeting points) and the formation of the five *Juntas de Buen Gobierno* ("Good Governance Councils," herein referred to as *Juntas*) to be seated in them. It was a major turning point for Zapatismo, signaling a transition from military to civilian governance and the formal end to their petition for state recognition of their collective right to autonomy. In the words of Comandanta Rosalinda in her speech at the ceremony, "The government didn't pay attention to us. *Que se queden con sus pendejadas.*[1] We know how to make our municipalities work." From now on, the Zapatista communities would govern themselves—without state recognition—through the *Juntas.* The capacity to define whether or not indigenous people have rights to engage in autonomous practices had been taken out of the hands of the state.

In August of 2003, the Zapatistas announced the establishment of the five *Juntas de Buen Gobierno* in the Zapatista autonomous region. These civilian governance bodies were specifically posited against established form of rule, which the Zapatistas call *mal gobierno,* or bad government, and, as the quotes above reflect, were intended to move Zapatista resistance forward, "improving the path of resistance" and creating new forms of local governance in order to "live their rights." In the process, they are redefining concepts such as "autonomy" and "rights" as existing prior to and regardless of their recognition by the state. The Zapatistas' assertion is that these rights exist in their *exercise,* not their establishment in the legal regimes of the state. By eliminating the state as the external referent for rights and tying them to alternative logics of power,

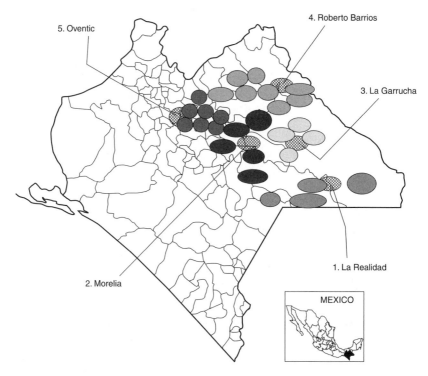

Map 7.1 Location of Zapatista autonomous municipalities in rebellion, *caracoles,* and *Juntas de Buen Gobierno.*

such conceptual reframings are challenging not only to the state, but also to liberal and neoliberal conceptualizations of rights and their relationship to the law. In this chapter, I explore how people in the Zapatista autonomous municipalities are appropriating globalized discourses such as human and indigenous rights, reconfiguring them based on their own experiences and needs, and representing them in ways that subvert the logics of the neoliberal state.

While this chapter is based on long-term research in the region, it does not include ethnographic descriptions of the working of the *Juntas* or the autonomous councils. In order to publish such material, I would have needed to obtain permission from Zapatista authorities. The Zapatistas have been scrupulously cautious about deciding what research projects could take place in regard to the regions and especially in the *Juntas*. Because the participant observation data I obtained while in *Junta*, council, or other official meetings did not form part of a previously approved research project, I have respectfully refrained from utilizing them as anything other than background material that guides my analysis. Indeed, even if I had had permission to publish such description, at this time it would not have been prudent. While tensions have calmed somewhat, the region is still in a state of war, and Zapatista communities are still the objects of counterinsurgency operations. Thus, descriptions of the workings of their authority structure, while they provide fascinating material for analysis, could put some people at greater risk. All descriptions contained in this chapter are from approved projects or public events.

From San Andrés to the National Congress: The Struggle for State Recognition

During his presidential campaign, Vicente Fox vowed that if elected, he would resolve the Chiapas conflict in fifteen minutes. While that time frame might have been overly ambitious, during his first months in office he did, in fact, make a number of moves that appeared to be aimed at creating conditions for a return to peace dialogues with the Zapatistas. Zapatista leaders, cautiously hopeful, set out three "signs" or conditions that the Mexican government would need to meet in order to consider the possibility of reinitiating dialogues. Those points were: (1) the release of Zapatista political prisoners; (2) removal of military checkpoints at key sites throughout the state and the reduction of troops, including the closure of seven specific military camps; and (3) the passage of the COCOPA law, as a sign of government commitment to honor and implement the San Andrés Accords. President Fox made significant efforts to satisfy these conditions: camps were dismantled and troops reduced within hours of his inauguration, many of the prisoners were released, and the COCOPA law was submitted to Congress within a couple of months.[2] While many Zapatista supporters in the communities remained skeptical, there was enough hope that the Zapatista liaison, Fernando Yañez, was able to remark to the press, "I think it is possible that dialogue could restart soon."[3]

As we have seen, the failure of the government to submit legislation to Congress for constitutional reform based on the San Andrés Accords, and particularly the "COCOPA debacle," which made clear that the government would not honor the agreements that had been signed, was a key turning point after which unilateral autonomy became the heart of the Zapatista project. The submission of the COCOPA bill to Congress thus held tremendous significance, not only because it signaled a new willingness by the government to honor its signed agreements (making return to dialogue possible), but also because it offered state recognition of the autonomy process that had been the focus of the movement and the communities' efforts for several years. Thousands of Zapatistas and their supporters marched to Mexico City to express their support for the bill. They were met by a crowd of 60,000 supporters in Mexico City.

Controversy surged when congresspeople of Fox's conservative National Action Party (PAN) disputed the legality of having Zapatistas address the Congress, suggesting instead that they should meet with legislators in back chambers. Nevertheless, they were granted the opportunity to speak before the Congress, by a narrow vote of 220 in favor and 210 against.[4] The *Panistas* threatened to boycott the session to display their distaste for the presence of the rebels and their objection to what they viewed as the president's capitulation.[5] In spite of the controversy, Tzeltal Comandanta Esther gave a moving speech in a historic special session of Congress. "My name is Esther, but that's not important. I'm a Zapatista, but that's not important either. What is important is that I am indigenous and I am a woman and I am speaking in this symbolic place," she said.[6] She received a standing ovation. Following the march, hope was strong that the law would soon be passed and peace dialogues could resume quickly. Fernando Yañez, when meeting with members of the COCOPA, optimistically announced, "Peace is closer every moment."[7]

Peace never came. The outcome of the legislative process was a bitter disappointment to indigenous peoples throughout Mexico. In April 2001, the Mexican Congress passed a greatly watered down version of the original accords.[8] Whether the president intended the law to go through intact or had some responsibility for the outcome is a matter of political debate. But the Zapatistas, and indigenous people more generally, certainly interpreted the law as a betrayal. The fact that the president supported the law as it went through the process of state ratification, a process itself marked by irregularities, made him at minimum party to the treachery.[9]

Rather than officially recognize indigenous autonomy at the federal level, the law places a series of restrictions on indigenous autonomy, including giving the authority for defining the specifics about how autonomy can be realized and by whom to individual state legislatures. This is problematic for a number of reasons, not the least of which is that it thwarts the autonomy prospects of the many indigenous groups whose territory comprises different states, as is often the case in southern Mexico. The altered legislation also omitted the right of the indigenous peoples to the collective use and enjoyment of the natural resources found on their lands and territories, "except under the terms [already] established by this Constitution," ensuring that decades of exploitation of the resources (including hydroelectric power, lumber, and oil) of indigenous lands

Figure 7.1 The celebration of the birth of the *caracoles* and the formation of the *Juntas de Buen Gobierno* in Oventic, August 2003. Shannon Speed.

by Mexico City could continue without impediment (Kennis 2002). Indigenous peoples throughout Mexico unanimously rejected the law, and the Zapatistas issued a communiqué calling it a "legislative joke" (Marcos 2001). Needless to say, peace dialogues never resumed.

From Guns to Shells: Toward an Autonomous Civilian Governance

It was one year after the disastrous Indigenous Law went into effect that the Zapatistas announced the creation of five *caracoles*.[10] The *caracoles* would replace the *Aguascalientes* (regional points of encounter with civil society) and would be the seats of five *Juntas de Buen Gobierno*. Each of the five *Juntas* includes one to three delegates from each of the already-existing Autonomous Councils in each zone. Thirty Zapatista autonomous municipalities in rebellion feed into the five *Juntas*. Among other things, the functions of the *Juntas* include monitoring projects and community works in Zapatista autonomous municipalities; monitoring the implementation of laws that have been agreed to by the communities within their jurisdiction; conflict and dispute resolution within their jurisdiction; and governing Zapatista territory under the logic of *mandar obedeciendo* (lead by obeying), a keystone of "good governance," which holds that authorities have a responsibility to carry out consensually arrived-at decisions, rather than a mandate to make decisions on behalf of the population they represent.

At the celebration for the new *Juntas de Buen Gobierno* in Oventic, Comandanta Esther, who had addressed the Mexican Congress two years earlier to urge them to implement the San Andrés Accords, expressed the Zapatistas' disillusionment with and rejection of the constitutional recognition process:

> The political parties conspired to deny us our rights when they passed [the Law on Indigenous Rights and Culture]. . . . Now, we have to exercise our rights ourselves. We don't need anyone's permission, especially that of politicians. . . . Forming our own autonomous municipalities, that's what we are doing in practice and we don't ask anyone's permission.[11]

With the formation of the *caracoles* and the *Juntas de Buen Gobierno*, the Zapatistas were signaling a new phase in their renegotiation of the relationship between indigenous peoples and the Mexican state. No longer willing to petition the state for recognition through the legal system, the Zapatistas were making a bold assertion that their rights to local autonomy as indigenous peoples already existed, even in the absence of the state's recognition of them. They existed because they were already being exercised in practice. Further, as Esther continued: "Even though the bad government does not recognize it, *for us it is our law*, and we shall defend ourselves with it" (emphasis mine). Thus in the Zapatista interpretation, rights exist in practice, and the law, too, had been wrested from the hands of the state. This interpretation has important implications for the meanings attached to rights, law, state power, and indigenous resistance, which I will consider below.

Rights in the Law

> What was lost in the promulgation of human rights theory in the 1990s was the connection between rights and subjects who can exercise those rights.
>
> *Chandler (2002:114)*

The notion of rights existing in their exercise challenges the positive law assumption that rights exist only once they have been established in law. To begin with, it reveals the erroneous nature of the assumption in positive law that states honor the laws established within their institutions. In practice, Mexico (like most states) selectively applies or enforces laws regarding the rights of citizens based on a gamut of the political exigencies of maintaining power. Thus, even though individual Mexican citizens have many rights established in the Mexican Constitution and its derivative laws and penal codes, their ability to exercise them is limited, in some cases severely. The state's development of particular discourses of rights—and even the establishment of those rights in law—are thus distinct matters from the realization of rights. So, the conceptual question of whether such rights exist prior to their establishment in law is compounded by the question of whether they can be exercised even after such establishment.

One fundamental aspect of the limitation of the exercise of rights is access of certain individuals and groups to the judicial system, thereby eliminating their recourse to the law. This is particularly the case for women, indigenous people, and political dissidents in Mexico (Azaola 1996; CNDH 1995; Human Rights Watch 1997). Access is denied in a number of ways: inadequate public defense, failure to provide translators (or inadequate translation), bureaucratic stonewalling,[12] and outright political bias on the part of judges in their decisions (i.e., lack of an independent judicial branch). For these reasons, victims of human rights violations are rarely able to seek justice, and if they do, rarely achieve it.[13] This problem is so widespread that on a visit to Mexico in 2001, the

U.N. Special Rapporteur on the Independence of Judges and Lawyers stated that Mexico suffers from 95 to 98 percent impunity and that Mexican citizens "do not believe in the possibility of justice."[14] This lack of access to the justice system means, in concrete terms, that they cannot exercise their rights; therefore, in practice, their rights do not exist.

One might argue that what is needed is simply a mechanism by which to compel states to fairly and evenly enforce the rights they have established. But the question is not that simple. States may also pass laws—as Mexico's Indigenous Law makes apparent—that are designed to limit the very rights they are supposed to establish. More dangerously, legal rights may function in such a way that the very act of exercising them contributes to reinforcing hegemonic power. Below I will briefly revisit this proposition, which I discussed in the introductory chapter to this book.

Law and the Neoliberal Logics of Rule

Neoliberalization requires states to reduce their social spending, which entails divestment of responsibility for mediating social inequality through social welfare and corporatist policies and programs. Relations between groups in society are left to market forces, with civil society organizations as mediators. Neoliberalization not only entails the reduction of government's social functions and the implementation of steps to "free" the economy, but also introduces a new set of governance practices. In neoliberalism, the state's primary responsibility is ensuring that the market operates freely. One of the principal ways that the state does this is by maintaining "stability," in particular through the maintenance of law and order. As Rose argues, the relationship between the state and the people has taken on new forms in the latest stage of capitalism, with the former "maintain[ing] the infrastructure of law and order" and the latter "promot[ing] individual and national well-being by their responsibility and enterprise" (1999:139). Thus on the one hand, the state maintains "law and order" (hence the new preeminence of the discourse of "rule of law" which we have seen was mobilized in Chiapas by both the government and ruling party supporters), while on the other it produces subjects who are autonomous and self-regulating. Rose argues, "To govern better, the state must govern less; to optimize the economy, one must govern through the entrepreneurship of autonomous actors—individuals and families, firms and corporations. Once responsibilized and entrepreneurialized, they would govern themselves within a state secured framework of law and order" (Rose 1999:139). The neoliberal state thus governs by creating "responsible" and "entrepreneurial" subjects, on the one hand, and maintaining the structure of law on the other. Neoliberalism, then, is not about "rolling back the state" but about inventing new strategies of governance that create "the legal, institutional and cultural conditions that will enable an artificial competitive game of entrepreneurial conduct to be played to best effect" (Burchell 1996:27). Because these two aspects of neoliberal governance, controlling law and the formation of subjects, are so key, it is worth considering the ways that they come together in what Trouillot calls "the reworking of processes and relations of power so as to create new spaces for the deployment of power" (2001:127).

Law, with its delimiting and regulating capacities, provides a privileged space for the state to engage in neoliberal subject making. Menon argues that "modern forms of power do not simply oppress, they produce and regulate identity [and] law is an important technique by which this is achieved" (2004:205). As I suggested in the last chapter, it is not really necessary for this regulation to be enforced by the state, because it fosters *self-regulation* on the part of those who seek to gain or retain legal rights as established by the state. Rights struggles, by encouraging a process in which the identities of the dissenters are "fixed" in legal regimes, may create a problematic need for subjects to continually fit themselves into these established legal categories, producing a self-regulatory policing of identity (see also Dugan 2003; Povinelli 2002).

Mexico's Law on Indigenous Rights and Culture provides an example of how neoliberal states use the law as a site for the production of subjects. In the Indigenous Law, the responsibility for determining both which indigenous people will be recognized and what form of autonomy of indigenous peoples will be granted is left in the hands of state-level legislatures. This interesting double move shifts responsibility from the centralized state, while retaining it within the purview of the state. Because these state-level legislatures can be expected to adopt restricted definitions of each, indigenous people would be placed in the position of attempting to "prove" to the lawmakers that they and their practices are "authentically" indigenous in order to access whatever rights these bodies might grant. The federal government is free of responsibility for this mediation. Perhaps the most transparent move to define indigenous subjects through the law resides in the clause that deems indigenous people to be "subjects of public interest" (*interés público*), a category also occupied by orphans, rather than "subjects of public right/law" (*derecho público*). This move meant that, even as rights for indigenous people were ostensibly being established, indigenous collectivities were being "undefined" as subjects of legal rights (see Adelfo Regino Montes, "Negación Constitucional," *La Jornada,* April 28, 2001). Thus, were indigenous people to embrace the law and seek their rights only within it, they would likely have to do considerable self-reconstruction and regulation in order to fit themselves within the parameters of what autonomy is and who can enjoy it. Further, if they were able to do so, they would find themselves in the uncomfortable position of becoming subjects of rights who are not subjects of rights. In the act of attempting to exercise their rights, they would contribute to the undermining of those rights (even as they reinforce state legitimacy and power).

Throughout this book, I have argued that definitions and interpretations of rights have shifted over time in accordance with shifting forms of governance. In the neoliberal era, the interpretation given to "rights" is distinct from that of the modern liberal era. Despite the reduction of the state's function for mediating social conflict, "rights" enjoy greater primacy today than in past eras. Law has become the privileged site of both contestation and regulation, and thus "rights" are the superlative mode for acceptable resistance. Neoliberalism reconfigures rights, taking collectives into the fold in the process of disciplining. Disciplined citizen-subjects appropriately mediate themselves, and the state is reinforced through the privileging of the legal system as the appropriate forum for dispute and the state as the appropriate arbiter.

Considering these characteristics of neoliberal rule, we can recognize the potential for rights-based claims to be seduced into a system where legal process is an empty signifier for the resolution of immediate conflict, while leaving the architecture of power that created those conflicts unquestioned. Similarly, the law's illusion that organized power can be exercised only through the state is combined with the desperation created by the social decay that accompanies the downsizing of the corporatist state, resulting in marginalized groups making claims to a sclerotic neoliberal state whose capacity to resolve social conflict is increasingly limited to its police function. Thus, although immediate conflict and violence may be temporarily resolved, this "resolution" may come at a heavy cost (see Agamben 1998; Guehenno 1995).

However, this does not mean that discourses of rights are always or inevitably proscribed. In many places, indigenous people (and others) are appropriating discourses of rights and reformulating them in ways that are radically challenging to the particular forms and logics of power at work in a neoliberal state: Bolivia is just one recent example (see Goldstein 2007; Goodale

2007; Postero 2004). In the following section, I will return to the Zapatistas' autonomy process and the formation of the *Juntas de Buen Gobierno*. The Zapatista movement has pursued social change largely through the dominant discourse of rights. Even early on, when many of their demands remained broad—for reform of the state, democratization—they were couched in the language of rights. The language of rights became more pronounced in their public discourse as the movement became increasingly focused on the struggle for indigenous autonomy. But what meanings do the Zapatistas invest in rights and law? What are the effects on the Zapatista movement of adopting this discourse? Is the movement inadvertently reinforcing the state's position as the purveyor of law by petitioning the state to recognize their rights? Do they waste valuable energy and resources on actions that further legitimate institutions and empty forms of social mediation that function to guarantee their ultimate subordination? In mobilizing the discourse of law, do they enter the ideal space of neoliberal subject making? I will argue that Zapatista autonomy, in particular the *Juntas de Buen Gobierno*, are an example of how local appropriations, reinterpretations, and redeployments of rights discourses can represent alternative forms of resistance.

Autonomy in Practice, Rights in Their Exercise: The Alternative Logics of Power in *Buen Gobierno*

As I stood listening to Comandanta Esther's words at the inauguration of the *caracoles*—"Now, we have to exercise our rights ourselves. We don't need anyone's permission, especially that of politicians"—the words of another indigenous woman, spoken a year earlier, came back to me. In the San Cristóbal office of the *Red*, "Celerina" commented on the newly passed law: "It doesn't matter. Our autonomy doesn't need permission from the government; it already exists." "Celerina's" comment presaged Comandanta Esther's and suggests that well before the establishment of the *Juntas*, even as they worked for the passage of the law, people in Zapatista communities were conceptualizing indigenous rights and autonomy as existing prior to and irrespective of their establishment in law. The sentiment, and certainly the autonomous structures and philosophies of Zapatista governance, were already in existence when the law was passed. As "Celerina's" comment suggested, the pursuit of constitutional recognition of indigenous rights was but one tactic in a much larger project of self-determination. The failure to gain adequate state recognition was unfortunate, but it was neither surprising nor debilitating to this project. In fact, I suggest that it strengthened the Zapatistas' autonomy project and weakened the state's position.

Since its inception, the Zapatista movement has continually maintained an alternative project to that of negotiating with the state. This project entailed distinct conceptualizations and structures of power, governance, and law (Speed and Reyes 2002, 2005). Since they were established, the autonomous municipalities have continued to grow and develop, gaining momentum after the state's abandonment of the San Andrés Accords. Even as they continued to petition the state for legal recognition of indigenous rights, particularly the right to autonomy, they were engaging in autonomous governance practices within the Zapatista regions. The EZLN had always maintained that the kind of social change needed in Mexico would not—could not—come about through the existing political system. With the failure of the Law on Indigenous Rights and Culture to produce substantive improvements for indigenous people, the Zapatistas dropped all pretense of petitioning the state as one avenue for pursuing social change. The autonomy project that had been in formation since 1994 was poised to demonstrate in practice their alternative logics of power and governance. With the establishment of the *caracoles* and the *Juntas*, this alternative project was formalized, setting in motion a new dynamic of resistance. There are several points worth taking into consideration about the significance of the Zapatista project for our understandings of rights, the law, and the state in neoliberal Mexico, as well as the broader issues of power and resistance in the dialogic global-local-state interaction.

The move to formally establish the *Juntas de Buen Gobierno* displaced and disempowered the state in important ways. First, because the neoliberal state's primary role is maintaining stability through the rule of law (a task the Mexican government had been failing at since the uprising began nearly ten years earlier), it was vital that stability be reinstated through the law, the state's principal site of legitimation and subject making. However, the state failed in this task. As we have seen, the law's content was drastically altered by legislators, and the end result was rejected by indigenous people and created an outpouring of resentment and social discord. An astonishing 330 constitutional challenges to the law were filed by individuals, communities, and organizations (Ramírez Cuevas 2002). Needless to say, stability was not restored, "law and order" were destabilized, and the state suffered yet another blow to its legitimacy before civil society. Further, the new indigenous subject of neoliberal multiculturalism that the law sought to create was never to be.

Even more significantly, the failed law was the final event that compelled the Zapatistas to openly disregard the state not just as a site for pursuing social change but also as the source of their rights and the law of the state as the site for establishing them. This presented a radical challenge to the state: not, as some national analysts claimed, by seeking to secede and form a new sovereign state (for the EZLN position on this see Marcos 2004b), but by unilaterally exercising their right to autonomy and self-determination—expressed as the capacity to control and affect their daily lives. This move effectively displaced the state as the sovereign power, which can grant or retract rights through the law, and delivered a direct hit to the primary site of both legitimation and subject-making processes of the neoliberal state.

Reconceptualizing Rights: The Power in *Potentia*

From the start of the uprising, the emission of the Revolutionary Laws suggested a challenge to the state/sovereign as the only source of rights and emphasized the constitutive power of social struggle. There is thus more to the current mode of Zapatista autonomy than simply a response to the intransigence of the government in instituting serious reform on indigenous rights. There is a distinct conceptualization of those rights that functionally eliminates the legal regimes of the state as the external referent for the existence of rights. Bearing some resemblance to a natural law conceptualization of rights as prior to and irrespective of the laws of states, the Zapatista interpretation also eliminates the notion of God/nature as the source of those rights. The source of rights in this conceptualization lies in the actors themselves, who are collectively exercising them. This does not mean that the state is irrelevant—Zapatista autonomy, even when completely disengaged from interaction with the state, is still forged in silent dialogue with the state. However, by refusing to grant the state the power to designate who are rights-bearers and what rights they may enjoy, the Zapatistas articulate a radically distinct discourse of rights.

As we have seen above, in the direct exercise of their right to self-determination, the Zapatista movement disengages from liberal conceptualizations of natural and positive law and redefines "rights" as existing *in their exercise*, not as designations from God/nature or the state/law. Further, they are exercised in Zapatista regions as a form of resistance, explicitly expressed in the term *Autonomous Municipalities in Rebellion*. This notion of "rights" as the product of particular relations of force / power is not exclusive to the Zapatistas. Theorists whose work on power is influenced by Spinoza (see Deleuze

1988b, 1993; Foucault 1980, 1989; Hardt and Negri 2000; Montag 1999; Negri 1990, 1999) have considered the potential of rights. Spinoza argued: "Nature's right and its order . . . forbid only those things that no one desires and *no one can do*" (cited in Deleuze 1993). That is, for Spinoza, a body's right was coextensive with what it could do. A "body" for Spinoza could be "anything; it can be an animal, a body of sounds, a mind or an idea; it can be a linguistic corpus, a social body, a collectivity" (Deleuze 1988b:127), though for our purposes here the most relevant is the notion of the social body or collectivity. In Spinoza's view, the only natural rights were those that were within a body's affect, its power to influence the world and be influenced by it. From this perspective, rights can exist only when they can be exercised—although "natural," they do not exist always at all times, but rather only when they can be enacted, and their granting by a sovereign is irrelevant (Speed and Reyes 2002). At a philosophical level, this conceptualization is obviously distinct from the legal discourses that underpin the state power in the current global order (and equally distinct for natural law discourses in which rights always exist, regardless of the creation by a state or their exercise).

In fact, it is not only distinct, it is radically challenging, if we think of it in Antonio Negri's terms. Negri's work analyzes how power permeates the social body, at the same time highlighting creative social forces and affirmative alternative practices. His understanding of Spinoza is key to this analytical project. In particular, he builds on Spinoza's argument that there are two types of power: *potestas* [Power] and *potentia* [power], and that they are fundamentally antagonistic.[15] In *The Savage Anomaly*, Negri argues that Spinoza's concept of *potentia* provides us with an effective "other" to Power: a radically distinct alternative for the organization of society. In Negri's analysis, Power refers to centralized authority, command, rule, whereas power is the creative activity or force of constitution (see also Agamben 1998). Hardt claims that "this distinction does not merely refer to the different capabilities of subjects with disparate resources and potentialities; rather, it marks two fundamentally different forms of authority and organization that stand opposed in both conceptual and material terms . . . in the organization of being as in the organization of society" (1990:xi).

This distinction echoed in Marcos's famous statement, "We the Zapatistas want to exercise power, not take it," is vital to understanding the meaning of the Zapatistas' reconceptualization. In Spinozan or Negrian terms, Marcos's statement signals that the power they are interested in is *potentia*, power constituted through the creative force of social struggle, not *potestas*, constituted power in the form of a new sovereign. Negri (1999) and Hardt and Negri (2000, 2004) extended the concept of *potentia* against *potestas* to a notion of the multitude against the sovereign (Hardt and Negri 2004; Negri 1999). They argued that the social body or the "multitude," even as it is imbued with the logics of capital and formed by state subject-making processes, is nevertheless capable of revolt, and the source of that capability lies in its constitutive power (see Cleaver 2007). The exercise of rights is part of that creative activity, that practice of constituting power, and is fundamentally antagonistic to sovereign power.

This is not to say, of course, that the members of the *Juntas* are sitting around in the *caracoles* debating Negri's interpretation of Spinoza as a basis for their conceptualization of rights. (Though this isn't out of the question, I have never heard such a discussion take place.) In fact, no Zapatista leader or base supporter has ever told me in such terms that they were consciously reconceptualizing rights. Their understanding of rights emerges from their experience and their particular political subjectivities, and is, in a sense, an organic reformulation, one that makes sense in terms of the history and their proposed project for the future.

Reordering Rule: The Power of *Buen Gobierno*

On the road to Oventic, there is a sign that reads: "You are in Zapatista Territory: Here the people rule and the government obeys." Almost a year after the formation of the Juntas, *I was again in Oventic, now home of the* Junta *de Buen Gobierno Corazón Céntrico de los Zapatistas delante del Mundo (Central Heart of the Zapatistas Before the World). During a seemingly interminable wait for a decision on a project, I chatted with some members of the* Junta. *We sat in their meeting room, built of pine wood slats and lamina, perched about halfway up the steep incline from the basketball court / amphitheater to the road—the central artery of the* caracol. *We talked about the* Juntas, *and "how things were going" in their first months. I couldn't resist interjecting a subtle complaint about the cumbersome process that seemed to be holding up approval—or even rejection—of my research project. One of the* Junta *members, looking me in the eye, said, "Well, yes. It's difficult. Sometimes things take time, because we make decisions, but we don't make them alone. We have to respond to others, we have to respond to el pueblo. That is our way."[16]*

This *Junta* member was pointing to a key Zapatista conceptualization of power and governance. Zapatista leadership style has been specifically constructed, both in discourse and practice, in a way that discourages the public role of individual leaders and heavily emphasizes collective processes. Through the structure of the CCRI, the Zapatistas elaborated a notion of authority that downplayed the role of the leaders themselves, and highlighted collective decision making and the subjection of individual leaders' power to the collective will. Aspects of the Zapatistas' philosophy of governance, especially that of "lead by obeying," reflect their commitment to giving priority to the decisions of the many, rather than the chosen few. All major decisions in the communities are made after extensive deliberations in which all members have had the opportunity to speak (though women are often excluded from this process). Zapatista authorities, rather than having a right to make decisions for the communities, have a responsibility to carry out the collective decisions of the communities. If they use their position to do anything other than execute the decision of the people, they are removed from their positions.

This alternative logic of power was given new impetus and new visibility with the formation of the *Juntas de Buen Gobierno*. The *Juntas*, which deal with a range of issues for their regions from local disputes to major political policy, represented the transfer of power from military to civilian authorities in the autonomous regions. The five *Juntas* are made up of groups of from seven to fifteen members who rotate on a weekly or biweekly basis. This means that for each *Junta*, there are between twenty-eight and sixty people participating in the decisions for their regions. The *Junta* draws its members from the councils of each autonomous township. Further, for each rotation of the *Junta*, there are *suplentes* (alternates), who are also present and actively engaged. Because the *Juntas* are staffed by a rotating structure of large groups and experience frequent turnover, the diffusion of leadership and authority is solidly built into the system.

There is no need to romanticize this process. The positing of alternative logics of governance and a distinct framework of rights is a tall order, and on the ground their application and their results are uneven. The inverted power relations of *mandar obedeciendo* lead to complicated decision-making processes, and the rotating leadership model of the *Juntas* does give rise to confusion and inconsistencies. The concentration of authority and decision-making power in the hands of a few individuals would undoubtedly facilitate decision-making processes. However, the goal of the EZLN's autonomy project is not to promote efficiency. Although collective decision making and the rotation of members can be cumbersome, they reduce corruption, abuses of power, and *protagonismo*, or individuals using their position to promote themselves and their interests. By positing these concepts as part of their autonomy project, Zapatistas articulate an alternative for social organization and rule.

Figure 7.2 A sign outside Oventic in the Highlands reads, "You are in Zapatista Territory. Here the people rule and the government obeys. Good Governance Council 'Heart Center of the Zapatistas Before the World.' " Shannon Speed.

The concept manifested in Zapatista philosophy as "lead by obeying" emerged from the communities themselves. "Lead by obeying" is one of the principal concepts of the Zapatistas' proposal for an alternative form of governance, which they call *buen gobierno*, distinct from that of the Mexican state, or *mal gobierno*. The assertion of these alternative democratic practices challenges the emergent discourse of electoral representative democracy in Mexico, one that promotes certain types of citizenship and acceptable forms of political participation, such as voting and expressing dissent through the law. While many celebrated this liberalizing discourse as Mexico emerged from decades of authoritarian rule, others, like the Zapatistas, have recognized that it also forms part of the process of hegemonic construction by the neoliberal state—part of a set of rationalities and cultural logics that interpolate subjects and inform practices. The Zapatistas' discourse asserts a very different kind of logic, one that does not lend itself well to market logics and to notions of rational-actor citizens out to maximize individual benefits, express their freedom of choice at the ballot box, and express their dissent in the courts of the state. Zapatista philosophy presents a challenge to the dominant discourse of the Mexican state, not with arms, but with alternatives: alternative logics, subjectivities, and forms of power and authority.

Conclusions: Reconfiguring Resistance

The Zapatistas have mobilized global discourses of rights and waged their struggle on the legal terrain of the state in strategic fashion. I have argued that, by withdrawing their claims to indigenous rights from the realm of legal contestation, they have appropriated the discourses of human and indigenous rights and are redeploying them with new significations in support of an alternative project that, rather than reinforcing state power, can be read as challenging it.

In the Zapatistas' alternative project, rights exist in their exercise. This is a distinct conceptualization from that of liberal and neoliberal theory. This interpretation exposes the myth of liberal conceptions of law and the state: that the state will attempt to mediate social inequalities through the law and the establishment and defense of rights (when it may be engaged in just the opposite), and that rights, once established in law, *exist*. Indigenous people in southern Mexico are well aware that many rights established in law are functionally nonexistent, precisely because the state refuses to enforce them, and thus they cannot be exercised. The Zapatista movement has consistently channeled global discourses through the Zapatistas' own local knowledge and understanding and has put them into practice in new ways. The Zapatistas continue to claim their rights, but do not do so on the legal terrain of the state. By deriving rights through community practice, they are "improving the paths of resistance," making their rights struggle contestatory rather than accommodating to neoliberal state power.

Not all rights-based forms of resistance are simply reproducing the structures of power that maintain neoliberal global rule. Neither are all contesting it. I suggest that the Zapatista movement is one example of potential alternatives that break with the normalizing characteristics of legal discourse. These retooled conceptualizations make indigenous autonomy in the form elaborated by Zapatistas and their supporters challenging to the neoliberal state—not because of the much-debated risk of "separatism," but rather by providing both symbolic and material alternatives to neoliberal rule. They offer an alternative structure of power that is based on distinct logics of rule, in collective and consensus decision making, the concept of *mandar obedeciendo,* and the assertion of pluriculturality or diversity within the collective. But in constructing their autonomy *en los hechos* (loosely, in practice) and outside state recognition, the Zapatistas can assert their own logic of rule, "good government" as posited against the "bad government" of the state, and in the process minimize the limiting, normalizing, and reproductive forces of the state and its legal regimes. Further, they mobilize a form of constitutive power in social struggle against the Power of the sovereign/state.

It is unclear what the limits of "rights in their exercise" would be. It is easy to celebrate such an argument when emanating from a movement one is sympathetic to, such as the Zapatista movement (which I am indeed sympathetic to). It might be less so if deployed by groups whose goals one finds abhorrent, for example, right-wing armed militia groups in the United States. But even in that case, it should be acknowledged that such deployments might also be challenging to neoliberal power. Further, the strength of the Zapatistas' claim—and the force of its challenge—lies in the alternative project it is deployed to defend—a project that seeks to reconfigure power relations—not to hold power themselves, but to exercise it in ways that are more socially just for all within their territory.

8

Rights in Rebellion: Rethinking Resistance in the Neoliberal Global Order

Empire creates a greater potential for revolution than did the modern regimes of power because it presents us, alongside the machine of command,
with an alternative: the set of all the exploited and the subjugated, a multitude that is directly opposed to Empire, with no mediation between them.
Hardt and Negri (2004)

IN THE COURSE OF THIS BOOK, I have made several interrelated arguments
regarding globalization, human rights, and indigenous resistance in Chiapas. I
have argued that the discourse of human rights has three conceptual and practical trajectories in Chiapas: natural law, positive law, and indigenous law. This
last, while it emerges from a historical dialogic engagement with the first two,
is an organic conceptualization that has important distinctions that may subvert dominant conceptualizations of rights and rule. I have also argued that
globalization, and particularly the globalization of the discourse of human
rights, produces the potential for the realization of increased diversity at the
local level. Local identities and the forms of resistance based on them emerge in
dialogic interactions with nonlocal actors and discourses, and because human
rights discourse has become globalized, today it is a primary discourse of those
dialogues. But the rearticulation of many discourses of resistance into the
dominant discourse of human rights reflects not their subsumption, but rather
the appropriation of the discourse of rights and the multiplication of its usage
based on distinct subjectivities. Finally, the practice of human rights law in defense of autonomy projects, when done by indigenous communities without
intermediaries and as part of a particular alternative project that has reconceptualized rights and law, represents a significant challenge to the legal order of
the state and in fact to the state and global forms of rule those legal systems underpin.

Reflections on Activist Research

It is my hope that throughout the chapters of this book I have demonstrated sufficiently the local complexities and abundant internal contradictions that Zapatistas, their support communities, and others elaborating their practices in a discourse of identity and rights confront. Having spent ten years doing research in Chiapas, I am conscious that there will be some who feel that I am romanticizing the Zapatista movement, who will be disposed to raise examples of poor decisions made by the *Juntas*, or times when authority was abused by one or another leader. I am as aware as anyone that such examples exist. My goal in this book was not to argue that the Zapatista movement is a perfect one, or that indigenous people in Chiapas can do no wrong. My purpose, rather, was to take a sustained look at the Chiapas conflict and see what lessons could be taken away regarding rights discourses and resistance in the current global juncture. Some of those lessons were hopeful ones, and I chose to end the book with them.

As I argued in the Preface, all researchers make decisions about what it is important to study and what we will write about that subject based on our own political and ethical positions, whether we choose to recognize this or not. One advantage of activist research, from my perspective, is that it compels us to make those positions explicit and to make our knowledge production part of our larger political goals. In choosing the material for this book, I have tried to remain true to my own political project and stay focused on the information that would contribute to a better future. I have left out some interesting materials that I felt could put people in jeopardy, and I have been disinclined to discuss others when the likely political effects of publishing about them were not ones I wished to participate in generating.

Throughout, I have tried to keep myself and my concerns present in the text, particularly when those concerns presented a conflict or contradiction to the work I was engaging in. Elsewhere (Speed 2006a) I have written about some of the contradictions I faced in discussing community identity with the *comuneros* of Nicolás Ruiz. As an anthropologist steeped in anti-essentialism, I wanted to view their identity as historically constructed, fluid, and changing. They, on the other hand, were adamant in emphasizing that the base of their identity—their *usos y costumbres*—were essential and had remained the same over time. This was vital to their understandings of themselves, but also, they pointed out, to their legal argument with the ILO and with the Mexican government. My anthropological analysis came into contradiction with their own and with the concrete realities of their daily political struggle. That contradiction, neverthe- less, brought me new understandings of identity construction that I might not otherwise have gained. Similarly, it was the contradictory nature of my work with the *Red* that led me to new understandings. I came to the work cognizant of the dangers of legalism as a form of struggle and all the risks that human rights work entailed. I could see the importance and potential for local "empower- ment" that the *Red* offered, even as I recognized the way in which such local em- powerment projects regularly construct indigenous subjects that are professional, entrepreneurial, and increasingly distanced from their communities, as it simul- taneously channels resistance into acceptable forms that reinforce state power through its legal regimes. Yet it was through my struggle with this contradiction that I began to gain a different understanding of the *defensores*' work as the wield- ing of a tool in defense of a larger and potentially more subversive project. There were many contradictions large and small throughout my activist work in Chia- pas. While I cannot know what I would have "known" if I had approached the work in a different way, it is my belief that my analysis benefited greatly from these very contradictions and the reflection that they necessitated.

Identity, Discourse, and Dialogisms

A variety of theorists have pointed to ways that identities are historically con- structed in relations of domination (e.g., C. R. Hale 1994). Hernández Castillo has argued that identity and rights-based discourses are "formulated and refor- mulated in a permanent dialogue with discourses of power" (2001b:20). In that dialogue, they may also challenge those relations of power and domination. The dialogic nature of discourse was implicit in its definition in Foucault's work (1989), and in this he followed on Bakhtin (1981), who argued that every speech act implies a dialogic process, a response to other speech acts that preceded it. Thus, discourse only exists in the context of previous or alternative discourses and is in dialogue with them. This conceptualization is useful to us here because it allows us to see how each usage of a discourse is shaped by the usages that came before it, but is itself a new discourse, with which each successive usage will auto- matically engage. In terms of discourses of rights, this implies that their origins as "Western" or as an aspect of neoliberal capitalism do not absolutely determine their potentialities as they are appropriated and utilized in ongoing dialogic fash- ion. Each appropriation of a discourse will produce a new meaning, and that new meaning is in dialogue with, and may be challenging to, other discourses.

Yet even as global discourses are affected by the subjectivities of the social groups who appropriate them, so too do these appropriations affect the subjectivities of the appropriators. We saw this dialogic relationship in Nicolás Ruiz, where community identity shifted over time in relation to the distinct discourses they were engaging. These effects are long-lasting: even as campesinist discourse is in decline in Mexico and is less important to Nicolás Ruiz in its land struggle, the *comuneros* continue to understand themselves as campesinos, while reasserting their indigenous identity (the two are of course not in contradiction). And even as Nicolás Ruiz has lessened its connection with the EZLN (many people in Nicolás Ruiz consider themselves "autonomous" but "independent" today, which is in itself an interesting dynamic), they have retained the discourse of indigenous rights, autonomy, and territory that emerged from that engagement, as well as the component of their identity produced by their collective memory of struggle (C. R. Hale 2002). Thus in January of 2007 the *comuneros*, in a press release meant to pressure the new governor, Juan Sabines, to resolve their land issues, described themselves in the following manner:

> Since 1994, after the uprising of our zapatista brothers, tired of the deceits of the PRI governments, as Nicolás Ruíz we decided to walk autonomously, as a community and as a municipality. And we continue to walk autonomously, obeying only the word of our *pueblo*. . . . Our municipality has decided since 1994 to function based on our *usos y costumbres,* like the indigenous people that we are. . . . Our *pueblo,* in its just struggles to recover our communal territory that is our inheritance from our Tzeltal ancestors, has suffered repressions, assassinations, imprisonment, and even bureaucratic wearing down.[1]

By redeploying these concepts in their engagements with the state, they have also contributed (along with other pressures) to altering the discourse as employed by the state. Over the course of the last decade, the state has backed off significantly in its assertion that language is the basic component of indigenous identity and indeed has generally accepted Nicolás Ruiz's assertion that it is indigenous. This dialogic engagement thus reshaped the discourse for all the actors involved.

Appropriating Empire's Rights

But how, then, precisely, can the appropriation and redeployment of discourses of rights become subversive? On one level it can be argued that both natural and positive law are historical constructions and normative orders that have underpinned relations of inequality, and that positive law—specifically in the context of the Mexican legal system—has also become the site of direct contestation of these relations of power (Hernández Castillo 2001b). As we have seen, the blending of natural law and positive law concepts in the discourse of human rights or indigenous rights has made for a powerful weapon wielded on the legal terrain of the state.

But there is more to this wielding than just a "retaking" of the legal terrain as a site of contestation or a "space of resistance" (Merry 1997). In the very dialogic act in which local people appropriate global discourses (or discourses of the nation-state, for that matter) and redeploy them based on their own subjectivities and to their own goals, they are engaging in resistance. In "Empire," Hardt and Negri posit reappropriation as one of the principal components necessary for the "multitude" to go "against Empire," that is, of resistance to the new global forms of rule. They state that the "right to reappropriation is really the multitude's right to self-control and autonomous self-production" (2000:407).

Reappropriation, when viewed in this way, is interestingly linked to those who do their "reappropriating" in the context of asserting their right to self-definition and autonomy, as many indigenous people in Chiapas are doing. Hernández Castillo argues that a significant aspect of the Zapatista autonomy movement is that its participants are "claiming the right to name" (2001a:215). Importantly, she notes that Zapatistas and other indigenous peoples are now engaging in a dialogue with the state, in which the terms of debate were not established by the state. In other words, while in most dialogic interactions one side brings considerably more force to the interaction, there nevertheless exists a potential for subverting that force in the appropriation of the "terms" or discourse of dialogue. What Hernández Castillo points to here is exactly what I have tried to demonstrate throughout this book: the process by which local indigenous people reappropriate global discourses of human rights (indigenous rights, self-determination) and redeploy them based on their own understandings and goals and, in so doing, reshape the very terms.

Taking this argument a step further, I would suggest that claiming the right to name (actually, "seizing the right to name" would be more appropriate: this is not simply a claim, but an act) subverts not only the discourses themselves, but also the structures of rule they uphold. Hence Hardt and Negri assert that "All the elements of corruption and exploitation are imposed on us by the linguistic and communicative regimes of production: destroying them in words is as urgent as doing so in deeds" (2000:404). Destroying or challenging the "communicative regimes" of production (discourses) is vital here to the purpose of eliminating the systems of exploitation they impose and enforce.

Autonomy in Practice and Rights in Their Exercise

But the reappropriation and subversion of communicative regimes or discourses (such as law, rights) are not the end of the challenge presented by Zapatista autonomy. This reappropriation, as I argued in regard to the *Red de Defensores*, is done "in defense of our rights, our autonomy," in the words of one *defensor*. The connection that Hardt and Negri make between reappropriation and the right to self-control and autonomous self-production is precisely the link between the two aspects of what is subversive in the impulse toward autonomy: the subversion of the discourse and the alternative form of the production of subjectivities (for Hardt and Negri "singularities") and of rule.

June Nash has argued that Zapatistas and their supporters, through their assertions of autonomy in their renegotiation of their relationship with the state, offer "indigenous counterplots" or "alternative visions" which are subversive to the "new global order" (2001:20, 246). Though I fear Nash falls into some essentializing of indigenous culture as inherently contestatory, such as in her claim that there is an indigenous "body of tradition embedded in a cultural logic that is *necessarily* opposed to Western practices" (2001:249, emphasis mine), I think Nash and I are in fundamental agreement that some "alternative visions" are challenging to the neoliberal state and the global order. For me, the subversive nature of indigenous autonomy and rights struggles in the form elaborated by Zapatistas and their supporters is twofold. It challenges the state by presenting and demanding the right to maintain an alternative structure of power. Furthermore, this alternative structure of power is based on alternative logics of rule, not in the sense of their indigenous cosmovision, but rather in collective and consensus decision making, the concept of "rule obeying," and the assertion of pluriculturality or diversity within the collective.[2] These aspects of organization vary from community to community, region to region, but the basic logic is there. It is historically constructed, emerging from decades or centuries of dialogic interactions, and it is the logic of those communities today. Understood as such, it is not open to attack from those who would undermine it on grounds of being "inauthentic" in the way that definitions are based on reference to a primordial essence or millenary culture.

I recognize that my argument contradicts what many people, including many indigenous proponents of autonomy themselves, have asserted: that

Indian autonomy does not undermine the established forms of rule. The debate in Mexico regarding Indian autonomy has circulated around this very question. Many—including ex-president Ernesto Zedillo—have claimed that giving indigenous people autonomy would mean "balkanization," or the breakup of the nation-state along ethnic lines. In fact, this was the principal argument provided by the Zedillo regime for its failure to respect the San Andrés Accords. Indigenous peoples responded by arguing that recognizing their autonomy did not challenge the nation-state, that autonomy represents, rather, a plan for peaceful coexistence in the pluricultural nation. For example, Adelfo Regino, a Mixtec Indian and a leader of the National Indigenous Congress, stated:

> There is no reason to fear. There are no reasons to enter the realm of mistrust or technical confusion . . . autonomy is the faculty that peoples have within the framework of the nation-state—and not out of it—to determine their living conditions in coordination with the state and federal governments. When we Mexican indigenous peoples claim our right to self-determination concretely in indigenous autonomy, we are not upsetting sovereignty.[3]

These are really debates about autonomy as secessionism: the threat to the nation-state posed by autonomy is secession or the breakup of an (illusory) coherent national identity and the loss of rule by the state over sections of its population. I can agree, in this context, that autonomy is not a challenge to the nation-state—not as secession. However, I argue that it does present a challenge on other levels, that it is "upsetting sovereignty" when this is understood as absolute rule by a sovereign power (be it king, state, or global Empire). I think, on the contrary, that it *is* challenging sovereignty, and that it is thus a form of antisystemic resistance that goes far beyond the legal reformism of most rights-based movements. While the debates focus on "balkanization," the fear that generates these debates may have more to do with this deeper challenge.

Human Rights—Subversive After All?

Although I find many of Hardt and Negri's theoretical propositions useful, I disagree with their discussion of the Chiapas uprising, in which they suggest that the Zapatista movement and other radically subversive localized struggles fail to join up into a global struggle because of a communication failure: the lack of a common language which links them together. The needs that they express cannot be "translated into different contexts." According to Hardt and

Negri, they have global significance, but "because all these local struggles are incommunicable and thus blocked from traveling horizontally . . . they are forced instead to leap vertically and touch immediately on the global level" (2001). While certainly such local struggles have not propelled world revolution, I think that the Chiapas uprising demonstrates precisely the capacity for "horizontal travel," linking up actors throughout the globe and garnering their participation in a movement that has a strongly subversive nature.

Further, I would like to suggest that, in fact, human rights provides a common language that facilitates those linkages. This is so precisely because it is a globalized discourse that can be reappropriated to many different kinds of struggles based on local understandings. Which means, of course, that globalization produces the very discourses that, when reappropriated, have the potential to bind diverse local subjectivities and the struggles based on them into the language of its own undoing. The process is quite the reverse of Hardt and Negri's suggested course, in which local struggles move toward the global struggle by moving into a common discursive regime (and staying there).

Human rights discourse and practice can simultaneously be a discourse of globalizing neoliberal capitalism, as well as an effective tool in its resistance. The widespread utilization of human rights as a discourse of resistance reflects the hegemonic position of both Western legal institutions and the liberal ideology of the global market that sustains them. It is within this contemporary structure of global power that identity-based rights claims arise. Yet, the context of their birth does not absolutely determine their value for resistance. "Human rights will not make us bless capitalism," to revisit Deleuze and Guattari's words.[4] Thus, while neoliberalism and its globalized discourses and forms of rule shape the way resistance is framed, in the reappropriation of the terms of globalization itself they become the "tools." Wielding them in defense of a project that posits alternative logics and structures of rule is one way to "hold them right."

The limited message of all that I have said regards human rights: If we understand human rights in the context of this interpretation, it is no longer critical to demonstrate their universality, or to reject them as cultural impositions. Theoretically, we can learn more by looking at the various reappropriations of the discourse of human rights, and the ways that they emerge in particular interactions: the way the tool is held by particular social actors in particular contexts. Politically, we can even embrace the discourse to support the people we work with when it is necessary, based on our own historically and politically contingent interpretations and understandings.

The broader message regards globalization and resistance. Whatever defects one might find in it, one gift of Empire was that it brought resistance back in. Since its publication, many more social analysts have moved away from conceptualizing the new global order *only* as a system of oppression and domination (though it is critical to understand how it works as one) and begin to recognize the potential for resistance to domination and oppression that globalization offers. In postmodernity, resistance is coterminous with power. Domination and rule are globalized: deterritorialized, a-cephalic, and diffused throughout the social body. That is its strength. However, resistance too is globalized, deterritorialized, and diffused through the social body, and this is also its potential and its power. This book has been an attempt to explore the ways that specific discursive practices in Chiapas harness that power to challenge the emergent global order and its particular configurations of power.

Epilogue: Horizontally Traveling Resistance?

Indigenous people in Chiapas have played an important role in resistance prior to and since the Zapatista uprising. At the time this study was being concluded (if it can ever really be concluded) in late 2005, the EZLN was launching "The Other Campaign," and Subcomandante Marcos was emerging from the *selva* (jungle), redubbed "Delegado Zero," to embark on a national tour. The purpose of this tour was to meet with groups throughout the country seeking alternatives to the options offered (or not) by the political parties in a contentious electoral year that would result in a new president, as well as a new governor in Chiapas. The movement had consolidated its autonomy in Chiapas and was apparently prepared to take the struggle back to the national terrain. It was claimed that the indigenous voice of the EZLN would be maintained, and whether it has been so far is debatable.

But perhaps more significantly, the "other campaign" was joined (and perhaps superseded in the public consciousness) by another important upsurge of resistance. In June 2006, in the Mexican state of Oaxaca, an annual teachers' strike for better wages held by the members of Section 22 of the Mexican National Educational Workers Union (SNTE) was repressed by government forces. A spontaneous social movement arose, harnessing the discontent of millions of Oaxacans chafing under neoliberal policies and a repressive authoritarian state government. The Popular Assembly of the Oaxacan People (APPO) was first convened on June 17, 2006, and included representatives of many of the state's regions and municipalities, unions (including the Section 22), NGOs, cooperatives, and others. The APPO called on Oaxacans to organize popular assemblies in neighborhoods, street blocks, towns, and communities. While the principal demand of the APPO is the removal of Governor Ulises Ruiz, the APPO has also called for broader social, political, and economic change. Included in the APPO resolutions are the recognition of indigenous rights and autonomy, gender equality, political accountability, and opposition to neoliberalism.

Interestingly, though its makeup is by no means entirely indigenous, the APPO has based its political practice in the indigenous *usos y costumbres* that have been functioning at the level of municipal government in Oaxaca. Much like those of many indigenous communities in Chiapas, these practices include open assembly meetings to make consensus-based collective decisions. Declaring itself the de facto governing body in the state, the APPO has applied the notion of the community assembly to a new form of state government. Calling itself a "movement of the bases, not of leaders," the APPO has elaborated a notion of authority that markedly resembles that of many indigenous communities and of the Zapatistas' *mandar obedeciendo*: one in which the assemblies oversee the execution of their resolutions by their municipal authorities. The authorities are charged with carrying out the collective decisions of the assembly and hold no power to make decisions on behalf of the group.

In Oaxaca, it seems, another "alternative logic," based on similar indigenous customs, is being offered. While people in Oaxaca have undoubtedly been influenced by Zapatismo, the discourse of the APPO is also organic, emerging from particular historical experience. The resistance that has surged there serves as one more example of the constitutive force (*potentia*) of social struggle and the resistance that, coterminous with power, is always present, ready to rise up and challenge the sovereign when the time is right.

Notes

Preface

1. One aspect of these critiques was a challenge to the term *research subject*. The term carries other meanings than subject as in topic, including "subject of power," which added to the sensitivity about the hierarchical relations of power that inhere in the relationship between researcher and the researched. I use the term purposefully in this text to remind us of the problematics of those power relations, though without the cumbersome quotation marks often used around the term to denote the author's recognition of the term's negative implications.

2. A notable example of this in the Americas is found in the Barbados Declarations. The First Declaration, written and signed by anthropologists and indigenous people, contained a strong argument in favor of committed anthropologists acting in collaboration with indigenous peoples toward their liberation. It nevertheless reflected some of the emergent critiques of the time:

> Anthropology took form within and became an instrument of colonial domination . . . it has rationalized and justified in scientific language the domination of some people by others. The discipline has continued to supply information and methods of action useful for maintaining, reaffirming, and disguising social relations of a colonial nature. (1971:5)

By the time of the Second Declaration six years later (1977), the critical stance being taken toward anthropology was strong enough that the document was drafted only by the indigenous participants and it omitted any mention of the relationship with committed anthropologists that had played prominently in the first declaration.

3. Lourdes Tíban, in activist research project meeting "Gobernar en (la) Diversidad," Mexico City, March 2004.

4. This work is discussed in Chapter 4. I analyze some aspects of my activist research in the community and the insights it provided, as well as the difficulties it implied, in Speed 2006a and Speed forthcoming.

5. Elio Henríquez and Angeles Mariscal, "*Invitan* a salir del país a 12 observdores europeos: Los acusan de participar en 'actos de apoyo' a Zapatistas en Chiapas," *La Jornada*, May 2, 1997.

6. See Global Exchange et al.'s 1999 report, *Foreigners of Conscience: The Mexican Government's Campaign Against International Human Rights Observers in Chiapas*. News articles discussing the expulsions include: *Los Angeles Times*, "Mexican Officials Seek to Deport 43 Foreigners Latin America," January 7, 2000; Reuters, "Mexico Defends Crackdown on Tourists in Chiapas," January 6, 2000; *New York Times*, "Mexico Expels 2 U.S. Supporters of Zapatistas Who Visited Chiapas," January 6, 1999; *La Jornada*, "A U.S. Citizen Is the First Person Expelled from Chiapas This Year," January 5, 2000; Associated Press, "Mexican Rebel Supporters Threatened," January 6, 2000. The Acteal massacre is discussed further in Chapter 3.

7. Even after I obtained a temporary residency status through my Mexican citizen husband and child, I was actively investigated by the immigration service. Agents visited our home unannounced on several occasions and questioned me at length. They went to my research institute, questioned the director about my activities, and told her the institute was in violation of the law by giving me an affiliation (which was untrue). I carried my infant daughter with me on all research trips, fearing that if I left her at home, I might be picked up by immigration and expelled from the country without her. Thankfully, that era ended after 2000, and it is far easier to conduct research today. And of course, any difficulties in doing research I might have encountered were pale reflections of the hardships being confronted by people in indigenous communities in the conflict zones on a daily basis in the context of military occupation and low-intensity warfare.

Chapter 1

1. I have never felt satisfied with how the term *mal gobierno*, or "bad government," used regularly by the Zapatistas to describe current forms of governance in Mexico, sounds in English. Nevertheless, there is no better translation for the term, so I use it throughout the book in this form.

2. Author's field notes, 2003.

3. Activist research is discussed at length in the Preface.

4. Conversation with the author, October 1996.

5. Conversation with the author, September 1996.

6. I utilize the term *discourse* in a Foucaultian sense (though Foucault, of course, defined discourse in a variety of ways). Discourses of power work by defining and regulating, setting the terms of what we can think about a particular set of relations. Discourse is not discernible from practice, but rather encompasses "ways of constituting knowl-

edge, together with the social practices, forms of subjectivity and power relations which inhere in such knowledges and relations between them. Discourses are more than ways of thinking and producing meaning. They constitute the 'nature' of the body, unconscious and conscious mind and emotional life of the subjects they seek to govern" (Weedon 1987:108). Thus, for Foucault, "discourse is a complex, differentiated *practice*" (Foucault 1979:211, emphasis mine), and meaning and meaningful practice are constructed through discourse.

7. Conversation with the author, December 1996, San Cristóbal de Las Casas. Notes in possession of the author.

8. Much theorizing of globalization invokes the now-familiar geography of globals and locals. Such analyses often invoke implicit assumptions about local knowledges, peoples, or communities, as rooted and fixed in some primordial place, and roving, transformative global ideas, movements, and claims (Hayden 2003). This imagined geography can suggest hierarchized levels of significance and unidirectional influence that obscure the fact that global and local ideas and understandings are often forged in dialogue with one another. They can also tend to overshadow the contributions to this dialogic interaction by, for example, nation-states. That dialogic interaction is the primary topic of this book. I view the terms as necessary shorthand for exploring the very kinds of interactions they are criticized for obfuscating: the ways in which local knowledges and identities take shape in dialogic interaction with decidedly translocal discourses and practices, how "globalizing" processes take shape and make sense through specific conditions of possibility in the context of the nation-state, and the ways in which local and global interactions can reshape those conditions of possibility. The obfuscation seems to me more a result of the unreflexive usage of the terms than a problem inherent in the terms themselves. Similarly, there have been numerous studies deconstructing "the state." Recognizing the problematics of state reification, I try to be clear about what aspect of the state I am referring to: the ruling party in government, be it federal or state; security forces; legal institutions; or sets of norms or ideas that emerge from these.

9. This process is discussed in greater detail in Chapters 3 and 4.

10. The history of the INI is more complex than presented here, and by the 1970s there were significant challenges to assimilationism from within the agency. For discussion, see Hernández Castillo (2001a).

11. For discussion of the debates, see Cowan, Dembour, and Wilson 2001; Nagengast and Turner 1997.

12. Perhaps not surprisingly, the anthropological work on human rights that did emerge beginning in the 1970s took the form of solidarity with and advocacy for indigenous peoples struggling for their cultural rights and their continued existence as culturally distinct groups. Indigenous peoples had been struggling against oppression and cultural annihilation for centuries, but it was in the latter part of the twentieth century that these began to take the form of struggles for rights. Work with this type of group was the

purview of anthropologists, and the notion of collective cultural rights fit well within the cultural relativist framework and was fundamentally anti-universalist. In fact, Messer (1995) posits anthropologists' support for indigenous rights as one of the perceived hindrances to engagement with universal rights.

However, by the 1980s, anthropologists made an increasingly significant contribution to documenting human rights violations in the areas in which they worked (e.g., Binford 1996; Manz 1988; Sanford 2003; Scheper-Hughes 1995; Wilson 1997). The emergence of forensic anthropology in documenting past mass abuses and seeking justice for them also constituted an important anthropological contribution to the field (see Joyce and Stove 1991; Koff 2004; Maples and Browning 1994). Anthropologists' collaboration in creating testimonials provided a unique, personalized perspective on the impact of rights violations for individuals and communities (e.g., Menchú and Burgos Debray 1987; Tula and Stephen 1994).

13. Term coined by Francis Fukuyama. Fukuyama's position on Western liberal democracies is discussed in Bell (2000:4).

14. The United Nations Economic Commission for Latin America and the Caribbean (ECLAC) reports that from 1980 to 1999, the percentage of households in poverty in Latin America grew from 34.7 percent to 35.3 percent. The percentage of individuals in poverty increased from 40.5 percent to 43.8 percent—meaning an increase of poor people from 136 million to 211 million. A later report by the U.N. Economics Commission for Latin America and the Caribbean (ECLAC, or CEPAL by its Spanish acronym [Comisión Económica para América Latina y el Caribe]) indicated that in 2003, there were 20 million more Latin Americans living in poverty than in 1997.

Economic inequality is a matter of much debate. While some analysts argue that it remains stable and others suggest it has grown in the neoliberal period (e.g., Londoño and Székely 2000), few report that it has decreased. Whether it has remained stable or grown, in Latin America the levels of inequality are often staggering. For example, in Brazil at the end of the 1990s the richest 10 percent of the population received 43.9 percent of the total income, while the poorest 70 percent had only 28.11 percent of the income. In Argentina, the top 10 percent held almost as large a share of the national income (34.8 percent) as the poorest 70 percent (37.6 percent) (ECLAC [CEPAL] report, cited in the *Miami Herald*, July 16, 2002). In Mexico, the poorest 20 percent held only 4.2 percent of the national income, while the richest 20 percent held 55 percent. According to Dr. Peter Piot, Executive Director of the U.N. HIV/AIDS Commission ONUSIDA, in 1995, the wealth of the richest single Mexican citizen was equivalent to that of the combined wealth of the 17 million poorest Mexicans.

15. The United Nations has specifically tied neoliberalization policies such as structural adjustment to human rights questions. A report by an independent expert to the United Nations High Commission of Human Rights (UNHCHR) discussed the effects of structural adjustment policies and foreign debt on the full enjoyment of human

rights, particularly economic, social, and cultural rights (E/CN.4/2003/10) and the UNHCHR passed a resolution recognizing the negative impact of such policies (Resolution 2003/21).

16. The term *neoliberal multiculturalism* was coined by C. R. Hale (2002).

17. Povinelli (2002) has shown how liberal multiculturalism in Australia perpetuates unequal systems of power by compelling aboriginal people to identify with impossible standards of authentic traditional culture. As in C. R. Hale's analysis, notions of who is properly indigenous become fixed in multicultural law and policy and ultimately mean that identity claims as a form of struggle put us on the terrain of authenticity and legality in ways that are divisive of struggle and that reinscribe certain discourses and regimes of power. Interestingly, Taylor's (1994) classic text on multiculturalism argues that the concept emerged through the historical trajectory of the concept of authenticity.

18. Notable was the reform of Article 27, ending land reform and opening communal lands to privatization. These reforms and their implications are discussed in greater depth in Chapter 2.

Chapter 2

1. Conversation with the author, July 30, 2001.

2. See Collier 2000; García Aguilar 1998a; interviews by Shannon Speed with Mercedes Olivera of the Center for Women's Research and Action (CIAM), July 2000; Marta Figueroa, human rights attorney of COLEM, May 1999 and June 2000; Miguel Angel de los Santos, human rights attorney, June 1998; and Marina Patricia Jímenez, executive secretary of the "Fray Bartolomé de Las Casas" Human Rights Center (CDHFBC), June 2000. All notes in possession of the author.

3. The diocese in 1960 covered the entire state of Chiapas. In 1964, the diocese was divided into three (San Cristóbal de Las Casas, Tapachula, and Tuxtla Gutiérrez) at the urging of Ruíz, who wanted to be able to devote more of the diocese's work to the indigenous populations of the state, virtually all of which were situated within the area of the Diocese of San Cristóbal (Womack 1998). This area, which covers 48 percent of the state, was then subdivided by the diocese into six ethnogeographic zones: the Zona Chol, Zona Sur, Zona Sureste, Zona Centro, Zona Tzotzil, and Zona Tzeltal (Leyva Solano 1995).

4. Unfortunately, "all men" for Las Casas apparently, at least for a significant period of time, did not include those of African origin, and he recommended that they rather than Indians be enslaved (de Las Casas 1974 [1542]). He later repented and came to believe that African slavery was equally unjust to Indian slavery.

5. Notably the *Centro de Derechos Indígenas A. C.* (CEDIAC), formed in 1992 by the Jesuit mission in Bachajón, and the *Centro de Derechos Humanos "Fray Pedro Lorenzo de la Nada,"* founded by Franciscans in Ocosingo in May 1994, a direct outcome of the uprising and the violence perpetrated by the army in that city.

6. Carozza (2003) argues that there was a heavy Rousseauian influence on Latin American constitutions that resulted in the notion of rights with corollary responsibilities characteristic of those documents.

7. These precepts are particularly notable in the post–World War II conceptualization, enshrined in the Universal Declaration of Human Rights, with its emphasis on rights aimed at protecting human dignity. In the Universal Declaration, a dignified life is conceptualized as requiring a degree of liberty, embodied by the civil and political rights of Articles 1–21, but also enjoying a measure of well-being, reflected in the list of welfare rights in Articles 21–28 such as social security, leisure, "food, clothing, housing and medical care and necessary social services" (Article 26), unemployment benefits, education, and cultural participation. In the modern liberal interpretation of rights, states—now charged with both creating rights through law and enforcing respect for them through law—also had a larger role to play in mediating economic and social relations, and in many cases placed controls on the economy. Carozza (2003) argues that Mexico and other Latin American countries played a significant role in ensuring that social rights were encompassed in the Universal Declaration.

8. The *Porfiriato*, the period of the dictatorship of Porfirio Díaz, represented the climax of the liberal period and immediately preceded the Revolution. At the end of the *Porfiriato*, the degree of land concentration in Mexico was greater than in any other Latin American country, and indigenous communities had lost up to 90 percent of their lands.

9. The reforms entailed a number of key components, including (1) ending the government's obligation to redistribute lands in favor of peasants who demand it; (2) establishing a structure through which *ejidatarios* can obtain individual title deeds or certificates over their parcels by participating in the Program for Certification of Ejidal Rights and Urban Patios (PROCEDE); (3) establishing the legal right of *ejidatarios* to rent or sell lands, hire a workforce, or use their land as loan collateral (the decision to authorize the sale of lands of the *ejido* to external persons must be approved by two-thirds of the general assembly's vote); (4) allowing common lands used by *ejidatarios* collectively as pastureland or forest resources to be sold for commercial development if the majority of *ejidatarios* are in favor; (5) eliminating *ejidatarios*' obligation to personally work their plots (Cornelius and Mhyre 1998).

10. In February 1990, a World Bank official drafted an agricultural policy document that recommended striving to eliminate the differences between private and *ejidal* property, with an emphasis on the security of land tenancy, the individualization of the collective functions of the *ejido,* and its destruction as a unit of production and organization (World Bank 1990). The text was later published under the official's name (Heath 1992). Teichman (2004) is an excellent discussion of the World Bank influence in the reform of agrarian policy in Mexico and Argentina.

11. Albores was one of the first people to obtain a grant from the Mexican Academy of Human Rights (AMDH), the first national organization with a broad human rights

agenda, formed in 1984. Albores received his grant in 1986–87 and produced a report on the violation of human rights in the prisons of Chiapas at that time (Neil Harvey, personal communication with the author, September 2006).

12. Neil Harvey, personal communication with the author, September 2006. A "*cacique*" in this context is a local political boss.

13. Collier (2000) cites at least ten more, though I was not able to independently verify their existence.

14. These included the *Comisión Mexicana de Defensa y Promoción de los Derechos Humanos* (CMDPDH), the *Academia Mexicana de Derechos Humanos* (AMDH), the *Centro de Derechos Humanos Miguel Agustín Pro* (Centro Prodh), *Centro de Derechos Humanos* "Fray Francisco de Vitoria O. P.," and the *Red Todos los Derechos para Todos*.

15. International organizations with offices in Chiapas were SIPAZ and Global Exchange. Others had a periodic presence through commissions or delegations; these included Human Rights Watch, Amnesty International, the Minnesota Advocates for Human Rights, the Humanitarian Law Project, the *Comisión Interamericana de Derechos Humanos* (CIDH), the *Federación Internacional de los Derechos del Hombre* (FIDH), and the *Instituto Interamericano de Derechos Humanos* (IIDH) (drawn in part from Collier 2000).

16. The state government formed the Comisión Estatal de Derechos Humanos (CEDH) in 1990, and the federal government's human rights agency, the Comisión Nacional de Derechos Humanos (CNDH), was formed in 1990 and opened offices in Chiapas in 1994.

17. This tendency within the movement changed in 2006, a period outside the scope of analysis in this book. In June and July 2005, the EZLN presented the Sixth Declaration of the Selva Lacandona. The "Sexta" provides an analysis of the history and struggle of the Zapatistas in the preceding eleven years. In it, the Zapatistas argue that "a new step forward in the indigenous struggle is only possible if the indigenous join together with . . . the workers of the city and the countryside." Suggesting that local autonomic processes were already consolidated, the EZLN proposed the creation of a broad front that would simultaneously construct "a national program of struggle, but a program which will be clearly of the left, or anti-capitalist." The Sexta, and "The Other Campaign" that followed it, brought the Zapatista movement back to a national and anti-neoliberal agenda that had been put on the back burner for several years as the consolidation of local autonomy was prioritized. This process is discussed further in the concluding chapter.

18. *El dedazo* means, literally, "the big finger," which the president figuratively points at his successor.

19. Federal prosecutors assert that Colosio was the victim of a plot, yet only one man has been convicted in the killing. Mario Aburto Martinez, a factory worker, confessed

to shooting the candidate. He was sentenced to forty-five years in prison. Many, including the prosecutors, clearly believed Aburto Martinez to be a scapegoat. Notably, Jesus Romero Magana, the first federal prosecutor to interrogate Aburto Martinez after he was detained, was shot and killed on August 17, 1996 (Ortiz Pardo and Puig Magana 1997). Police suspect Romero may have known his assailants.

20. Muñoz Rocha disappeared, presumed a fugitive from justice, though many suspected he had also been killed.

21. On March 3, 2005, Ruíz Massieu was arrested in a Newark, New Jersey, airport while en route to Spain from Houston for failing to declare that he was carrying more than $10,000 in cash. His arrest came just two days after he was questioned for eight hours by Mexican authorities trying to determine whether his investigation into his brother's murder covered up the involvement of Raul Salinas.

22. Anthony De Palma, "Crisis in Mexico: The Overview, with Peso Freed, Mexican Currency Drops 20% More," *New York Times*, December 23, 1994.

23. This document may be obtained from the Counterpunch Institute for Policy Studies, 1601 Connecticut Avenue Northwest, Washington, DC 20009.

24. He was acquitted in 2005.

25. Though there were tensions between the EZLN and Bishop Ruíz, and the relationship between them was not as close as some people asserted at the time (suggestions that the diocese was directly responsible for the uprising are examined in the next chapter), the EZLN clearly trusted this negotiating body more than the other and publicly supported Bishop Ruíz when he came under public attack. For example, in the closing words of the EZLN-COCOPA-CONAI meeting in October 1996, the Zapatista leadership eloquently expressed its support for the bishop:

> Through my voice speaks as well the quiet and efficient work of the National Commission of Intermediation. We especially salute the noble attitude of its president, Bishop Samuel Ruíz García who, in spite of threats, persecution, slander and insults, perseveres in opening paths of peace which we would have chosen before had they existed. Though he is the nightmare of the power which badly governs this country, Mr. Samuel Ruíz has learned to walk amidst the intrigues and the traps which are intended to eliminate him and follow the path which, long before January 1 of '94, he walked through example; the path of peaceful struggle for justice in this life. The paradoxes which mark our history as a nation reproduce themselves in the life of this man whose greatest defect is to speak the truth, regardless of whether it pleases the powerful. . . . Those who want the war ask for the head of Samuel Ruíz García. Those who want peace will have to learn there will be none without him.

Document can be accessed at http://flag.blackened.net/revolt/mexico/ezln/1996/ccri_closing_words_oct.html. Last accessed January 10, 2007.

26. CONAI press release, April 10, 1995. Document in possession of the author.

27. See Clarke and Ross 1994 for an English compilation of early declarations by the EZLN.

28. In Mexico, the vast majority of legislation is submitted to the congress by the executive branch.

29. *La Jornada*, January 1997.

30. On June 8, 1997, the CONAI issued the following statement: "The CONAI, expression of civilian participation in the construction of a just and dignified peace, directs to the Mexican people the following considerations and proposals:

1. The failure to implement the agreements of San Andrés has placed not only the dialogue between the EZLN and the federal government in crisis, but also the path of political negotiation itself as a road toward the peaceful solution of all conflicts. If what is agreed upon is not implemented, then trust becomes affected and makes any advance impossible. It is for this reason that it becomes urgent to recover and reestablish, with concrete deeds, the conditions of trust and credibility such that the path of dialogue and negotiation remains that which will lead to a solution to the real causes of conflict. Without all this, it will not be possible to re-establish the Dialogue of San Andrés.

2. Furthermore, the constant appearance of provocations and tensions in different municipalities of the state of Chiapas has profoundly damaged the sociocultural fabric of these communities. On this subject, the following actions stand out:

   a. the growing military presence which deepens the scenario of a latent war;
   b. the method of provoking conflicts so as to create divisions within a community and justify the intervention of police and paramilitary forces;
   c. the unilateral measures taken by the executive, judicial, and legislative powers of the state of Chiapas which are attempting to create the baseless appearance of the implementation of the commitments derived from San Andrés.

31. For example, the National Assembly of Indigenous Peoples for Autonomy (ANIPA) formed in early 1995, and its assemblies brought together various autonomy groups from throughout the country.

32. These debates were principally focused on whether autonomy would be best realized at the community, municipal, or regional level. Organizations such as ANIPA have supported regional models such as the *Regiones Autónomas Pluriétnicas* (RAP), while others have focused on cummunal autonomy. The Zapatistas have frustrated some by not taking a strong position in favor of any one model, utilizing both community and regional models and maintaining a degree of flexibility in their approach to their autonomy project.

33. See Falcón 1994.

34. The "municipalities in rebellion" became a target of the federal and state governments, resulting in numerous massive raids on municipal seats during 1998 by the joint

forces of the federal army, federal police, and state security police. The raids were designed to dismantle the seats of autonomous government and, in several cases, were successful (López Monjardín and Rebolledo Millán 1998; Stephen 1999). The raids are discussed further in Chapter 3. The state government developed its own initiative to create new municipalities in contested regions, but many analysts have shown that this "remunicipalization" was designed to dismember the existing "municipalities in rebellion" by establishing municipal seats in population centers loyal to the national ruling party, the PRI (Burguete Cal y Mayor, 1999b). Today there are thirty autonomous municipalities.

Chapter 3

1. The organizations involved in *Estación Norte* were CONPAZ, the Fray Bartolomé Human Rights Center, SIPAZ, Global Exchange, and the *Centro de Derechos Indígenas A. C.* (CEDIAC).

2. In Chiapas, particularly in indigenous communities but elsewhere as well, people use the term *human rights* to alternately refer to the rights themselves and human rights organizations or individual human rights workers.

3. January 1997. Notes in possession of the author. I have purposefully withheld the names of the men and the community for reasons of privacy.

4. *La Jornada*, February 10, 11, and 12, 1995.

5. The Cañadas refers to the canyons of the Lacandón jungle, in the municipality of Ocosingo.

6. That project, the *Red de Defensores Comunitarios por los Derechos Humanos*, is the subject of Chapter 6.

7. The Interamerican Human Rights Commission also made a ruling in the case of three Zapatista supporters from the community of Morelia—Severiano Santiz Gómez, Hermelindo Santiz Gómez, and Sebastián Santiz López—who were detained and murdered by the Mexican Army on January 7, 1994 (Informe #48/97), which recommended criminal charges against those involved and compensation of the family members.

8. Actually, the capital moved back and forth between Tuxtla Gutiérrez and San Cristóbal several times during the nineteenth century as the rivaling liberals and conservatives vied for control. On February 9, 1834, the capital was first moved to Tuxtla Gutiérrez, only to return the following year to San Cristóbal. In January of 1858, the capital again relocated to Tuxtla, returning to San Cristóbal in 1861, where it remained until February of 1864. In 1867 San Cristóbal again regained the status of capital city. The capital was relocated to Tuxtla for the fourth and final time in August 1892 by Governor Emilio Rabasa (Benjamin 1989).

9. It is the case in much of the region—and as we shall see in relation to indigenous communities later in the chapter—that *foreigners* refers not only to non-Mexicans, but to any nonlocals. The term in Spanish, *extranjero*, means both foreigner and stranger.

10. Doña Concepción, in conversation with the author, July 1995. Note her use of the term *Indito*, meaning "little Indian," a common depreciative term that infantilizes Indians.

11. Doña Marina, in conversation with the author, November 1996.

12. This interpretation, openly expressed here with all its racist content, is argued with only slightly more restraint by the Mexican scholar Enrique Krauze (1999).

13. This view was expressed to me, for example, by Marina Patricia, executive secretary of the Fray Bartolomé Human Rights Center, when I interviewed her on August 3, 2000, as well as by many "peace campers" I spoke with between 1995 and 1998.

14. Samuel Sánchez Sánchez was imprisoned in 2001, after the ruling party left power in the state, for his participation as a leader of *Paz y Justicia*.

15. Document in possession of the author.

16. This was a social process that took place in indigenous communities throughout the state. It is discussed at length in relation to the community of Nicolás Ruiz in Chapter 4.

17. *Ni Derechos, Ni Humanos en la Zona Norte de Chiapas: La otra verdad de los sucesos en la zona ch'ol, como respuesta a la versión difundida por el Centro de Derechos Humanos "Fray Bartolomé de Las Casas"* was published by *Desarrollo, Paz y Justicia* in 1997. As the title indicates, it was a direct response to the 1996 publication *Ni Paz, Ni Justicia: Informe amplio acerca de la guerra civil que sufren los ch'oles en la zona norte de Chiapas*, by the *Centro de Derechos Humanos "Fray Bartolomé de Las Casas."*

18. In fact, this latter interpretation ("If human rights butts in, it will provoke more violence. We do not tolerate human rights here.") was so strongly held that ultimately the *Estación Norte* withdrew from the zone, fearing that human rights accompaniment, rather than deterring violence, was likely to exacerbate it.

19. I thank Jane Collier for generously sharing her thoughts on this meeting with me.

20. Article 10, which opens the section on the administration of justice, establishes that "the customs and ancestral traditions of indigenous communities constitute the fundamental basis for the resolution of their conflicts. These customs and traditions . . . will be applied within the limits of their habitat, as long as they do not constitute a violation of human rights" (State Government of Chiapas 1999).

21. Translation by the author.

22. Elio Henríquez, "Desmantelan otro cabildo zapatista mil soldados y policías," *La Jornada*, May 2, 1998:1.

23. Ibid.

24. Ibid.

25. ACNUR officials were ordered by the *Secretaria de Gobernación* not to go to Amparo Aguatinta. The government opposed ACNUR's negotiating with the Autonomous Council because it considered such negotiation a "recognition of the Council's legitimacy." An official from ACNUR, however, stated, "On several occasions, for different

problems, we have come to engage in dialogue with the Council to resolve issues relating to refugees. They even have some documents signed by us." The ACNUR official also observed, "The ambiguity of the situation here does not allow ACNUR to define who is the competent authority. What we recommend is that members of the Guatemalan community decide for themselves the best way to resolve their problems. If they had recourse to the Autonomous Council, or to some other authority, then that's what they should do" (Carlos Zaccagnini, chief of the office of ACNUR–Chiapas, quoted in Hermann Bellinghausen, "No Pidió ACNUR Acción Policial en Aguatinta," *La Jornada*, May 3, 1998:7).

26. U.N. Universal Declaration on Human Rights, Art. 9; International Convention on Civil and Political Rights, Art. 9; Mexican Constitution, Art. 14, Art. 21.

27. Declaration of Pascual Gómez Domingo, Official Record, File 132/998 Juzgado Tercero de Primera Instancia, State of Chiapas, 1999. Copy of file in possession of the author.

28. Declaration of Pascual Gómez Domingo, Official Record, File 132/998 Juzgado Tercero de Primera Instancia, State of Chiapas, 1999. Copy of file in possession of the author.

29. Aureliano Lopez Ruiz, president of the Autonomous Council, stated in his declaration,

[I] was elected by the authorities of the communities of Amparo Aguatinta [names twenty communities], among others, as President of the Autonomous Municipal Council of Tierra y Libertad. My primary function is to reach agreements with each community and then to carry out these agreements as they are stipulated, such as fixing fines regarding [crimes such as] the sale and consumption of alcohol, as well as theft, and beating or harming women. [I] would like to clarify, we also call "fines" the days that one is locked up in the jail of Aguatinta—from two to ten days maximum, depending on the infraction.

—Official record, file #132/998, Juzgado Tercero Penal de Primera Instancia, State of Chiapas

Expert witness Yuri Escalante testified that the ceremony in which newly elected authorities take office places a strong emphasis on the obligation of the authorities to respect *usos y costumbres* as they conduct their official duties.

30. The election process for autonomous authorities, which is based on consensus decisions taken in community assemblies, is discussed as a form of *usos y costumbres* by Yuri Alex Escalante, ethnohistorian and head of the Department of Juridical Customs of the National Indigenous Institute, when giving expert testimony in the Tierra y Libertad case. Official Record, file #132/998, Juzgado Tercero Penal de Primera Instancia, State of Chiapas (1999).

31. Official Record, file #132/998, Juzgado Tercero Penal de Primera Instancia, State of Chiapas (1999).

32. Daniel Pensamiento, "Liberan a cinco indígenas de Tierra y Libertad: La acción, para reencauzar las negociaciones de paz," *Expreso,* September 15, 1999:1.

Chapter 4

1. Letter to Governor Juan Sabines Guerrero, signed by the authorities of *Bienes Comunales* of Nicolás Ruiz, Marco Antonio López Díaz (Comisariado), Benito Alfredo López López (Secretario), and Constantino López Ramírez (Tesorero). January 20, 2007.

2. Nicolás Ruiz, community assembly meeting, June 30, 2001.

3. The only published article I know of is one on the fiesta de San Agustín in Nicolás Ruiz and Acala (Lisbona Guillén 1992). A recent dissertation by Inés Castro Apreza (2006) will undoubtedly make a significant contribution to our knowledge of current dynamics in the community.

4. The community, originally named San Diego, was made a municipality in 1868. At that time it was renamed La Reforma, though it was generally called San Diego de la Reforma. The name was changed to Nicolás Ruiz when the utilization of saints' names for towns was outlawed by Governor Victórico Grajales in 1934, though for many years residents continued to call it by its former name and, until very recently, many official documents contained the parenthetical clause "(formerly San Diego de la Reforma)."

5. I utilize data from the 1990 census because they are the most recent census data available for this municipality. Nicolás Ruiz did not participate in the 2000 Federal Census as part of its resistance to government control.

6. Hernández Castillo (2002) discusses the different meanings concepts such as "customary law" and "traditional authorities" have in different regions of the state, depending on the local history.

7. The divisions among the women of the assembly are the subject of Chapter 5.

8. As we saw in Chapter 3 some communities have faced problems when their authorities, elected through customary practices, are not recognized as legitimate by the state. As was the case in Tierra y Libertad, these authorities are open to legal charges of "usurping the functions" of authorities chosen through "official" electoral processes (see also Speed and Collier 2000a).

9. The *títulos primordiales* are colonial-era indigenous-language documents containing lengthy and complex descriptions of community boundaries. These and a series of other Spanish-language documents related to this land, bound in deer-hide, were in the possession of the authorities of Nicolás Ruiz until June 3, 1998. On that date, the documents were taken by a masked man, assumed to be a local *priísta,* who was accompanied by state security police, during the joint military-police raid on the town. This event is discussed further in the text. The documents had been partially transcribed by the historian Jan de Vos at the petition of municipal authorities in 1989. He considered them so valuable he later referred to them as "the Treasure of Nicolás Ruiz." After the

documents were stolen, the authorities contacted Jan de Vos for copies of the transcriptions, which is all they have today. It was this set of transcriptions that I utilized in the study of their recent history. I also base this section on documents in the Archive of the Diocese of San Cristóbal de Las Casas and the Registro Agrario Nacional in Tuxtla Gutiérrez.

10. Records in the Archive of the Diocese of San Cristóbal de Las Casas.

11. According to Morales Avendaño (1974), Ostuta was formed in 1540, when the emperor Carlos V ordered by royal decree that small indigenous communities be gathered into large ones. Ostuta was made up of various small communities of the region. The exact reason for the disappearance of Ostuta is not known. It is speculated that an outbreak of malaria, spread by the mosquitoes and biting flies that were abundant on the banks of the river where Ostuta was located, wiped out the population.

12. Document in possession of *Bienes Comunales*, Nicolás Ruiz.

13. A *caballería* is roughly equivalent to 42.25 hectares.

14. Document in possession of *Bienes Comunales*, Nicolás Ruiz.

15. This price included the land and buildings on San Diego, along with a small chapel and altarpiece, for 500 pesos, the uninhabited lands of San Lazaro for 300 pesos, 45 head of cattle for 5 pesos, 17 bulls for 3 pesos, 17 horses for 5 pesos, 30 ponies for 3 pesos, 2 burros for 8 pesos, 36 pesos owed by the indentured servants living on San Diego, and 10 pesos for the tables, chairs, and other goods in the house on San Diego. The original document was broken in places and thus some information about goods and purchases is lost.

16. A *cacique* in this context was a larger landholder and political strongman, and the term is frequently associated with abuses of power.

17. Letter dated January 14, 1857, signed by Jose Antonio Larrainzar. Archive of the Diocese of San Cristóbal.

18. His petition was supported by the parish priest, Antonio Sabino Avilés, who seemed rather anxious to "discharge himself of its administration." Letter dated January 19, 1857, signed by Anto. Sabino Avilés. Archive of the Diocese of San Cristóbal.

19. Letter dated October 13, 1862, signed by Anto. Sabino Avilés. Archive of the Diocese of San Cristóbal. The petition to return San Diego to Teopisca was not honored as quickly as Larrainzar's had been. In February of 1865, the *Corporación Municipal* of Teopisca held a special session because "the entire town struck against this body" demanding the return of San Diego to the Parish of Teopisca (letter dated February 6, 1865, signed by representatives of the Corporación Municipal de Teopisca. Archive of the Diocese of San Cristóbal). The request of the Teopiscans was not respected either— as late as 1891, when San Diego completed its church, it was still annexed to the parish of San Bartolomé (letter dated 1891, signed by Jose Fernando Macal, the parish priest of San Bartolomé, to the bishop in San Cristóbal, reporting the completion of the construction of the church at San Diego).

20. This incident is also notable because Larrainzar moved the town from its former location onto a hill, which is the present-day location of the town.

21. Documents in possession of *Bienes Comunales* of Nicolás Ruiz.

22. *Carrancistas* were followers of revolutionary Venustiano Carranza from 1913 to 1914, then became the government army from 1914 until Carranza's death in 1920.

23. Periódico Oficial del Estado, October 31, 1914. Cited in Benjamin 1996 (1989).

24. The landholders were Braulio Coello (San Juanito), Abraham Castro, Vicente Franco (La Lanza), Arcadio Garcia (Finca Concepción Valunhuitz), and Doña Petra Bermúdes (widow of Paniagua—Santa Lucia).

25. Transcription of "telefonema" from General J. A. Castro and letter dated November 21, 1914, signed by "Jefe Político y Comandante Militar del Departamento," documents in possession of *Bienes Comunales*, Nicolás Ruiz.

26. Letter from Secretaría General del Gobierno Preconstitucional del Estado de Chiapas, Sección de Fomento, comunicaciones, y obras públicas, Mesa de fomento. Número 1157, dated June 5, 1915, in possession of *Bienes Comunales*, Nicolás Ruiz.

27. Like most rural parts of the state, San Diego de la Reforma suffered a good deal during the years of the Revolution. Both *Carrancista* forces and the *Mapaches* who rebelled against them wreaked havoc on the countryside, robbing, raping, and pillaging as they went (Benjamin 1996 [1989]). According to documents in the archives of the diocese of San Cristóbal and oral history in Nicolás Ruiz, the population of San Diego concentrated in the town for protection at this time. This relocation did little to help them, since the town was repeatedly attacked by the marauding bands and according to oral history was sacked and burned on May 14, 1917.

28. For example, letter dated November 18, 1918, from the Síndico Municipal of San Diego de la Reforma Julián Rodríguez to Ciudadano Juez Primera Instancia del Departamento de La Libertad, reiterating the results of the redrawn boundaries and pleading the "rights of my people." Document in possession of *Bienes Comunales*, Nicolás Ruiz.

29. As was the case of the *ejido* Nuevo Leon.

30. Archives of the *Registro Civil* de Nicolás Ruiz.

31. This discourse emerged as early as 1780, according to Montemayor (1997), who cites Francisco Xavier Clavijero's *Historia Antigua de México* as the first example.

32. Cited in Falcón 1994.

33. In the Highlands, as Rus (1994b) demonstrates, the *Centro Coordinador* played an important role in the reconfiguration of local governments to convert them into "*Comunidades Revolucionarios Institucionales*" (a play on the *Partido Revolucionario Institucional*—PRI—party name), that is, in linking the communities organically to the state project and the ruling party.

34. Diario Oficial, August 19, 1980, "Declaración de Resolución Presidencial 5 de Agosto 1980" page 14; Documento Num. 11914 de la Secretaría de la Reforma Agraria,

Presidencia de la Republica Acuerdos y Decretos. Copy in the Archive of *Bienes Comunales*, Nicolás Ruiz.

35. Information provided by a special commission of *Bienes Comunales* in interview with the author, August 2004.

36. Documents in the archive of the Registro Agrario Nacional.

37. I discuss them in slightly more depth in Speed (2006b).

38. Jorge Ozuna, Manuel Villatoro, and Ariosto Madrigal.

39. An *ejidatario* is a member of an *ejido*, a communal land grant by the government through the agrarian reform. A *comunero* is a member of a rural community that holds communal lands that do not have *ejido* status. Nicolás Ruiz is not an *ejido*, having gained its lands through a private purchase in 1734.

40. *Comunero* in interview, July 2004.

41. *Comunero* Juán Pérez Jiménez, July 2004.

42. A "restitution" of communal lands implies a recognition that the lands were once in communal possession of the rural community. An *ejidal* land grant does not necessarily carry this implication. Documents in possession of *Bienes Comunales*, Nicolás Ruiz. This PRA purchase is also noted in Villafuerte et al. (1999:118).

43. List with the stamp of the *Secretario de Gobierno del Estado de Chiapas*, in possession of *Bienes Comunales* of Nicolás Ruiz.

44. CCRI of the EZLN, "On the Capture, Condemnation, and Sentencing of Division General Absalón Castellanos Domínguez," *La Jornada*, January 13, 1994.

45. Interview, October 2004.

46. The dead were José Alfonso Lara Sántiz, José Alfonso Moreno Álvarez, and Gilibaldo Ramírez Reynosa.

47. A *comunero*, in conversation with the author in October 2004. Notes in possession of the author.

48. A *comunero*, in conversation with the author in October 2004. Notes in possession of the author.

49. Leopoldo Díaz García, Antonio Serafín López Díaz, Ignacio Ramírez López, Juan Juárez Gómez, Juan Méndez Thon, and Filadelfo Juárez López.

50. Comments to the author in June 1999.

51. Full quote is in chapter 2 (*Cuarto Poder*, June 2, 1998).

52. Comments to the author, July 1999.

53. Comments to the author, August 1999.

54. I discuss the *Red de Defensores* here not because it is the most important of the organizations that work with the community of Nicolás Ruiz, but rather because it is the organization I work with, and thus the one I know the most about. I leave the other organizations working there unnamed out of respect for their privacy and security.

55. De los Santos has done defense work for the community since the battle at El Gran Poder in 1996.

56. A complaint regarding a violation of an ILO Convention by a signatory state is called a representation, and it is presented only through an established labor union. The *Red de Defensores* worked in coordination with the *Frente Auténtico del Trabajo* (Authentic Labor Front, or FAT by its Spanish acronym) to present the representation.

57. Some of the lands lost by Nicolás Ruiz over the last two centuries are currently occupied by communities that formed years or decades ago. The people of Nicolás Ruiz are not interested in displacing these communities; thus they are not pursuing the recuperation of these lands. They are, however, pursuing the recuperation of lands held by large landowners.

58. President Vicente Fox, addressing Korean and Japanese business leaders (Juan Manuel Venegas, "Somos un Gobierno de Negocios: expresa Vicente Fox a la cúpula empresarial Coreana," *La Jornada*, June 5, 2001 and "PEMEX, anzuelo lanzado por Fox para captar capitales japoneses," *La Journada*, June 6, 2001.

Chapter 5

1. "Rosalina" in interview with the author, July 2001.

2. The Women's Revolutionary Law is republished in Speed, Hernández Castillo, and Stephen 2006.

3. Available in English online at http://www.infoshop.org/news_archive/mex_woman .html. Last accessed April 2006.

4. Available in English online at http://www.zmag.org/chiapas1/estmar28.htm. Last accessed April 2006.

5. Ignacion Burgoa, cited in Jaime Avilés, "Burgoa: Los acuerdos de San Andrés, inexistentes" *La Jornada*, March 4, 1997.

6. *Cuarto Poder*, June 2, 1998. Full quote appears in chapter 3.

7. It is worth noting that the state has done very little until now to protect individual indigenous women from suffering violations of their rights implied by particular customs, such as those I have mentioned. Moreover, it is not at all clear that the judicial system of the Mexican state is entirely willing or able to protect any women's rights, even those established in law (see Azaola 1996).

8. Other cases are discussed in Speed and Collier 2000a.

9. Interview, "Doña Matilde," June 1999.

10. "Francisca," in conversation with the author, 2000.

11. "María," conversation with the author, 2000.

12. Conversation with the author, August 2001.

13. Conversation with the author, August 2001.

14. Interview with *comunero*, September 2001.

15. Hernández Castillo (2006) notes that this perspective has been accepted by some Mexican academic feminists (as it has by many academic feminists in other parts of Latin America and in the United States). However, in both the United States and Latin

America, academic or "hegemonic" feminism has remained focused largely on the specific goals of reproductive rights and domestic violence. While these issues are relevant to indigenous women, their dominance continues to marginalize and exclude indigenous women's specific demands from the feminist agenda.

16. Comandanta Esther's complete speech of March 8, 2001, is available at www .infoshop.org/news_archive/mex_woman.html. Also reprinted in Speed, Hernández Castillo, and Stephen 2006.

Chapter 6

1. Interview, April 2001.

2. The term *"autogestión"* means carrying out their own processes autonomously.

3. This section is adapted from Speed and Reyes (2002). I gratefully acknowledge the contribution of Alvaro Reyes to my thinking on the issues addressed in this section and throughout this chapter.

4. The *Ministerio Público* is somewhat akin to a district attorney. It is the institution that receives complaints, assigns detectives to investigate crimes, and presents evidence on behalf of the state against a suspect at a preliminary hearing and during trial.

5. Field notes in possession of the author.

6. Water and electricity are two of the most volatile issues in Chiapas. The state has ample water resources and produces 35 percent of the hydroelectric energy for the entire country. However, only 71 percent of households in Chiapas have running water, and that percentage is as low as 19 percent in some indigenous areas (INEGI 2005). Of those households that do have running water, the quality is often so poor that it is unfit for human consumption. One study of high-poverty areas of Chiapas showed that only 30 percent of households that have running water receive water of adequate quality for human consumption (Sánchez-Pérez et al. 2000). In 2002, the World Bank gave Conagua (the National Water Commission) a $250 million loan to create a program called PROMAGUA (Program for Modernizing Water Utilities). PROMAGUA is part of a new infrastructure financing fund that provides loans to municipalities to upgrade and expand their water systems if they negotiate public-private partnerships (i.e., privatization), reform their state water laws, and impose full cost recovery. People fear this will lead to a situation similar to that they face regarding electricity. Statistics of the government National Institute for Statistics, Geography and Data Analysis (INEGI) indicate that 93 percent of the population had electricity in their homes in 2005, though in indigenous areas this number may be as low as 57.3 percent. But the most contentious issue is that those that do have electricity are charged exorbitant rates by the Federal Electricity Commission (CFE), resulting in many individuals, neighborhoods, communities, and even entire municipalities refusing to pay and engaging in long-term resistance through boycott. Occasionally, violence has resulted when CFE workers attempted to cut power, but more frequently people have learned to reconnect it themselves after the workers leave.

7. This and all quotes in this subsection are from unstructured interviews with *defensores* by Shannon Speed or Alvaro Reyes between late 1999 and early 2001.

8. Interview with the author, July 2000. Notes in possession of the author.

9. In this case I have used Méndez's real name. Because he is a public figure, his security is not likely to be (further) jeopardized by the publication of his name here. His comments were made to the author in June 2000.

10. This will be discussed in greater depth in Chapter 7.

Chapter 7

1. Colloquial phrase meaning, roughly, "They can keep their bullshit."

2. Reported on CNN.com World Report, December 1, 2000. Available at http://archives.cnn.com/2000/WORLD/americas/12/01/mexico.fox.04/index.html. Last accessed April 2006.

3. Victor Ballinas and Andrea Becerril, "La paz, cada vez más cerca: Fernando Yáñez," *La Jornada*, April 11, 2001:1.

4. Ciro Pérez Silva and David Aponte, "220 diputados abrieron la tribuna al EZLN," *La Jornada*, March 23, 2001:1.

5. Jo Tuckman, "Zapatistas, Minus Marcos, Have Their Day in Parliament," *The Guardian*, March 29, 2001.

6. Text of speech available in English at http://www.zmag.org/chiapas1/estmar28.htm. Last accessed May 2006.

7. Victor Ballinas and Andrea Becerril, "La paz, cada vez más cerca: Fernando Yáñez," *La Jornada*, April 11, 2001:1.

8. Of the voting breakdown, Kennis (2002) writes, "In the passage of the transformed legislation, somewhat surprising was that the center-left party, the Party of the Democratic Revolution (PRD), voted unanimously in favor of the bill in the senate." The official explanation was a hope to be able to bring about changes to the legislation in the future. Nevertheless, it is arguable that a more accurate explanation for the PRD's Senate vote can be found in a statement from one of its leading senators, Demetrio Sodi de Tijera, who is a member of the COCOPA commission. Sodi de Tijera suggested that the changes made to the indigenous law—and the indigenous law itself—simply were not that important, since "Indian peoples practically do not exist" today, and among those who do, very few are organized in just a handful of "small communities." Whatever the motive for the PRD in the Senate, the PRD's bench in the Chamber of Deputies (the other congressional body in Mexico) did not accede to such thinking and voted unanimously against the gutted legislation (along with three Workers Party deputies and five PRI deputies from the southern and highly indigenous populated state of Oaxaca). Nevertheless, the chamber still passed the legislation on April 28, as the PAN unanimously voted along with many PRI deputies in favor of the law (the final vote count was 386–60).

9. Regarding the state approval process (a legal requisite for the constitutionality of the reforms), Ramírez Cuevas (2002) cites Abigail Zuñiga, advisor for the municipality of Tlaxiaco: "After Congress approved the reform, the PRI and the PAN speeded up the process in the state legislatures. . . . On July 18, the Permanent Commission made the official count of the results, despite the fact that not all the legislatures had finished voting, and that two states had not even discussed the issue. The Commission totaled 19 state congresses in favor, and nine against (those with a majority indigenous population). Of the 19 states that voted in favor, irregularities and legal violations had been documented in eight. Chihuahua sent its results after the official count, and, despite that, it was included."

10. Subcomandante Marcos introduced the concept of *caracol* in July of 2003: "They say that the most ancient ones said that others, more ancient than they, appreciated the figure of the *caracol*. They say that they say that they said that *the* caracol *represented entering the heart*, that this was what the first to have knowledge said. And they say that they say that they said that *the* caracol *also represented the heart going forth to walk through the world*, that was what they said, the first to live. And not only that, they say that they say that they said that *with the* caracol *they called to the collective so that the word would be one and agreement would be born*. And they also say that they say that they said that the *caracol* helped the ear to hear even the most distant word. That is what they say that they said" ("Chiapas, la treceava estela: Un caracol." *La Jornada*, Thursday July 24, 2003). Thus the Zapatista *caracol* represents a place for going into the heart of the Zapatista regions, and one from which their heart "walks forth into the world," and it is a place to call together the collective so that agreement can be attained. The word itself refers to both a conch seashell and a snail shell. While the reference to shells for communication is for conch shells, which were once used to call people to public meetings, in the Tzeltal communities of Chiapas, people use the word *pu'y*, which means snail.

11. English text (translation may vary slightly from mine) available at: indymedia .org.uk/en/2001/03/2641.html. Last accessed March 5, 2006.

12. Refusal to take a rape complaint from a woman, for example, or to accept complaints of rights violations that are handwritten and/or in nonlegal language. It is also common to make the process of making a complaint so lengthy, arduous, and costly that it is no longer viable to the victim.

13. For example, victims of paramilitary violence in Chiapas have yet to see the perpetrators—aligned with the former ruling party PRI—brought to justice.

14. Victor Ballinas, Jesus Aranda, and Rosa Elvira Vargas, "La impunidad registra en Mexico un nivel de 95–98 por ciento, afirma Relator de la ONU," *La Jornada*, May 15, 2001:1.

15. In the English translation of the *Savage Anomaly*, Hardt utilizes the capitalized Power for *potestas* and the lowercase power for *potentia*.

16. Conversation with the author, June 2004. Notes in possession of the author. Za-

patista leaders meet with an astonishing number of people from national and international civil society. In one communiqué, Marcos reports that according to authorities in Oventic, in one year they had attended 2,921 persons from other countries and 1,537 from Mexico (outside Chiapas) (Marcos 2004a).

Chapter 8

1. Press release by the *comuneros* of Nicolás Ruiz, dated January 28, 2007.

2. I recognize that this inclusiveness is in many cases more of an ideal concept than an unfailing practice and that tolerance of diversity at the local level is uneven. Nevertheless, by positing these concepts as part of their autonomy project, Zapatistas do offer this up as an aspect of their alternative for social organization and rule.

3. From *La Jornada*, January 19, 1997:10, cited in Hernández Castillo (2001a). Translation is by Hernández Castillo.

4. Cited on page 16.

Bibliography

Adams, Abigail. 1998. "Gringas, Ghouls and Guatemala: The 1994 Attacks on North American Women Accused of Body Organ Trafficking," *Journal of Latin American Anthropology* 4(1):112–33.

Adams, Vincanne. 2002. "Suffering the Winds of Lhasa: Politicized Bodies, Human Rights, and Humanism in Tibet," in *The Anthropology of Globalization: A Reader*. Jonathan Xavier Inda and Renato Rosaldo, eds. Oxford: Blackwell.

Agamben, Giorgio. 1998. *Homo Sacer, Sovereign Power and Bare Life*. Stanford, CA: Stanford University Press.

———. 2005. *State of Exception*. Chicago: University of Chicago Press.

Aguirre Beltrán, Gonzalo. 1953. *Formas de gobierno indígena*. México: Imprenta Universitaria.

———. 1957. *El proceso de aculturación y el cambio sociocultural en México*. México: UNAM.

———. 1967. *Regiones de refugio*. México: INI.

Alejos García, Jose. 1988. "Lak Oñel: Praxis y discurso en el agrarismo ch'ol." MA thesis in Social Anthropology, ENAH.

Alonso, Ana Maria. 1995. *Thread of Blood: Colonialism, Revolution, and Gender on Mexico's Northern Frontier*. Tucson: University of Arizona Press.

———. 2004. "Conforming Disconformity: Mestizaje, Hybridity, and the Aesthetics of Mexican Nationalism," *Cultural Anthropology* 19(4):459–90.

Alvarez, Sonia E., Evelina Dagnino, and Arturo Escobar. 1998. *Cultures of Politics, Politics of Cultures: Re-Visioning Latin American Social Movements*. Boulder, CO: Westview Press.

American Anthropological Association. 1947. "Statement on Human Rights," *American Anthropologist* 49(4).

Amnesty International. 1986. *Mexico: Human Rights in Rural Areas: An Exchange of*

Documents with the Mexican Government on Human Rights in Oaxaca and Chiapas. London: Amnesty International Publications.

Anaya, S. James. 1993. "The Capacity of International Law to Advance Ethnic or Nationality Rights Claims," *Iowa Law Review* 75:837–44.

Anderson, Benedict. 1983. *Imagined Communities: Reflections on the Origin and Spread of Nationalism*. London: Verso.

Anderson, Elizabeth. 2006. "Feminist Epistemology and Philosophy of Science," in *The Stanford Encyclopedia of Philosophy*. Edward N. Zalta, ed. Available at: http://plato .stanford.edu/archives/fa112006/entries/feminism-epistemology/.

An'Naím, Abdullahi Ahmed. 1992. *Human Rights in Cross-Cultural Perspective: A Quest for Consensus*. Philadelphia: University of Pennsylvania Press.

Anzaldúa, Gloria. 1987. *Borderlands/La Frontera: The New Mestiza*. San Francisco: Spinsters / Aunt Lute.

———. 1990. "Haciendo cara, una entrada," in *Making Face, Making Soul / Haciendo Caras: Creative and Critical Perspectives by Feminists of Color*, xxi. Gloria Anzaldúa, ed. San Francisco: Aunt Lute Books.

Appadurai, Arjun. 1990. "Disjuncture and Difference in the Global Cultural Economy," *Public Culture* 2(2).

———. 1996. *Modernity at Large: Cultural Dimensions of Globalization*. Minneapolis: University of Minnesota Press.

Arias Perez, Jacinto. 1994. *El arreglo de los pueblos indios: La incansable tarea de reconstitucion*. Chiapas: Secretaria de Educacion Publica.

Arizpe, Lourdes. 1993. "Scale and Interaction in Cultural Processes: Towards an Anthropological Perspective of Global Change." Paper presented at ICAES, July.

Asad, Talal, ed. 1973. *Anthropology and the Colonial Encounter*. Ithica, NY: Ithica Press.

Assies, Willem, Gerrit Burgwal, and Ton Salman. 1990. *Structures of Power, Movements of Resistance: An Introduction to the Theories of Urban Movements in Latin America*. Amsterdam: Center for Latin American Research and Documentation.

Assies, Willem, Gemma van der Haar, and Andre Hoekema, eds. 2000. *The Challenge of Diversity: Indigenous Peoples and Reform of the State in Latin America*. Amsterdam: Thela Thesis.

Azaola, Elena. 1996. *El delito de ser mujer*. Mexico, D. F.: CIESAS and Plaza y Valdes.

Bakhtin, Mikhail Mikhailovich. 1981. *The Dialogic Imagination: Four Essays*. Michael Holquist, ed. Austin: University of Texas Press.

Balokrishnan, Gopal. 2003. *Debating Empire*. London: Verso.

Barranco Avilés, María del Carmen. 1996. *El discurso de los derechos: Del problema terminológico al debate conceptual*. Madrid: Instituto de Derechos Humanos "Bartolomé de Las Casas," Universidad Carlos III de Madrid, Dykinson.

Barsh, Russell Lawrence. 1996. "Indigenous Peoples and the U.N. Commission on

Human Rights: A Case of the Immovable Object and the Irresistible Force," *Human Rights Quarterly* 18:782–813.

Bartra, Armando. 1991. "Debate sobre el ejido," *Cuadernos Agrarios* No. 3, Nueva Epoca, Setiembre–Diciembre. Mexico City.

Bartra, Roger. 1997. "Violencias indígenas," *La Jornada Semanal* 130:8–9.

Basch, Linda, et al. 1993. *Nations Unbound: Transnational Projects, Postcolonial Predicaments and Deterritorialized Nation-States*. Langhorne, PA: Gordon and Breach.

Baudrillard, Jean. 1988. "Simulacra and Simulation," in *Jean Baudrillard, Selected Writings*, 166–84. Mark Poster, ed. Stanford, CA: Stanford University Press.

Bedregal, Ximena. 1994. "Reflexiones desde nuestro feminismo," in *Chiapas, ¿y las mujeres, qué?* 1:43–56. Rosa Rojas, ed. México, D.F.: La Correa Feminista.

Bell, Daniel. 2000. *East Meets West: Human Rights and Democracy in East Asia*. Princeton, NJ: Princeton University Press.

Beller, Jonathan. 1996. "Desiring the Involuntary," in *Global/Local: Cultural Production and the Transnational Imaginary*. Rob Wilson and Wimal Dissanayake, eds. Durham, NC: Duke University Press.

Benford, David A., and Robert D. Snow. 1988. "Ideology, Frame Resonance, and Participant Mobilization," *International Social Movement Research* 1:197–217.

Bengoa, José, ed. 2000. *La emergencia indígena en América Latina*. Santiago de Chile: FCE.

Benhabib, Seyla, ed. 1996. *Democracy and Difference: Contesting the Boundaries of the Political*. Princeton, NJ: Princeton University Press.

Benjamin, Thomas. 1989. *Rich Land, Poor People: Politics and Society in Modern Chiapas*. Albuquerque: University of New Mexico Press.

Berreman, John. 1981. *The Politics of Truth: Essays in Critical Anthropology*. Madras: South Asia Publishers.

Berting, Jan, and Peter R. Baehr et al., eds. 1987. *Human Rights in a Pluralist World, Individuals and Collectivities*. The Hague: UNESCO.

———. 1990. *Human Rights in a Pluralist World: Individuals and Collectivities*. Westport, CT: Meckler.

Bhavnani, Kum Kum. 2000. *Feminism and "Race."* New York: Oxford University Press.

Binford, Leigh. 1996. *The El Mozote Massacre: Anthropology and Human Rights*. Tucson: University of Arizona Press.

Bonfil Batalla, Guillermo. 1987. *México Profundo*. México: SEP.

Brown, Wendy. 1995. *States of Injury: Power and Freedom in Late Modernity*. Princeton, NJ: Princeton University Press.

Brown, Wendy, and Janet Halley, eds. 2002. *Left Legalism / Left Critique*. Durham, NC: Duke University Press.

Brydon-Miller, M., D. Greenwood, and P. Maguire. 2003. "Why Action Research?" *Action Research* 1(1):9–28.

Brysk, Alison. 1994. "From Above and Below: Social Movements, the International System, and Human Rights in Argentina," *Comparative Political Studies* 26(3).

———. 1996. "Turning Weakness into Strength: The Internationalization of Indian Rights," *Latin American Perspectives* 23(2).

———, ed. 2002. *Globalization and Human Rights.* Berkeley: University of California Press.

Burbach, Roger. 1994. "Roots of the Postmodern Rebellion in Chiapas," *New Left Review* 205, May–June.

———. 1996. "A Zapatista Postmodern Perspective," *Monthly Review* 27(10):34–41.

Burchell, Graham. 1996. "Liberal Government and Techniques of the Self," in *Foucault and Political Reason: Liberalism, Neoliberalism, and Rationalities of Governance,* 19–36. A. T. Barry and N. Rose Osburne, eds. London: UCL Press.

Burguete Cal y Mayor, Araceli. 1994. "Chiapas: Maya Identity and the Zapatista Uprising," *Abya Yala News* 8(1 & 2).

———. 1997. "Procesos de autonomías de facto en Chiapas: Nuevas jurisdicciones y gobiernos paralelos en rebeldía." Unpublished manuscript.

———. 1998a. "Chiapas: Autonomías indígenas: La construcción de sujetos autónomos," *Quorum* VII(May–June):60.

———. 1998b. "Remunicipalización en Chiapas: Los retos," *Revista CEMOS-Memoria,* 114.

———. 1999a. "Poder local y autonomía indígena en Chiapas: Rebeliones comunitarias y luchas municipalistas," in *Espacios disputados: Transformaciones rurales en Chiapas.* M. E. Reyes et al., eds. México, D. F.: UAM-Xochimilco and ECOSUR.

———, ed. 1999b. *México: Experiencias de autonomía indígena.* Copenhagen: IWGIA.

———. 2000. "Poder local y gobiernos paralelos: Cambios jurídico-politicos y remunicipalización en los altos de Chiapas." Unpublished manuscript.

Burguete, Araceli, and Xochitl Leyva. 2000. *Los nuevos municipios en Chiapas: Un análisis de coyuntura.* San Cristóbal de Las Casas, Chiapas: Proyecto de investigación financiado por la Fundación Ford y el CIESAS.

Carbado, Devon W., ed. 1999. *Black Men on Race, Gender, and Sexuality: A Critical Reader.* New York: NYU Press.

Carozza, Paolo. 2003. "From Conquest to Constitutions: Retrieving a Latin American Tradition of the Idea of Human Rights," *Human Rights Quarterly* 25(2):281–313.

Carton de Grammont, Humberto, and Sara Lara Flores. 1982. "Algunas ideas acerca de la integración de un grupo indígena a la economía nacional: El caso de los Choles de Chiapas," *Revista Textual* 9:53–76.

Castells, Manuel. 1989. *The Informational City: Information Technology, Economic Restructuring and the Urban-Regional Process.* Oxford, UK and Cambridge, MA: Blackwell.

Castells, M., and G. Henderson, eds. 1987. *Global Restructuring and Territorial Development.* London: Sage.

Castro Apreza, Inés. 2006. "Las transformaciones políticas contemporáneas frente a los usos y costumbres: Minorías políticas y mujeres en Nicolás Ruiz, Chiapas." Tesis doctoral presentada en el programa de doctorado en Ciencias Políticas y Sociales en la Facultad de Ciencias Políticas y Sociales de la Universidad Nacional Autónoma de México (Mayo).

Ce Acatl. 1996. *Los primeros acuerdos de Sacam Ch'en: Compromisos propuestas y pronunciamientos de la mesa de trabajo 1: "Derechos y cultura Indígena."* México, D. F.: Número Especial 78–79 del 11 de marzo al 19 de abril.

Centro de Derechos Humanos "Fray Bartolomé de Las Casas" (CDHFBC). 1996. *Ni paz, ni justicia: Informe amplio acerca de la guerra civil que sufren los ch'oles en la zona norte de Chiapas.* San Cristóbal de Las Casas: Centro de Derechos Humanos "Fray Bartolomé de Las Casas."

Centro de Información y Análisis de Chiapas (CIACH) et al. 1997. *Para entender Chiapas: Chiapas en cifras.* México, D. F.: Imprentei.

Chandler, David. 2002. *From Kosovo to Kabul: Human Rights and International Intervention.* London: Pluto Press.

CIEPAC. 1999. *Militarization and Paramilitarization in Chiapas.* Available at: http://www.ciepac.org/analysis/militar.html.

Clarke, Ben, and Clifton Ross, eds. 1994. *Voice of Fire: Communiques and Interviews from the Zapatista National Liberation Army.* Berkeley, CA: New Earth Publications.

Cleaver, Harry. 2007. "Deep Currents Rising: Some Notes on the Global Challenge to Capitalism," in *Subverting the Present, Imagining the Future: Insurrection, Movement, Commons.* New York: Autonomedia. Available at: http://www.eco.utexas.edu/facstaff/Cleaver/DeepCurrentsRisingFina12.htm. Last accessed January 2007.

Clifford, James, and George E. Marcus, eds. 1986.*Writing Culture: The Poetics and Politics of Ethnography.* Berkeley, CA: University of California Press.

Cobo, Rosario, Adriana López Monjardín, y Sergio Sarmiento Silva, eds. 1998. *Poder local, derechos indígenas y municipios.* Mexico: Cuadernos Agrarios 16.

Collier, George. 1994a. *Basta! Land and the Zapatista Rebellion in Chiapas.* Oakland, CA: Food First Books.

———. 1994b. "The New Politics of Exclusion: Antecedents to the Rebellion in Mexico," *Dialectical Anthropology* 19(1).

———. 1994c. "Reforms on Mexico's Agrarian Code: Impacts on the Peasantry," *Research in Economic Anthropology* 15:105–28.

———. 2000. "Emergent Identities in Chiapas." Paper presented at the 2000 meetings of the Latin American Studies Association (LASA), Miami, FL.

Collier, Jane Fishburne, Bill Maurer, and Liliana Suarez-Navaz. 1995. "Sanctioned Identities: Legal Constructions of Modern Personhood," *Identities: Global Studies in Culture and Power* 2(1).

Collins, Patricia Hill. 1991. *Black Feminist Thought: Knowledge, Consciousness, and the Politics of Empowerment.* Boston: Unwin Hyman.

Comandanta Esther. 2001. "Speech Before the Congress of the Union." Available at: fzlnnet.org. Last accessed March 24, 2005. Also reprinted in Shannon Speed, Rosalva Aída Hernández Castillo, and Lynn Stephen, eds. 2006. *Dissident Women: Gender and Cultural Politics in Chiapas*. Austin: University of Texas Press.

Comisión Nacional de Derechos Humanos (CNDH). 1995. *El problema de las expulsiones en las comunidades indígenas de Chiapas y los derechos humanos*. México, D. F.: CNDH.

Constitución política de los Estados Unidos Mexicanos. 2000. México, D. F.: Instituto Federal Electoral.

Cornelius, W., and D. Mhyre, eds. 1998. *The Transformation of Rural Mexico: Reforming the Ejido Sector*. San Diego: University of California, San Diego, Center for U.S.-Mexican Studies.

Corrigan and Sayer. 1986. *The Great Arch: English State Formation as Cultural Revolution*. Oxford: Blackwell.

Corro, Salvador. 1998. "Asesinatos por consigna de simpatizantes zapatistas: Una familia de políticos chiapanecos armó una red de sicarios al servicio de empresarios, finqueros y caciques." *Proceso* No. 1123 (May 9).

Cowan, Jane K., Marie-Bénédicte Dembour, and Richard A. Wilson. 2001. *Culture and Rights: Anthropological Perspectives*. Cambride: Cambridge University Press.

Crenshaw, Kimberle. 1991. "Mapping the Margins: Intersectionality, Identity Politics, and Violence Against Women of Color," *Stanford Law Review* 43(6):1241–99.

Cruz Burguete, Jorge Luis, and Gabriela Robledo. 1989. "Vivier la diversidad en Betania y Nuevo Zinacantan: Las nuevas identidades comunitarias entre desplazados religiosos," *Gaceta Mensual* 4:10–14.

Davies, Maureen. 1987. "International Developments in Indigenous Rights," *Law and Anthropology* 2.

Davis, Angela. 1983. *Women, Race and Class*. New York: Vintage Press.

Dean, Bartholomew and Jerome M. Levi. 2003. *At the Risk of Being Heard: Identity, Indigenous Rights, and Postcolonial States*. Ann Arbor: University of Michigan Press.

Declaration of Barbados. 1971. Available at: http://www.nativeweb.org/papers/statements/state/barbados1.php. Last accessed May 15, 2007.

Declaration of Barbados II. 1977. Available at: http://www.nativeweb.org/papers/statements/state/barbados2.php. Last accessed May 15, 2007.

Deere, Carmen Diana and Magdalena Leon De Leal. 2001. *Empowering Women: Land and Property Rights in Latin America (Pitt Latin American Series)*. Pittsburg: University of Pittsburg Press.

———. 2002. "The Gender Asset Gap: Land in Latin America." Paper prepared for Latin America Regional Workshop on Land Issues, 19–22 (May), Pachuca, Hidalgo, Mexico.

deGaay Fortman, Bastiaan. 1987. "The Dialectic of Western Law in a Non-Western World," in *Human Rights in a Pluralist World: Individuals and Collectivities*. Jan Burting and Peter R. Baehr, eds. The Hague: UNESCO.

de la Fuente, Julio. 1968 (1952). "Ethnic and Communal Relations," in *Heritage of Conquest*. Sol Tax, ed. New York: Copper Square Publishers.

De la Peña, Guillermo. 2006. "A New Mexican Nationalism? Indigenous Rights, Constitutional Reform and the Conflicting Meanings of Multiculturalism," *Nations and Nationalism* 12(2):279–302.

De las Casas, Fray Bartolomé. 1974 (1542). *In Defense of the Indians*. Stafford Poole, ed. DeKalb: Northern Illinois University Press.

Deleuze, Gilles. 1988a. *Foucault*. Minneapolis: University of Minnesota Press.

———. 1988b. *Spinoza: Practical Philosophy*. San Francisco: City Lights Books.

———. 1993. *Expressionism in Philosophy: Spinoza*. London: Zone Books.

———. 1994. "Postscript on Societies of Control," in *Negotiations*. New York: Columbia University Press.

Deleuze, Gilles, and Felix Guattari. 1994. *What Is Philosophy?* New York: Columbia University Press.

Desarrollo, Paz y Justicia. 1997. *Ni derechos ni humanos en la Zona Norte de Chiapas: La otra verdad de los sucesos en la zona ch'ol, como respuesta a la versión difundida por el Centro de Derechos Humanos "Fray Bartolomé de Las Casas."* Tila, Chiapas: Publisher anonymous.

De Vos, Jan. 2002. *Una tierra para sembrar sueños: Historia reciente de la selva lacandona (1950–2000)*. Mexico City: Fondo de Cultura Económica.

Díaz de Salas, Marcelo. 1995. *San Bartolomé de los Llanos en la escritura de un etnógrafo, 1960–1961: Diario de Campo Venustiano Carranza, Chiapas*. Chiapas: Gobierno del Estado de Chiapas, UNICACH, Tuxtla Gutiérrez.

Díaz-Polanco, Hector. 1985. *La cuestion etnico-nacional*. Mexico City: Editorial Linea.

———. 1987. *Etnia, nacion y politica*. México: Juan Pablo Editorial.

———. 1991. *Autonomía regional: La autonomía de los pueblos indígenas*. México: Siglo XXI.

———. 1997. *La rebellion Zapatista y la autonomía*. México: Siglo XXI.

Donnelly, Jack. 1989. *Universal Human Rights in Theory and Practice*. Ithaca: Cornell University Press.

Doughty, Paul L. 1988. "Crossroads for Anthropology: Human Rights in Latin America," in *Human Rights and Anthropology*. Theodore E. Downing and Gilbert Kushner, eds. Cambridge, MA: Cultural Survival.

Downing, Theodore E., and Gilbert Kushner, eds. 1988. *Human Rights and Anthropology*. Cambridge, MA: Cultural Survival.

Dugan, Lisa. 2003. *The Twilight of Equality: Neoliberalism, Cultural Politics, and the Attack on Democracy*. Boston: Beacon Press.

Eber, Christine, and Christine Kovic, eds. 2003. *Women of Chiapas: Making History in Times of Struggle and Hope*. London: Routledge.

Echohawk, Crystal. 1998. "Chiapas: Massacre in Acteal," *Abya Yala News* (Spring).

Engle, Karen. 2005. "International Human Rights and Feminisms: When Discourses Keep Meeting" in *International Law: Modern Feminist Approaches*. Doris Buss and Ambreena Manji, eds. Oxford: Hart Publishing.

Escobar, Arturo, and Sonia Alvarez, eds. 1992. *The Making of Social Movements in Latin America: Identity, Strategy, and Democracy*. Boulder, CO: Westview Press.

Falcón, Romana. 1994. "Force and the Search for Consent: The Role of the Jefaturas Políticas of Coahuila in National State Formation," in *Everyday Forms of State Formation: Revolution and the Negotiation of Rule in Modern Mexico*. Gilbert M. Joseph and Daniel Nugent, eds. Durham, NC: Duke University Press.

Falk, Richard. 1988. "The Rights of Peoples (in Particular Indigenous Peoples)," in *The Rights of Peoples*. J. Crawford, ed. Oxford: Clarendon.

———. 1992. "Cultural Foundations for the International Protection of Human Rights," in *Human Rights in Cross-Cultural Perspective: A Quest for Consensus*. Abdullahi Ahmed An'Naím, ed. Philadelphia: University of Pennsylvania Press.

———. 2002. "Interpreting the Interaction Between Global Markets and Human Rights," in *Globalization and Human Rights*. Alison Brysk, ed. Berkeley: University of California Press.

Fals Borda, O. 1979. "Investigating Reality in Order to Transform It: The Colombian Experience," *Dialectical Anthropology* 4(March):33–55.

Fals Borda, O., and M. A. Rahman. 1991. *Action and Knowledge: Breaking the Monopoly*. New York: Apex Press.

Favre, Henri. 1973. *Cambio y continuidad entre los mayas de México*. México: Siglo XXI.

Featherstone, Mike, ed. 1990. *Global Culture: Nationalism, Globalization and Modernity*. London: Sage.

Feldman, Shelley. 1997. "NGOs and Civil Society: (Un)stated Contradictions," *Annals of the American Academy of Political and Social Science* 554(November):46–65.

Foss, Daniel A., and Ralph Larkin, eds. 1986. *Beyond Revolution: A New Theory of Social Movements*. South Hadley, MA: Bergin and Garvey.

Foucault, Michel. 1979. *Discipline and Punish: The Birth of the Prison*. New York: Vintage Books.

———. 1980. "Two Lectures," in *Power/Knowledge: Selected Interviews and Other Writings*. Colin Gordon, ed. New York: Random House.

———. 1989. *The Archaeology of Knowledge*. London: Routledge.

———. 1991. "Governmentality," in *The Foucault Effect: Studies in Governmentality*. G. Burchell, C. Gordon, and P. Miller, eds. London: Harvester Wheatsheaf.

———. 1993. "The Subject and Power," in *Michel Foucault: Beyond Structuralism and Hermenuetics*. Hubert Dreyfus and Paul Rabinow, eds. Chicago: University of Chicago Press.

———. 1997. *Essential Works of Foucault, 1954–1984, Volume 1, Ethics: Subjectivity and Truth*. Paul Rabinow, ed.; Robert Hurley et al., trans. New York: The New Press.

Foweraker, Joe, and Anne L. Craig, eds. 1990. *Popular Movements and Political Change in Mexico*. Boulder, CO: Lynne Reinner.

Freire, P. 1982. "Creating Alternative Research Methods: Learning to Do It by Doing It," in *Creating Knowledge: A Monopoly?*, 29–37. B. Hall, A. Gillette, and R. Tandon, eds. New Delhi: Society for Participatory Research in Asia.

Friedlander, Judith. 1974. *Being Indian in Hueyapan: A Study of Forced Identity in Contemporary Mexico*. New York: St. Martin's Press.

Galenkamp, M. 1993. *Individualism vs. Collectivism: The Concept of Collective Rights*. Rotterdam: Rotterdam Filosofiche Studies.

Gamio, Manuel. 1916. *Forjando patria*. Porrúa Hnos, Mexico.

García Aguilar, María del Carmen. 1998a. "Las organizaciones no gubernamentales en los espacios rurales de Chiapas: Reflexiones en turno a su actuacion política," in *Espacios disputadoas: Transformaciones rurales en Chiapas*. María Eugenia Reyes Ramos, Reyna Moguel Viveros, y Gemma van der Haar, eds. México, D. F.: UAM-Xochimilco and ECOSUR.

———. 1998b. "Las organizaciones no gubernamentales en Chiapas: Alcances y límites de su actuación política," in *ANUARIO 1997*. Tuxtla Gutiérrez, Chiapas: Gobierno del estado de Chiapas y UNICACH.

García Canclini, Néstor. 1989. *Hybrid Cultures: Strategies for Entering and Leaving Modernity*. Minneapolis: University of Minneapolis Press.

García de León, Antonio. 1985. *Resistencia yutopía*. Mexico, D. F.: Era.

Garza Caligarís, Anna María. 2002. *Género, interlegalidad y conflicto en San Pedro Chenalho*. San Cristóbal de Las Casas: IEI/UNAM/UNACO.

Gill, Lesley. 2000. *Teetering on the Rim: Global Restructuring, Daily Life, and the Armed Retreat of the Bolivian State*. New York: Columbia University Press.

Gledhill, John. 1997. "Liberalism, Socio-economic Rights and the Politics of Identity: From Moral Economy to Indigenous Rights," in *Human Rights, Culture and Context: Anthropological Perspectives*. R. Wilson, ed. London: Pluto Press.

Global Exchange et al. 1998. *On the Offensive: Intensified Military Occupation in Chiapas Six Months Since the Massacre at Acteal*. Available at: http://www.globalexchange.org/campaigns/mexico/OntheOffensive.html.

———. 2000. *Las fuerzas armadas de México: Siempre cerca, siempre lejos*. México: Global Exchange, CIEPAC y CENCOS.

Goldstein, Daniel. 2007. "Human Rights as Culprit, Human Rights as Victim: Rights and Security in the State of Exception," in *The Practice of Human Rights: Tracking the Law Between the Global and the Local*, 49–99. Mark Goodale and Sally Engle Merry, eds. Cambridge: Cambridge University Press.

Gómez Rivera, Magdalena, ed. 1997. *Derecho indígena*. México: INI.

González Hernández, Miguel, and Elvia Quintanar Quintanar. 1999. "La reconstrucción de la región autónomo norte y el ejercicion del gobierno municipal," in *México: Expe-*

riencias de autonomía indígena. Araceli Burguete Cal y Mayor, ed. Copenhagen: IWGIA.

Goodale, Mark. 2005. "Empires of Law: Discipline and Resistance within the Transnational System," *Social & Legal Studies* 14(4). London: Sage.

———. 2007. "The Power of Right(s): Tracking Empires of Law and New Modes of Social Resistance in Bolivia (and elsewhere)," in *The Practice of Human Rights: Tracking Law Between the Global and the Local*, 130–62. Mark Goodale and Sally Engle Merry, eds. Cambridge: Cambridge University Press.

Gordon, Edmund T. 1991. "Anthropology and Liberation," in *Decolonizing Anthropology: Moving Further toward an Anthropology of Liberation*, 149–67. Faye Harrison, ed. Washington, DC: American Anthropological Association.

Gough, Kathleen. 1968. "Anthropology and Imperialism," *Monthly Review* 19(11):12–27.

Gourevitch, Alex. 2004. "Are Human Rights Liberal?" Available at: http://www.columbia.edu/cu/polisci/pdf-files/gourevitch.pdf. Last accessed October 15, 2005.

Gramsci, Antonio. 1971. *Selections from the Prison Notebooks*. New York: International Publishers.

Grandin, Greg. 2004. *The Last Colonial Massacre: Latin America in the Cold War*. Chicago: University of Chicago Press.

Greenwood, Davydd, and Morton Levin. 1998. *Introduction to Action Research: Social Research for Social Change*. London: Sage.

Guehenno, Jean Marie. 1995. *The End of the Nation State*. Minneapolis: University of Minnesota Press.

Gupta, Akil, and Jim Ferguson. 1992. "Beyond 'Culture': Space, Identity, and the Politics of Difference," *Cultural Anthropology Theme Issue* (February).

Gurguha, Francisco. 2000. "Nicolás Ruiz: Tierra sin ley." *Areópago* 275(March 6):6–9.

Gustafson, Bret. 2002. "Paradoxes of Liberal Indigenism: Indigenous Movements, State Processes, and Intercultural Reform in Bolivia," in *The Politics of Ethnicity: Indigenous Peoples in Latin American States*, 267–306. David Maybury-Lewis, ed. Cambridge, MA: Harvard University Press.

Hale, Charles A. 1990. *The Transmission of Liberalism in Late Nineteenth-Century Mexico*. Princeton, NJ: Princeton University Press.

———. 2000. "The Civil Law Tradition and Constitutionalism in Twentieth-Century Mexico: The Legacy of Emilio Rabasa," *Law and History Review* 18(2):257–80.

Hale, Charles R. 1994. *Resistance and Contradiction: Miskito Indians and the Nicaraguan State*. Stanford, CA: Stanford University Press.

———. 1997. "Consciousness, Violence, and the Politics of Memory in Guatemala," *Current Anthropology* 38(5):817–38.

———. 1999. "Activist Research." Talk presented at the Fellow's Conference of the SSRC-MacArthur Fellowship on Peace and Security in a Changing World. New Delhi, India.

———. 2002. "Does Multiculturalism Menace? Governance, Cultural Rights and the Politics of Identity in Guatemala," *Journal of Latin American Studies* 34(3):485–524.

———. 2004. "Rethinking Indigenous Politics in the Era of the 'Indio Permitido.'" *NACLA* 38(2):16–21.

———. 2006. "Activist Research vs. Cultural Critique: Indigenous Land Rights and the Contradictions of Politically Engaged Anthropology," *Cultural Anthropology* 21(1):96–120.

———. 2007. "In Praise of 'Reckless Minds': Making a Case for Activist Anthropology," in *Anthropology Put to Work*. L. W. Field and R. Fox, eds. Gordonsville, VA: Berg Publishers.

Hall, Stuart. 1991. "Old and New Identities, Old and New Ethnicities," in *Culture, Globalization and the World-System: Contemporary Conditions for the Representation of Identity*. Anthony King, ed. Binghamton: State University of New York.

———. 1994. "Cultural Identity and Diaspora," in *Colonial Discourse and Post Colonial Theory*. P. Williams and S. Chrisman, eds. New York: Columbia University Press.

Hamelink, C. 1983. *Cultural Autonomy in Global Communications*. New York: Longman.

Hannerz, Ulf. 2002. "Notes on the Global Ecumene," in *The Anthropology of Globalization: A Reader*. Jonathan Xavier Inda and Renato Rosaldo, eds. Oxford: Blackwell.

Haraway, Donna. 1988. "Situated Knowledge: The Science Question in Feminism as a Site of Discourse on the Privilege of Partial Perspective." *Feminist Studies* 14(3):575–99.

———. 1989. *Primate Visions*. New York: Routledge.

Harding, Sandra. 1986. *The Science Question in Feminism*. Ithaca, NY: Cornell University Press.

Hardt, Michael. 1990. "Translator's Foreword," in *The Savage Anamoly: The Power of Spinoza's Metaphysics and Politics*. Antonio Negri. Minneapolis: University of Minnesota Press.

———. 1998. "The Withering of Civil Society," in *Deleuze and Guattari: New Mapping in Politics and Philosophy*, 23–39. Eleanor Kaufman and Kevin Jon Heller, eds. Minneapolis: University of Minnesota Press.

Hardt, Michael, and Antonio Negri. 2001. *Empire*. Cambridge, MA: Harvard University Press.

———. 2004. *Multitude*. New York: Penguin Press.

Harrison, Faye Venecia, ed. 1991. *Decolonizing Anthropology: Moving Further Toward an Anthropology for Liberation*. Washington, DC: AAA Association of Black Anthropologists.

Harvey, David. 1989. *The Condition of Postmodernity and Enquiry into the Origins of Cultural Change*. Oxford: Blackwell.

———. 1993. "Class Relations, Social Justice and the Politics of Difference," in *Place and the Politics of Identity*. M. Keith and S. Pile, eds. London: Routledge.

Harvey, Neil. 1998. *The Chiapas Rebellion: The Struggle for Land and Democracy.* Durham, NC: Duke University Press.

Hayden, Cori. 2003. *When Nature Goes Public: The Making and Unmaking of Bioprospecting in Mexico.* Princeton, NJ: Princeton University Press.

Heath, John Richard. 1992. "Enhancing the Contribution of Land Reform to Mexican Agricultural Development," *World Development* 20:695–711.

Henríquez, Elio. 1998. "Detectó: a CIDH serias anomalías en el juicio a 16 detenidos en Taniperlas," *La Jornada*, June 29.

Hernández Castillo, Rosalva Aída. 1995. "De la sierra a la selva: Identidades étnicas y religiosas en la frontera sur," in *Chiapas, los rumbos de otra Historia.* Juan Pedro Siquiera and Mario Humberto Ruz, eds. México: UNAM, CIESAS, CEMCA, Universidad de Guadalajara.

———. 1998a. "Construyendo la utopia: Esperanzas y desafios de las mujeres Chiapanecas de frente al siglo XXI," in *La otra palabra: Mujeres y violence en chiapas antes y después de acteal.* Aída Hernández, ed. México: CIESAS.

———, ed. 1998b. *La otra palabra: Mujeres y violence en chiapas antes y después de acteal.* México: CIESAS.

———. 2001a. *Histories and Stories from Chiapas: Border Identities in Southern Mexico.* Austin: University of Texas Press.

———. 2001b. "Indigenous Law and Identity Politics in Mexico: Indigenous Women Recreate Multiculturalism," in *Political and Legal Anthropology Review (PoLAR)* 25(1):90–109.

———. 2002. "Indigenous Law and Identity Politics in Mexico: Indigenous Men's and Women's Struggles for a Multicultural Nation," *Political and Legal Anthropology Review (PoLAR)* 24(2):90–109.

———. 2006. "Between Feminist Ethnocentricity and Ethnic Essentialism: The Zapatistas' Demands and the National Indigenous Women's Movement," in *Dissident Women: Gender and Cultural Politics in Chiapas*, 57–74. Shannon Speed, Rosalva Aída Hernández Castillo, and Lynn Stephen, eds. Austin: University of Texas Press.

Hernández Castillo, Rosalva Aída, and Ronald Nigh. 1997. "Global Process and Local Identity: Indians of the Sierra Madre of Chiapas and the International Organic Market," *American Anthropologist* 100(1):1–12.

Hernández Castillo, Rosalva Aída, Sarela Paz, and María Teresa Sierra, eds. 2004. *El estado y los indígenas en tiempos del PAN: Neoindigenismo, legalidad e identidad.* México D. F.: CIESAS-Porrúa.

Hernández Navarro, Luis. 1998. "Ciudadanos iguales, ciudadanos diferentes," in *Los Acuerdos de San Andrés.* Luis Hernández Navarro and Ramón Vera Herrera, eds. México: ERA.

Hernández Navarro, Luis, and Ramón Vera Herrera. 1998. *Los Acuerdos de San Andres.* México: ERA.

Herskovits, Melville. 1947. "Statement on Human Rights," *American Anthropologist* 49(4):539–43

Hewlitt de Alcántara, Cynthia. 1984. *Anthropological Perspectives on Rural Mexico*. London: Routledge.

Hobsbawm, Eric, and Terence Ranger, eds. 1983. *The Invention of Tradition*. Cambridge, UK: Cambridge University Press.

hooks, bell. 1984. *Feminist Theory from Margin to Center*. Boston, MA: South End Press.

———. 1995. "The Oppositional Gaze: Black Female Spectators," in *Feminism and Tradition in Aesthetics*, 142–59. Peggy Zeglin Brand and Carolyn Korsmeyer, eds. State College: Pennsylvania State University Press.

Horowitz, Irving. 1967. *The Rise and Fall of Project Camelot: Studies in the Relationship Between Social Science and Practical Politics*. Cambridge, MA: MIT Press.

Human Rights Watch. 1997. *Implausible Deniability*. New York: Human Rights Watch.

Humphrey, Brett M. 2000. "The Post-NAFTA Mexican Peso Crisis: Bailout or Aid? Isolationism or Globalization?" *Hinckley Journal of Politics* 2(1):33–40.

Ignatieff, Michael. 2001. *Human Rights as Politics and Idolatry*. Princeton, NJ: Princeton University Press.

Instituto Nacional de Estadística, Geografía y Informática (INEGI). 1990. *XI Censo general de población y vivienda*. Available at: www.inegi.gov.mx.

———. 2000. *XII Censo general de población y vivienda*. Available at: www.inegi .gov.mx.

———. 2005. *II Conteo de Población y Vivienda*. Available at: www.inegi.gov.mx.

Jackson, Jean, and Kay Warren. 2005. "Indigenous Movements in Latin America, 1992–2004: Controversies, Ironies, New Directions," in *Annual Review of Anthropology* 34:549–73.

Jameson, Fredric. 1983. "Postmodernism and Consumer Society," in *The Anti-Aesthetic: Essays in Postmodern Culture*. H. Foster, ed. Port Townsend, WA: Bay Press.

———. 1991. *Postmodernism, or the Cultural Logic of Late Capitalism*. Durham, NC: Duke University Press.

———. 1999. "Notes on Globalization as a Philosophical Issue," in *The Cultures of Globalization*. Fredric Jameson and Masao Miyoshi, eds. Durham, NC: Duke University Press.

Jameson, Fredric, and Masao Miyoshi, eds. 1998. *The Cultures of Globalization*. Durham, NC: Duke University Press.

Jelin, Elizabeth, and Eric Hershberg. 1996. *Constructing Democracy: Human Rights, Citizenship, and Society in Latin America*. Boulder, CO: Westview Press.

Jenkins, J. Craig, and Kurt Schock. 1992. "Global Structures and Political Processes in the Study of Domestic Political Conflict," *Annual Review of Sociology* 18:161–85.

Joseph, Gilbert M., and Daniel Nugent. 1994. *Everyday Forms of State Formation: Revo-*

lution and the Negotiation of Rule in Modern Mexico. Durham, NC: Duke University Press.

Joseph, Miranda. 2002. *Against the Romance of Community.* Minneapolis: University of Minnesota Press.

Joyce, Christopher and Eric Stove. 1991. *Witnesses from the Grave: The Stories Bones Tell.* Boston: Little, Brown.

Kamenka, E. 1988. "Human Rights; People's Rights," in *The Rights of Peoples.* J. Crawford, ed. Oxford: Clarendon.

Kampwirth, Karen. 2002. *Women and Guerrilla Movements: Nicaragua, El Salvador, Chiapas, Cuba.* University Park: Pennsylvania State University Press.

Kapur, Ratna. 2002. "The Tragedy of Victimization Rhetoric: Resurrecting the 'Native' Subject in International / Post-Colonial Feminist Legal Politics," in *Harvard Human Rights Journal* 15 (Spring):1–37.

Kearney, Michael. 1991. "Borders and Boundaries of Self and State at the End of Empire," *Journal of Historical Sociology* 4(1).

———. 1995. "The Local and the Global: The Anthropology of Globalization and Transnationalism," *Annual Review of Anthropology* 24:547–65.

———. 1996. *Reconceptualizing the Peasantry: Anthropology in Global Perspective.* Boulder, CO: Westview Press.

Kearney, Michael, and Carol Nagengast. 1989. "Anthropological Perspectives on Transnational Communities in Rural California." *Farm Labor and Rural Policy*, No. 3. Davis: California Institute for Rural Studies.

Keck, Margaret, and Kathryn Sikkink. 1998. *Activists Beyond Borders: Advocacy Networks in International Politics.* Ithaca, NY: Cornell University Press.

Kennis, Andrew. 2002. "Peace in Chiapas: Farther Away Now Than Ever Before," *Synthesis/Regeneration* 27 (Winter).

Knight, Alan. 1986. *The Mexican Revolution.* 2 Vols. New York: Cambridge University Press.

Koff, Clea. 2004. *The Bone Woman: A Forensic Anthropologist's Search for Truth in the Mass Graves of Rwanda, Bosnia, Croatia, and Kosovo.* New York: Random House.

Kovic, Christine. 1997. *Walking with One Heart: Human Rights and the Catholic Church Among the Maya of Highland Chiapas.* Ph.D. dissertation in Anthropology submitted to the City University of New York.

———. 2005. *Mayan Voices for Human Rights: Displaced Catholics in Highland Chiapas.* Austin: University of Texas Press.

Kovic, Christine, and Christine Eber. 2003. "Introduction," in *Women of Chiapas: Making History in Times of Struggle and Hope.* London: Routledge.

Krauze, Enrique. 1999. "Chiapas: The Indians' Prophet," *New York Review of Books* (December 16):65–73.

Kuhn, Thomas S. 1962. *The Structure of Scientific Revolutions*. Chicago: University of Chicago Press.

Kymlicka, W. 1997. *Multicultural Citizenship: A Liberal Theory of Minority Rights*. Oxford: Oxford University Press.

Lewis, Tessa. 2002. "Agrarian Change and Privatization of *Ejido* Lands in Northwestern Mexico," *Journal of Agrarian Change* 2(3):402–20.

Ley de Derechos y Cultura Indígena del Estado de Chiapas. 1994. Gobierno del Estado de Chiapas. Chiapas: Tuxtla Gutiérrez.

Leyva Solano, Xochitl. 1995. "Catequistas, misioneros y tradiciones en Las Cañadas," in *Chiapas, rumbos de otra Historia*. Juan Pedro Viquiera and Mario Humberto Ruz, eds. México, D. F.: Centro de Estudios Mayas del Instituto de Investigaciones Filológicas y Coordinacion de Humanidades (UNAM), CIESAS, CEMCA, Universidad de Guadalajara.

Leyva Solano, Xochitl, and Gabriel Ascencio Franco. 1996. *Lacandonia al Filo del Agua*. México: CIESAS, CIHMECH, UNACH, UNICACH y Fondo de Cultura Economica.

Leyva Solano, Xochitl, and Shannon Speed. 2001. "Los derechos humanos: Un '*discurso globalizado*' con 'gramatica moral,' " in *Derechos humanos en el area maya*. Pedro Pitarch and Julián López García, eds. Madrid: Sociedad Española de Estudios Mayas and Universidad Complutense de Madrid.

Lisbona Guillén, Miguel. 1992. "Un intercambio ritual entre dos pueblos de Chiapas: Totolapa y Nicolás Ruiz," *Revista del CONSEJO*, No. 6. Chiapas: Consejo Estatal de Fomento a la Investigación y Difusión de la Cultura, Gobierno del Estado de Chiapas, Tuxtla Gutiérrez.

Lomnitz-Adler, Claudio. 1992. *Exits from the Labyrinth: Culture and Ideology in the Mexican National Space*. Berkeley: University of California Press.

Londoño, Juan Luis, and Miguel Székely. 2000. "Persistent Poverty and Excess Inequality: Latin America, 1970–1995," *Journal of Applied Economics* 3(May):93–134.

López Astrain, Marta Patricia. 1996. *La guerra de baja intensidad en México*. Mexico City: Universidad Iberoamericana and Plaza and Valdés.

López Monjardín, Adriana, and Dulce María Rebolledo Millán. 1998. "La resistencia en los municipios zapatistas" in *Poder local, derechos indígenas y municipios*, Cuadernos agrarios 16. Rosario Cobo, Adriana López Monjardín, and Sergio Sarmiento Silva, eds. Mexico: Cuadernos Agrarios A.C.

Lorde, Audre. 1984. *Sister/Outsider*. Freedom, CA: Crossing Press Books.

Lowe, Lisa. 1991. "Heterogenity, Hybridity, Multiplicity: Marking Asian American Differences," *Diáspora* 1(1):24–44.

Lukes, Stephan. 1991. *Moral Conflict and Politics*. Oxford: Clarendon Press.

———. 1993. "Five Fables about Human Rights," in *On Human Rights: The Oxford Amnesty Lectures*. S. Shute and S. Hurley, eds. New York: Basic Books.

Lutz, Ellen L. 2005. "Cultural Survival: A Human Rights Organization," *Cultural Survival Quarterly* 28.2 (June 15).

Magnarella, P. J. 1994. "Anthropology, Human Rights and Justice," *International Journal of Anthropology* 9(1):3–7.

Mallon, Florencia. 1994. "Reflections on the Ruins: Everyday Forms of State Formation in Nineteenth Century Mexico," in *Everyday Forms of State Formation: Revolution and the Negotiation of Rule in Modern Mexico*. Gilbert M. Joseph and Daniel Nugent, eds. Durham, NC: Duke University Press.

———. 1995. *Peasant and Nation: The Making of Postcolonial Mexico and Peru*. Berkeley: University of California Press.

———. 1996. "Constructing *Mestizaje* in Latin America: Authenticity, Marginality and Gender in the Claiming of Ethnic Identities," *Journal of Latin American Anthropology* 2(1):170–181.

Mannheim, Bruce, and Dennis Tedlock, eds. 1995. *The Dialogic Emergence of Culture*. Chicago: University of Illinois Press.

Manz, Beatria. 1988. *Refugees of a Hidden War: The Aftermath of Counterinsurgency in Guatemala*. Albany: State University of New York Press.

Maples, William and Michael Browning. 1994. *Dead Men Do Tell Tales: The Strange and Fascinating Case of a Forensic Anthropologist*. New York: Doubleday.

Marcos, Subcomandante. 2001. Communiqué from the Clandestine Revolutionary Indigenous Committee-General Command of the Zapatista Army of National Liberation. Mexico (April 29). Available at: fzlnnet.org. Last accessed October 15, 2005.

———. 2004a. "Four Fallacies about the Juntas de Buen Gobierno" (August). Available at: http://flag.blackened.net/revolt/mexico/ezln/2004/marcos/amessageAUG.html. Last accessed May 2007.

———. 2004b. "Three Shoulders" (August). Available at: http://flag.blackened.net/revolt/mexico/ezln/2004/marcos/amessageAUG.html. Last accessed May 2007.

Marcus, George. 1995. "Ethnography In/Of the World System: The Emergence of Multi-Sited Ethnography," *Annual Review of Anthropology* 24(95):117.

Marín, Carlos. 1998. "Plan del ejército en Chiapas, desde 1994: Crear bandas paramilitares, desplazar a la población, destruir las bases de apoyo del EZLN," *Proceso* No. 1105 (January 4).

Mato, Daniel. 1994. "Transnational and International Relations and the Fights for Cultural Rights in Latin American Countries," *Abstracts* 239.

———. 1996. "The Indigenous Uprising in Chiapas: The Politics of Institutionalized Knowledge and Mexican Perspectives," *Identities*. Special Issue: Indigenous Peoples, Global Terrains 3(1–2).

Mattelart, A. 1983. *Transnationals and the Third World: The Struggle for Culture*. South Hadley, MA: Bergin and Garvey.

Mattiace, Shannan L. 1997. " 'Zapata Vive!': The EZLN, Indigenous Politics, and the Autonomy Movement in Mexico," *Journal of Latin American Anthropology* 3(1):32–71.

———. 2003. *To See with Two Eyes: Peasant Activism and Indian Autonomy in Chiapas, Mexico.* Albuquerque: University of New Mexico Press.

Maybury-Lewis, David H. P. 1990. "A Special Sort of Pleading: Anthropology at the Service of Ethnic Groups," in *Advocacy and Anthropology: First Encounters.* Robert Paine, ed., 130–48. St. John's: Memorial University of Newfoundland.

McQuown, Norman, and Julian Pitt-Rivers, eds. 1970. *Ensayos de antropología en la Zona Central de Chiapas.* México: INI.

Menchú, Rigoberta and Elizabeth Burgos Debray. 1987. *I, Rigoberta Menchu: An Indian Woman in Guatemala.* London: Verso.

Menon, Nivedita. 2004. *Recovering Subversion: Feminist Politics Beyond the Law.* Chicago: University of Chicago Press.

Merry, Sally Engle. 1992. "Anthropology, Law, and Transnational Processes," *Annual Review of Anthropology* 21:357–79.

———. 1997. "Legal Pluralism and Transnational Culture: The *Ka Ho'okolokolonui Kanaka Maoli* Tribunal, Hawai'i, 1993," in *Human Rights, Culture and Context.* Richard A. Wilson, ed. London: Pluto Press.

———. 2003. "Human Rights Law and the Demonization of Culture (and Anthropology along the Way)" *Political and Legal Anthropology Review (PoLAR)* 26(1):55–77.

———. 2006. *Human Rights and Gender Violence: Translating International Law into Local Justice.* Chicago: University of Chicago Press.

Messer, Ellen. 1993. "Anthropology and Human Rights," *Annual Review of Anthropology* 221:224–25.

———. 1995. "Anthropology and Human Rights in Latin America," *Journal of Latin American Anthropology* 1(1):48–97.

Meyer, Birgit, and Peter Geschiere. 1999. "Introduction," in *Globalization and Identity: Dialectics of Flow and Closure.* Birgit Meyer and Peter Geschiere, eds. Oxford: Blackwell Publishers.

Meyer, Jean, et al. 2000. *Samuel Ruiz en San Cristóbal.* México, D. F.: Tusquets Editores.

Mignolo, Walter. 1998. "Globalization, Civilization Processes, and the Relocation of Languages and Cultures," in *The Cultures of Globalization.* Fredric Jameson and Masao Miyoshi, eds. Durham, NC: Duke University Press.

Minh-ha, Trinh T. 1989. *Woman, Native, Other: Writing Postcoloniality and Feminism.* Indianapolis: Indiana University Press.

Minnesota Advocates. 1992. *Report on the Independence of the Judiciary in Mexico.* Minneapolis: Minnesota Advocates.

Miyoshi, Masao. 1993. "A Borderless World? From Colonialism to Transnationalism and the Decline of the Nation-State," *Critical Inquiry* 19:726–51.

Moguel, Julio, Carlota Botey, and Luis Hernández, eds. 1992. *Autonomía y nuevos sujetos sociales en el desarrollo rural*. México: Siglo XXI.

Mohanty, Chandra. 1988. "Under Western Eyes: Feminist Scholarship and Colonial Discourses," *Feminist Review* 30(Autumn):61–88.

———. 2003. *Feminism Without Borders: Decolonizing Theory, Practicing Solidarity*. Durham, NC: Duke University Press.

Molina, Virginia. 1976. *San Bartolomé de los Llanos: Una urbanización frenada*. México: SEP-INAH.

Molyneux, Maxine. 1985. "Mobilization without Emancipation?: Women's Interests, State and Revolution in Nicaragua," *Feminist Studies* 2(2):227–54.

Moncada, María. 1983. "Movimiento campesino y estructura de poder: Venustiano Carranza, Chiapas," in *Revista Textual* 13:65–76.

Montag, Warren. 1999. *Bodies, Masses, Power*. London: Verso Press.

Montemayor, Carlos. 1997. *Chiapas: La rebelión indígena de México*. México, D. F.: Joaquín Moritz.

Moraga, Cherie, and Gloria Anzaldúa. 2002 (1989). *This Bridge Called My Back: Writings by Radical Women of Color*. Berkeley: Third Woman Press.

Morales, Patricia, ed. 2001. *Pueblos indígenas, derechos humanos, e interdependencia global*. México: Siglo XXI.

Morales Avendaño, Juan María. 1974. *Rincones de Chiapas: Ensayo monográfico sobre San Bartolomé de los Llanos*. Chiapas: Venustiano Carranza.

———. 1977. *Rincones de Chiapas: Evolución de la tenencia de la tierraen San Bartolomé de los Llanos*. Chiapas: Venustiano Carranza.

———. 1985. *San Bartolomé de los Llanos en la historia de Chiapas*. Chiapas: UNACH, Tuxtla Gutiérrez.

Mutua, Kagendo, and Beth Swadener. 2004. *Decolonizing Research in Cross-Cultural Contexts: Critical Personal Narratives*. New York: State University of New York Press.

Nagengast, Carol. 1994. "Violence, Terror, and the Crisis of the State," *Annual Review of Anthropology* 23:109–36.

Nagengast, Carol, and Michael Kearney. 1990. "Mixtec Ethnicity: Social Identity, Political Consciousness, and Political Activism." *Latin American Research Review* 25(2).

Nagengast, Carol, and Terence Turner. 1997. "Introduction: Universal Human Rights Versus Cultural Relativity," *Journal of Anthropological Research* 53(Fall):269–72.

Nash, June. 1995. "The Reassertion of Indigenous Identity: Mayan Responses to State Intervention in Chiapas," *Latin American Research Review* (December).

———. 1997. "Press Reports of the Maya Rebellion: Towards a Transnationalized Communication," *Journal of Latin American Anthropology* 2(2):42–75.

———. 2001. *Mayan Visions: The Quest for Autonomy in an Age of Globalization*. New York and London: Routledge.

Negri, Antonio. 1989. *The Politics of Subversion: A Manifesto for the Twenty-first Century.* Cambridge, UK: Polity Press.

————. 1990. *The Savage Anomaly: The Power of Spinoza's Metaphysics and Politics.* Minneapolis: University of Minnesota Press.

————. 1999. *Insurgencias: Constituent Power and the Modern State.* Minneapolis: University of Minnesota Press.

Nelson, Diane. 1999. *A Finger in the Wound: Body Politics in Quincentennial Guatemala.* Berkeley: University of California Press.

Nordstrom, Carolyn, and JoAnn Martin. 1992. *The Paths to Domination, Resistance and Terror.* Berkeley: University of California Press.

Nugent, Daniel. 1996. "Northern Intellectuals and the EZLN," *Monthly Review* 37(3):124–38.

Okin, Susan Moller. 1999. *Is Multiculturalism Bad for Women?* Princeton, NJ: Princeton University Press.

Olivera, Mercedes. 1997. "Acteal: Los efectos de la guerra de baja intensidad," in *La otra palabra: Mujeres y violencia en Chiapas, antes y despues de Acteal.* Rosalva Aída Hernández Castillo, ed. México, D. F.: CIESAS, COLEM, CIAM.

————. 1998. "Práctica feminista en el movimiento zapatista de liberación nacional," in *Chiapas, y las mujeres, qué?* 2:168–84. Rosa Rojas, ed. México, D. F.: La Correa Feminista.

Ortiz Pardo, Francisco, and Carlos Puig. 1997. "El narco mexicano: La sangrienta guerra entre cárteles, el asesinato de Posadas, la colusión de policías, la compra de autoridades," *Revista proceso* 1083 (August 3). México, D. F.

Otzoy, Irma. Forthcoming. "Indigenous Law and Gender Dialogues," in *Human Rights in the Maya Region: Global Politics, Moral Engagements, and Cultural Contentions.* Pedro Pitarch, Shannon Speed, and Xochitl Leyva Solano, eds. Durham: Duke University Press.

Pannikar, R. 1992. "Is the Notion of Human Rights a Western Concept?" in *Law and Anthropology.* Peter Sack and Jonathan Aleck, eds. Aldershot, UK: Dartmouth Publishing Co.

Paris Pombo, María Dolores. 2000. "Identidades Excluyentes en San Cristóbal de Las Casas," *Nueva Antropología. Revista de Ciencias Sociales* 58:89–100. México.

Patton, Paul. 2000. *Deleuze and the Political.* London: Routledge.

Pitach, Pedro, and Julián López García, eds. 2001. *Los derechos humanos en tierras mayas: Politica, representaciones, y moralidad.* Madrid: Sociedad Española de Estudios Mayas and Universidad Complutense de Madrid.

Pitt-Rivers, Julian. 1973. "Race Latin America," *Archives of European Sociology* 19:3–31.

Postero, Nancy Grey. 2001. "Constructing Indigenous Citizens in Multicultural Bolivia." Available at: geocities.com. Last accessed February 2005.

————. 2002. "Rationalizing Indigenous Politics: Multiculturalism and Neoliberalism in Bolivia." Paper presented at the American Anthropology Association Meetings, New Orleans (November).

———. 2004. "Indigenous Responses to Neoliberalism: A Look at the Bolivian Uprising of 2003," in *Political and Legal Anthropology Review (PoLAR)* 28(1). Special Issue, Shannon Speed and Teresa Sierra, eds.

———. 2006. *Now We Are Citizens: Indigenous Politics in Postmulticultural Bolivia.* Stanford, CA: Stanford University Press.

Postero, Nancy, and Leon Zamosc, eds. 2004. *The Struggle for Indian Rights in Latin America.* London: Sussex Academic Press.

Povinelli, Elizabeth. 2002. *The Cunning of Recognition: Indigenous Alterities and Multiculturalism.* Durham: Duke University Press.

Pozas, Ricardo. 1958. *Chamula: Un pueblo indio de los altos de Chiapas.* México: INI.

Price, David. 2000. "Anthropologists as Spies," *Nation* 271(16):24–27.

Ramírez Cuevas, Jesús. 1997. "Mapa de la contrainsurgencia," *Masiosare: La Jornada* (January 13).

———. 2002. "The Mexican State on Trial," *Masiosare: La Jornada* (May 7).

Renard, María Cristina. 1998. *Los llanos en llamas; San Bartolomé, Chiapas.* México: Universidad Autónomo de Chiapas.

Renteln, Alison Dundes. 1988. "Relativism and the Search for Human Rights," *American Anthropologist* 90.

———. 1990. *International Human Rights: Universalism versus Relativism.* London: Sage.

Reyes Ramos, María Eugenia, Reyna Moguel Viveros, and Gemma van der Haar, eds. 1998. *Tranformaciones rurales en Chiapas.* México: UAM Xochimilco.

Robertson, Roland. 1990. "Mapping the Global Condition: Globalization as the Central Concept," *Theory, Culture and Society* 7:15–30.

Rojas, Rosa. 1995a. "De la Primera Convención Nacional de Mujeres a la Consulta Nacional del EZLN," in *Chiapas, ¿y las mujeres, qué?*, Vol. 2, 3–70. México, D. F.: La Correa Feminista.

———, ed. 1995b. *Chiapas, y las mujeres, qué?* Vols. 1 & 2. México, D. F.: La Correa Feminista.

Ronfeldt, David, and John Arquilla. 1998. *The Zapatista Social Netwar in Mexico.* Santa Monica, CA: E.U. International Studies Group, RAND.

Rorty, Richard. 1993. "Human Rights, Rationality and Sentimentality," in *On Human Rights.* Steven Schute and Susan Hurley, eds. New York: Basic Books.

Rose, Nikolas. 1999. *Powers of Freedom: Reframing Political Thought.* Cambridge, UK: Cambridge University Press.

Roseberry, William. 1994. "Hegemony and the Language of Contention," in *Everyday Forms of State Formation: Revolution and the Negotiation of Rule in Modern Mexico.* Durham, NC: Duke University Press.

Rouse, Roger. 1991. "Mexican Migration and the Social Space of Postmodernism," *Diaspora* 1(1).

———. 1995a. "Questions of Identity: Personhood and Collectivity in Transnational Migration to the United States," *Critique of Anthropology* 15(4):351–80.

———. 1995b. "Thinking through Transnationalism: Notes on the Cultural Politics of Class Relations in the Contemporary United States," *Public Culture* 7.

Rovira, Guiomar. 1996. *Mujeres de maíz*. México: Era.

Ruíz García, Samuel. 1999. *Mi trabajo pastoral en la diocesis de San Cristóbal de Las Casas: Principios teológicos*. México, D. F.: Ediciones Paulinas.

Rus, Jan. 1994a. " 'Jelavem Skotol Balamil—The Whole World Has Changed': The Reordering of Native Society in Highland Chiapas, 1974–1994." Unpublished manuscript, San Cristóbal de Las Casas, INAREMAC.

———. 1994b. "The 'Comunidad Revolutionaria Institucional': The Subversion of Native Government in Highland Chiapas, 1936–1968," in *Everyday Forms of State Formation: Revolution and the Negotiation of Rule in Modern Mexico*. G. M. Joseph and D. Nugent, eds. Durham, NC: Duke University Press.

Rus, Jan, and George Collier. 2003. "A Generation of Crisis in the Central Highlands of Chiapas: The Cases of Chamula and Zinacantan, 1974–2000," in *Mayan Lives, Mayan Utopias: The Indigenous People of Chiapas and the Zapatista Rebellion*, 33–61. Jan Rus, Aída Hernández Castillo, and Shannon Mattiace, eds. Lanham, MD: Rowman and Littlefield.

Rus, Jan, Rosalva Aída Hernández Castillo, and Shannan Mattiace, eds. 2003. *Mayan Lives, Mayan Utopias: The Indigenous People of Chiapas and the Zapatista Rebellion*. Lanham, MD: Rowman and Littlefield.

Said, Edward W. 1978. *Orientalism*. New York: Vintage.

Salovesh, Michael. 1972. *Politics in a Maya Community: V. Carranza, Chiapas*. Thesis, Department of Anthropology, Northern Illinois University, Dekalb, IL.

San Andrés Accords on Indigenous Rights and Culture. 1999. Lynn Stephen and Jonathan Fox, trans. *Cultural Survival Quarterly* 12(1):33–38.

Sánchez-Pérez, H. J., M. G. Vargas-Morales, and J. D. Méndez-Sánchez. 2000. "Bacteriological Quality of Human Drinking Water in High-Marginalization Zones in Chiapas," *Salud Publica Mexicana* 42(5):397–406.

Sandoval, Chela. 1991. "US Third World Feminism: The Theory and Method of Oppositional Consciousness." *Genders* (Spring):1–24.

Sanford, Victoria. 1999. "Between Rigoberta Menchu and La Violencia: Deconstructing David Stoll's History of Guatemala," *Latin American Perspectives* 109(26):38–46.

———. 2001. "From *I, Rigoberta* to the Commissioning of Truth: Maya Women and the Reshaping of Guatemalan History," *Cultural Critique* 47.

———. 2003. *Buried Secrets: Truth and Human Rights in Guatemala*. New York: Palgrave Macmillan.

Santos, Boaventura. 1998. *Por una concepción multicultural de los derechos humanos*. México: UNAM.

Santos, Boaventura, and César A. Rodríguez-Garavito. 2005. *Law and Globalization from Below: Towards a Cosmopolitan Legality*. Cambridge, UK: Cambridge University Press.

Sassen, Saskia. 1998. *Globalization and Its Discontents: Essays on the New Mobility of People and Money*. New York: New Press.

Scheper-Hughes, Nancy. 1995. "The Primacy of the Ethical: Propositions for a Militant Anthropology." *Current Anthropology* 36(3):409–20.

Schirmer, Jennifer. 1988. "The Dilemma of Cultural Diversity and Equivalency in Universal Human Rights Standards," in *Human Rights and Anthropology*. Theodore E. Downing and Gilbert Kushner, eds. Cambridge, MA: Cultural Survival.

Scott, Craig. 1996. "Indigenous Self-Determination and Decolonization of the International Imagination: A Plea," *Human Rights Quarterly* 18:814–20.

Scott, James C. 1976. *The Moral Economy of the Peasant: Rebellion and Subsistence in Southeast Asia*. New Haven, CT: Yale University Press.

———. 1985. *Weapons of the Weak: Everyday Forms of Peasant Resistance*. New Haven, CT: Yale University Press.

Secretaría de la Reforma Agraria. 2003. "Informe de Ejecución 2001–2003 del Programa Nacional de Población 2001–2006." Available at: www.conapo.gob.mx/micros/infavance/2003/24.pdf.

Seider, Rachel, ed. 2003. *Multiculturalism in Latin America: Indigenous Rights Diversity and Democracy*. New York: Palgrave MacMillan.

———. Forthcoming. "Legal Globalization and Human Rights: Constructing the 'Rule of Law' in Post-Conflict Guatemala?" in *Human Rights in the Maya Region: Global Politics, Moral Engagements, and Cultural Contentions*. Pedro Pitarch, Shannon Speed, and Xóchitl Leyva Solano, eds. Durham: Duke University Press.

Sierra, María Teresa. 1998. "Esencialismo y autonomía: Paradojas de las revindicaciones indígenas," *Alteridades* 14.

———. 2001. "Human Rights, Gender and Ethnicity: Legal Claims and Anthropological Challenges in Mexico," *PoLAR* 23(2):76–92.

Smith, Carol A., ed. 1990. *Guatemalan Indians and the State: 1540–1988*. Austin: University of Texas Press.

———. 1991. "Maya Nationalism," in *Report on the Americas*. Washington, DC: NACLA.

———. 1996. "Myths, Intellectuals and Race/Class/Gender Distinctions in the Formation of Latin American Nations," *Journal of Latin American Anthropology* 2(1).

Smith, Linda Tuhiwai. 1999. *Decolonizing Methodologies: Research and Indigenous Peoples.* Berkeley: Zed Books.

Smith, Michael Peter. 1987. "Global Capital Restructuring and Local Political Crises in US Cities," in *Global Restructuring and Territorial Development.* M. Castells and G. Henderson, eds. London: Sage.

———. 1994. "Can You Imagine? Transnational Migration and the Globalization of Grassroots Politics," *Social Text* 39.

Soysal, Yasemin Nuhoglu. 1994. *Limits of Citizenship: Migrants and Postnational Membership in Europe.* Chicago: University of Chicago Press.

Speed, Shannon. 2000. "Mujeres indígenas y resistencia de género a raíz de acteal: Las acciones dicen más que las palabras," in *Identidades indígenas y género: Cuaderno de trabajo no. 1—Research Project CONACYT-UNACH* (May). San Cristóbal de Las Casas: Facultad de Ciencias Sociales, UNACH.

———. 2002. "Global Discourses on the Local Terrain: Human Rights and Indigenous Identity in Chiapas," *Cultural Dynamics* 14(2):205–28.

———. 2003. "Indigenous Women and Gendered Resistance in the Wake of Acteal," in *Women of Chiapas: Making History in Times of Struggle and Hope.*

———. 2004. "Dangerous Discourses: Human Rights and Multiculturalism in Mexico," *Political and Legal Anthropology Review (PoLAR)* 28(1):29–51.

———. 2005a. "Critical Perspectives on Human Rights and Multiculturalism in Latin America: an Introduction," *Political and Legal Anthropology Review (PoLAR)* 28(1):1–9.

———. 2005b. "Luchas de tierra y reemergencia de identidad indigena: La étnohistoria y étnopresente de Nicolás Ruiz," in *Chiapas: La perspectiva de las investigadoras.* Maya Lorena Perez Ruiz, ed. México: INAH.

———. 2006a. "At the Crossroads of Human Rights and Anthropology: Toward a Critically Engaged Activist Research," *American Anthropologist,* In Focus Issue, "Human Rights in a New Key" 108(1):66–77.

———. 2006b. *Bajo la Lanza: Lucha por la tierra e identidad comunitaria en Nicolás Ruiz.* Tuxtla Gutiérrez: Consejo Estatal para la Cultura y las Artes de Chiapas (CONECULTA).

———. Forthcoming. "Forged in Dialogue: Toward a Critically Engaged Activist Research," in *Engaging Contradictions: Activist Scholarship in Interdisciplinary Perspective.* Charles R. Hale, ed. Berkeley: University of California Press.

Speed, Shannon, and Jane Collier. 2000a. "Limiting Indigenous Autonomy: The State Government's Use of Human Rights in Chiapas," *Human Rights Quarterly* 22(4):877–905.

———. 2000b. "Autonomía indígena, derechos humanos, y el estado: Dos casos en Chiapas," *Memoria* (September). Mexico, D. F.

Speed, Shannon, Rosalva Aída Hernández Castillo, and Lynn Stephen, eds. 2006. *Dissident Women: Gender and Cultural Politics in Chiapas*. Austin: University of Texas Press.

Speed, Shannon, and Alvaro Reyes. 2002. "In Our Own Defense: Globalization, Rights and Resistance in Chiapas," *Political and Legal Anthropology Review (PoLAR)* 25(1).

———. 2005. "Rights, Resistance, and Radical Alternatives: The Red de Defensores Comunitarios and Zapatismo in Chiapas," *Humboldt Journal of Social Justice* 29(1):47–82.

Spivak, Gayatri. 1988. "Can the Subaltern Speak?" in *Marxism and the Interpretation of Cultures*, 271–316. Cary Nelson and Lawrence Grossberg, eds. Urbana and Chicago: University of Illinois Press.

State Government of Chiapas. 1999. Ley de derechos y cultura indígena del estado de Chiapas, Periodico Oficial, Secretaría de Gobierno, Torno 1 (Jueves 29).

Stavenhagen, Rodolfo, et al. 1988. *Derecho indigena y derechos humanos en América Latina*. México: Instituto Interamericano Derechos Humanos.

———. 1990. "The Right to Cultural Identity," in *Human Rights in a Pluralist World: Individuals and Collectivities 39*. Jan Berting et al., eds. Westport, CT: Greenwood Press.

———. 1992. "Challenging the Nation-State in Latin America," in *Journal of International Affairs* 45(2).

———. 1996. "Indigenous Rights: Some Conceptual Problems," in *Constructing Democracy: Human Rights, Citizenship, and Society in Latin America*. Elizabeth Jelin and Eric Hershberg, eds. Boulder, CO: Westview Press.

———. 2003. "Indigenous Peoples and the State in Latin America: An Ongoing Debate," in *Multiculturalism in Latin America: Indigenous Rights Diversity and Democracy*. Rachel Seider, ed. New York: Palgrave MacMillan.

Stephen, Lynn. 1996a. "Redefined Nationalism in Building a Movement for Indigenous Autonomy in Mexico: Oaxaca and Chiapas." Paper presented at the 95th Annual Meeting of the American Anthropological Association, San Francisco (November).

———. 1996b. "The Creation and Recreation of Ethnicity: Lessons from the Zapotec and Mixtec of Oaxaca," in *The Politics of Ethnicity*, 50. Howard Campbell, ed. Nashville, TN: Vanderbilt University Publications in Anthropology.

———. 1997. *Women and Social Movements in Latin America: Power from Below*. Austin: University of Texas Press.

———. 1999. "Indigenous Rights and Self-Determination in Mexico," *Cultural Survival Quarterly* 23(1):23–53.

———. 2000. "The Construction of Indigenous Suspects: Militarization and the Gendered and Ethnic Dynamics of Human Rights Abuses in Southern Mexico," *American Ethnologist* 26(4):822–42.

———. 2002. "In the Wake of the Zapatistas: U.S. Solidarity Work Focused on Militarization, Human Rights, and Democratization in Chiapas," in *Cross-Border Dia-*

logues: U.S.-Mexico Social Movement Networking, 303–28. David Brooks and Jonathan Fox eds. La Jolla: University of California, San Diego, Center for U.S.-Mexican Studies.

Sudbury, Julia. 1998. *Other Kinds of Dreams: Black Women's Organizations and the Politics of Transformation (Gender, Racism, Ethnicity)*. London: Routledge.

Swepston, Lee. 1989. "Indigenous and Tribal Peoples International Law: Recent Developments," *Current Anthropology* 30(2).

Tavanti, Marco. 2002. *Las Abejas*. New York: Routledge.

Taylor, Charles. 1994. "The Politics of Recognition," in *Multiculturalism*, 25–73. Amy Gutmann, ed. Princeton, NJ: Princeton University Press.

Teichman, Judith A. 2004. "The World Bank and Policy Reform in Mexico and Argentina," *Latin American Politics & Society* 46(1):39–74.

Tello, Carlos. 1995. *La rebelión de las Cañadas*. México: Cal y Arena.

Terrazas, Carlos R. 1996. *Los derechos humanos en las constituciones políticas de México*. México: Miguel Angel Porrua Editorial.

Tíban, Lourdes. 2004. Activist research project meeting, "Gobernar en (la) Diversidad," Mexico City (March).

Trouillot, Ralph. 2001. "The Anthropology of the State in the Age of Globalization: Close Encounters of the Deceptive Kind," *Current Anthropology* 42(1).

Tula, María Teresa and Lynn Stephan. 1994. *Hear My Testimony: María Teresa Tula, Human Rights Activist of El Salvador*. Boston: South End Press.

Van Cott, Donna Lee. 2000. *The Friendly Liquidation of the Past: The Politics of Diversity in Latin America*. Pittsburgh: University of Pittsburgh Press.

Van Den Berghe, Pierre. 1994. *The Quest for the Other: Ethnic Tourism in San Cristóbal, Mexico*. Seattle: University of Washington Press.

Van der Haar, Gemma. 2004. "Autonomía a ras de tierra: Algunas implicaciones y dilemas de de la autonomia zapatista en la práctica," in *Tejiendo historia: Chiapas en la mirada de las mujeres*. Maya Lorena Pérez Ruiz, ed. México, D. F.: Instituto Nacional de Antropologia e Historia (INAH).

Varese, Stefano. 1988. "Multiethnicity and Hegemonic Construction: Indian Plans and the Future," in *Ethnicities and Nations*. Remo Guidieri, Francesco Pellizzi and Stanley Tambiah, eds. Austin: University of Texas Press.

———. 1994. "Think Locally, Act Globally," *NACLA Report on the Americas* 34(July–August):29–33.

———. 1997. "Identidad y destierro: Los pueblos indígenas ante la globalización," *Revista de critica literaria latinoamericana* 23(46).

Verduzco, Carlos. 1976. *Los factores que han propiciado e inhibido el proceso de aculturación en V. Carranza, Chiapas*. Thesis. Centro Coordinador Tzotzil, INI. ENAH.

Villafuerte Solís, Daniel, and Maria del Carmen García Aguilar. 1998. "El campo chiapaneco en la encrucijada neoliberal," in *Transformaciones rurales en Chiapas*. Maria

Eugenia Reyes Ramos, Reyna Mogel Viveros, and Gemma Van der Haar, eds. México: Universidad Autonoma de Mexico (UAM) Xochimilco and Colegio de la Frontera Norte (COLEF).

Villafuerte Solís, Daniel, Salvador Meza Díaz, Gabriel Ascencio Franco, María del Carmen García Aguilar, Carolina Rivera Farfán, Miguel Lisbona Guillén, and Jesús Morales Bermúdez. 1999. *La tierra en Chiapas: Viejos problemas nuevos*. México: Plaza y Valdés.

Viquiera, Juan Pedro, and Mario Humberto Ruz. 1995. *Chiapas, los rumbos de otra historia*. UNAM, CIESAS, CEMCA, eds. México: Universidad de Guadalajara.

Warren, Kay. 1998. *Indigenous Movements and Their Critics: Pan-Maya Activism in Guatemala*. Princeton, NJ: Princeton University Press.

Warren, Kay, and Jean Jackson, eds. 2002. *Indigenous Movements, Self-Representation, and the State in Latin America*. Austin: University of Texas Press.

Wasserstrom, Robert. 1989. *Clase y sociedad en el centro de Chiapas*. México: Fondo de Cultura Económica.

Weedon, C. 1987. *Feminist Practice and Poststructuralist Theory*. London: Basil Blackwell.

Wilson, Richard A. 1997. *Human Rights, Culture and Context: Anthropological Perspectives*. London: Pluto Press.

Wilson, Rob, and Wimal Dissanayake. 1996. *Global/Local: Cultural Production and the Transnational Imaginary*. Durham, NC: Duke University Press.

Wing, Adrien Katherine. 2000. *Global Critical Race Feminism: An International Reader*. New York: New York University Press.

Wolf, Eric. 1969. *Peasant Wars of the Twentieth Century*. New York: Harper and Row.

———. 1982. *Europe and the People without History*. Berkeley: University of California Press.

Wolf, Eric, and J. Jorgeson. 1970. "Anthropology on the Warpath in Thailand," *New York Review of Books* (November 19).

Womack, John, Jr. 1998. *Chiapas, el Obispo de San Cristóbal y la revuelta zapatista*. México, D. F.: Cal y Arena.

World Bank. 1990. "Enhancing the Contribution of Land Reform to Mexican Agricultural Development," John Richard Heath, Agricultural and Rural Development and Latin American and the Caribbean Regional Office, World Bank Policy Research Working Paper #285 (February).

Yashar, Deborah. 2005. *Contesting Citizenship in Latin America: The Rise of Indigenous Movements and the Postliberal Challenge*. Cambridge Studies in Contentious Politics. Cambridge, UK: Cambridge University Press.

Yúdice, George, Jean Franco, and Juan Flores, eds. 1992. *On Edge: The Crisis of Contemporary Latin American Culture*. Minneapolis: University of Minnesota Press.

Index